WOMAN AND NATION IN IRISH LITERATURE AND SOCIETY, 1880–1935

How Happy Could She be with Neither.

"Arrah, don't be moidherin' me with your 'where are ye goin', my pretty maid?' I'm goin' me own way; an' let me tell you both that me opinion of the pair o' yer politics is what Docthor Johnson said was 'the last refuge of a scoundrel.'"

'How happy could she be with neither.' Erin ignores the advances of both the Home Rulers and The Devolutionaries.

Woman and Nation in Irish Literature and Society, 1880–1935

WITHDRAWN

C.L. Innes

Catherine

Professor of Post-Colonial Literatures

University of Kent, Canterbury

The University of Georgia Press
Athens

Published in the United States of America in 1993 by
the University of Georgia Press
Athens, Georgia 30602

First published in Great Britain in 1993
by Harvester Wheatsheaf
A division of
Simon & Schuster International Group

Typeset in 10/12 Plantin
Printed and bound in Great Britain

1 2 3 4 5 C 97 96 95 94 93
1 2 3 4 5 p 97 96 95 94 93
ISBN 0-8203-1597-4
ISBN 0-8203-1598-2 (pbk)

Library of Congress Cataloging in Publication Data
is available on request

Clitheroe.   You have a mother, Langdon.
Lieut. Langdon.   Ireland is greater than a mother.
Capt. Brennan.   You have a wife, Clitheroe.
Clitheroe.   Ireland is greater than a wife.

Sean O'Casey, *The Plough and the Stars*

Our desire to have a voice in directing the affairs of Ireland is not based on the *failure of men* to do so properly, but is the inherent right of women as loyal citizens and intelligent human souls.

Editorial in *Bean na h-Eireann*

For my mother, Myriam Innes
and my sisters, Evelyn and Sylvia

Contents

List of Illustrations

Frontispiece. 'How happy could she be with neither.' Erin ignores the advances of both the Home Rulers and The Devolutionaries.

Introduction

The ambition of Stephen Dedalus as he prepares to leave Ireland at the end of *A Portrait of the Artist as a Young Man* to 'forge in the smithy of my soul the uncreated conscience of my race' was not unique to Dedalus, or to Joyce. It was an ambition shared by many Irish writers of his generation and the preceding one, who sought to define or proclaim the qualities which would make the content and expression of their work peculiarly Irish, and hence distinctively non-Anglo-Saxon. Indeed, all of Joyce's fiction, from the urban realism of *Dubliners* to the dream worlds of *Finnegans Wake*, can be read in part as a response to what he viewed as earlier misrepresentations or false creations of the Irish 'conscience', through the 'Celtic Twilight' made fashionable by Thomas Moore, to the 'dream of the noble and beggarman' proclaimed by Yeats, and the 'peasant thing' for which Synge is best remembered. The word 'conscience' (rather than 'consciousness') is carefully chosen, for the struggle to define the 'consciousness' of the race could not in those times be divorced from the desire to awaken its 'conscience', its moral sense, and so help shape the values, social relationships and structures of the future nation. For all these writers, the definition of Irish consciousness also involved a wrestling with and denial of English representations of Irishness, representations which were generally either derogatory or patronizing, or both.

Nor is Stephen Dedalus alone in his conceptualizing of the Irish race, and Ireland, as feminine rather than masculine. In an earlier

1

but related passage in *A Portrait of the Artist*, he coalesces images of working and peasant women with the image of the young woman who inspires his adolescent poetry, Emma Cleary. She in turn becomes in his mind an embodiment of the Irish soul:

> And yet he felt that, however he might revile and mock her image, his anger was also a form of homage. He had left the classroom in disdain that was not wholly sincere, feeling that perhaps the secret of her race lay behind those dark eyes upon which her long lashes flung a quick shadow. He had told himself bitterly as he walked through the streets that she was a figure of the womanhood of her country, a batlike soul waking in the consciousness of itself in darkness and secrecy and loneliness, tarrying awhile, loveless and sinless, with her mild lover and leaving him to whisper of innocent transgressions in the latticed ear of a priest. His anger against her found vent in coarse railing at her paramour, whose name and voice and features offended his baffled pride: a priested peasant, with a brother a policeman in Dublin and a brother a potboy in Moycullen.[1]

Later in this same final section of *A Portrait*, the association between the Irish race, woman and bats recurs:

> And under the deepened dusk he felt the thoughts and desires of the race to which he belonged flitting like bats, across the dark country lanes, under trees by the edges of streams and near the poolmottled bogs. A woman had waited in the doorway as Davin had passed by at night and, offering him a cup of milk, had all but wooed him to her bed; for Davin had the mild eyes of one who could be secret. But him no woman's eyes had wooed.[2]

Joyce here presents with irony the contest between would-be artist, priest and nationalists (here embodied by Davin), all male contestants courting 'the Irish race'. There are also other contestants, and Joyce draws upon a long tradition of representation. Throughout the history of its colonization, Ireland has been represented by British imperialists as well as Irish nationalists and artists as female: she is Hibernia, Eire, Erin, Mother Ireland, the Poor Old Woman, the Shan Van Vocht, Cathleen ni Houlihan, the Dark Rosaleen. British as well as Irish cartoons of the nineteenth and early twentieth century depict Ireland as a young maiden besieged, but the nature and nationality of the enemies differ.

A great deal has been written about individual Irish writers of the late nineteenth and early twentieth century – Yeats, Synge, Joyce and O'Casey in particular. A smaller but significant proportion of those studies has sought to see those writers in the context of Irish history and the struggle for Irish nationality and identity. What has received comparatively little attention until the last decade, however, is the role of Irish women in that struggle and how they themselves defined and sought to shape 'the conscience of [the] race'. Irish historians and literary scholars have generally given at best a passing mention to those women most actively involved in the political and literary movements, and have found it difficult to include them in their overall narratives of the nation.

Locked into confrontation with Britain and contestation over the motherland, Irish literature and Irish history have created males as national subjects, woman as the site of contestation. Liberators, Uncrowned Kings and would-be Messiahs abound in the rolls of honour, but women tend to be ignored except as muses or mates, such as Sarah Curran, Maud Gonne, and Kitty O'Shea. Those women who have sought involvement in national liberation have been dismissed as 'pretty ideologues', as William Irwin Thompson designates Maud Gonne, or as fanatics, and viragos.[3] Similarly critics have tended to ignore Irish women writers. The recent Field Day Anthology, despite its inclusion of other marginalized writings, found room for only a small group of women and generally ignored their journalistic contributions. In this it is symptomatic of a long tradition of Irish critical writing which focuses almost obsessively on Yeats, Joyce, Synge, O'Casey and Beckett, with a sprinkling of more recent male poets. Even the most recent cultural and literary studies, which one might have expected to be responsive to the work of women critics such as Toni O'Brien Johnson, Patricia Coughlan, Margaret Ward, and Mary Cullen, who have begun to recover the contributions of women to Irish history and culture, continue to uphold the impression that women do not exist except as passive icons. Of the ten figures who feature in Norman Vance's *Irish Literature: A Social History*, published in 1990, none is a woman. Roy Foster's *Modern Ireland 1600–1972* (London: Allen Lane, 1988) generally includes women only as footnotes; he does not find a place for them in the historical narrative. Thus Maud Gonne is given six footnotes, one of which lists her activities and biography quite extensively, but she does not appear in the main text. Although Foster devoted a whole chapter to Fanny and Anna Parnell in his study, *The Parnell Family* (Hemel Hempstead: Harvester Wheatsheaf, 1976), where the Ladies' Land League is assessed as having considerable significance for political and landlord–tenant relations in Ireland, he manages to give the sisters only very brief passing mention in this new history, which turns from a focus on family to a focus on historical narrative. Seamus Deane's *A Short History of Irish Literature* (London: Hutchinson, 1986), mentions only a half dozen woman writers in his account of the last hundred years, and some of these are given a mere mention amidst a list of other names. On the other hand, he devotes considerable attention to Maria Edgeworth and Lady Morgan, whom he posits as the 'mothers' of Irish fiction in the nineteenth century. To some extent, the exclusion of women writers in his account of the twentieth century is related to the focus he shares with most Irish critics on Irish modernism, and their interest in the obsessive intertwining by Yeats and Joyce of their own unfolding identities with the creation of an Irish identity. Many Irish women writers have worked within realist modes of fiction and drama, and have been content either to efface or play down their own personalities and identities as authors, or to allow their identities to be absorbed into symbolic constructs such as Erin. Male critics and male writers alike have also been absorbed in the 'family romance' which becomes linked to the colonial relationship; their concern is to challenge the authority of the father – the colonial power and the colonial cultural hegemony and tradition. Women writers and critics have often been marginalized in this contestation and struggle for authority.

Nor has much attention been given to how the mythicization of Ireland itself as female may have influenced male writers in their choices of subjects, their perception and portrayal of Irish women, of male–female relations, and of the interaction between the writer and his audience. How did women themselves respond to those images and that rhetoric? Did they endorse and adapt to them? Did they seek to modify them and use them in their own ways? During the first part of this century when the suffragette movement was at its peak in Ireland, did women see a conflict between nationalism and feminism? And how did both these concerns relate to the powerful images of motherhood and maidenhood promoted by the Catholic Church in Ireland? Some of the women centrally concerned with these issues – Maud Gonne, Constance Markievicz, Lady Gregory – have been written about by Yeats and in relation to him; others, such as Katharine Tynan, Alice Milligan, Hannah Sheehy-Skeffington, Anna Parnell, Elizabeth and Lily Yeats, also played an important part in the creation of the Irish literary and artistic revival, in the political debates concerning the nationalist struggle, as well as in the nationalist struggle itself.[4]

This book sets out to begin an exploration of these questions, first by sketching the 'consciousness' created by male writers, politicians and rhetoricians, with particular reference to gendered discourse and imagination, and then by examining in more detail the writings and speeches of the women concerned. I concentrate chiefly on the period between 1880 and 1935 when the cultural and political nationalist struggle and its immediate aftermath was particularly intense, and when the feminist campaign for civil rights also impinged strongly upon Ireland. It was not my intention to provide a survey of the literature produced by men or women over those years, and there is much work to be done in exploring and bringing to notice the extensive writings and activities of Irish women during this period of cultural nationalist activity. Originally I had planned to include chapters on Somerville and Ross, and on Mary Lavin, to refer in some detail to writers such as Kate O'Brien, Sarah Grand and George Egerton, but the space allotted me did not allow for this. Nor was there room to follow up the groundbreaking work of Elizabeth Coxhead in her *Daughters of Erin* on the role of women actresses and artists. Instead, this book provides a series of essays linked by my interest in the questions raised above, and particularly seeking to explore the role played by women in the creation of 'the conscience' of the Irish race. Part I focuses on the historical, cultural and literary context in which women were constructed as representations of Ireland or Irishness; Part II looks at the ways in which particular women, or groups of women, responded to such male constructions, and sought to redefine Irish consciousness.

I wish to thank the many colleagues who have encouraged and helped me at all stages in the writing of this book. Sue Roe first suggested the project to me; Sandra Siegel, Elizabeth Butler Cullingford, Declan Kiberd, and Janet Montefiore have read or heard sections of the book in its earlier stages and their suggestions have been of great value. I owe much to their published and unpublished work in this area, and also to the work and advice of Margaret Ward, Angela Bourke, Carol Coulter, Marjorie Hows, Bernard Sharratt, Toni Van Marle, Shaun Richards and David Cairns.

Parts of Chapters Six and Eight have been published in different form – Chapter Six in *Text and Context* no. III as 'Yeats Female Voices', and Chapter Eight in *Irish Writing: Exile and Subversion* (edited by Paul Hyland and Neil Sammells, London: Macmillan, 1991) as 'A Voice in Directing the Affairs of Ireland'. The chapter on Elizabeth Bowen has its origin in a paper delivered at the International Association for the Study of Anglo-Irish Literature Conference in Leiden in 1991.

PART I

Greater Than a Mother

CHAPTER ONE

Mother Country:

The Feminine Idiosyncrasy

. . . No doubt the sensibility of the Celtic nature, its nervous exaltation, have something feminine in them, and the Celt is thus peculiarly disposed to feel the spell of the feminine idiosyncrasy; he has an affinity to it; he is not far from its secret. Again, his sensibility gives him a peculiarly near and intimate feeling of nature and the life of nature . . .

(Matthew Arnold)[1]

In his linking of Celtic culture and sensibility to 'the feminine', Matthew Arnold himself is by no means idiosyncratic. He takes up a characterization which recurs frequently in nineteenth-century journalism and political discourse. Ernest Renan asserted that the Celtic races were feminine in nature. Lady Gregory reports in her diary for 24 August 1882 meeting in Holland an Anglo-Irish supporter of English rule who claimed that the countries of Europe were either male or female, and that the Celtic countries, along with Italy, comprised the female ones with 'their soft, pleasing quality and charm of a woman, but no capacity for self-government'. He believed that it was necessary for male countries like England to 'take the female countries in hand'.[2] Englishmen generally assumed their right as a 'masculine and virile race' to control feminine and childlike races such as Celts and Africans. That this characterization was shared also by Anglo-Irishmen is revealed by a letter from Sir Horace Plunkett to Lady Betty Balfour soon after her husband's resignation and replacement by George Wyndham as Chief Secretary: 'Lady Grosvenor's charming, the view is glorious and the day is fine – but it is the differences which

I feel, and all associations are pain. I am more like a woman than a man, I fear, but that's Irish.'[3] English critics of Oscar Wilde associated his 'effeminacy' with his Irishness. In Ulster a distinction was made between those of Scotch–Irish lineage, described as 'masculine', and their Southern neighbours who were seen as softer and weaker.[4] The Northern Irish poet, W.R. Rodgers (1909-1969), in a poem entitled 'The Character of Ireland', contrasted the speech of his people with that of the Southerners:

> an abrupt people
> who like the spiky consonants of speech
> and think the soft ones cissy;

Seamus Heaney continues the traditional gender distinction between England as male and Ireland as female in this analysis of how his poems are born:

> I think the process [of creating a poem] is for me a kind of somnambulist encounter between masculine will and intelligence and feminine clusters of image and emotion.
> I suppose the feminine element for me involves the matter of Ireland, and the masculine strain is drawn from the involvement with English literature. I teach English literature, I publish in London, but the English tradition is not ultimately home.[5]

Heaney's well-known poem, 'Act of Union', draws more self-consciously on the political implications of this trope.

The examples cited above are all references to racial characteristics – to the supposedly feminine or childlike qualities of the Celts or Irish as a race. While the distinction between race and *nation* is often blurred (sometimes deliberately), nevertheless such a distinction does exist. However, as a nation also, both in English and Irish writing and representation, Ireland is frequently allegorized as a woman, and the allegories are ones in which family or gender relationships are metaphors for political and economic relationships with a male England. One of the earliest, most sustained and detailed of these allegories is Jonathan Swift's first Irish pamphlet which, although not published in England until 1746, appears by its allusions to contemporary events to have been written about 1707.[6] Entitled *The Story of the Injured Lady*, this pamphlet, written in the form of a letter from the lady (Ireland) to a male friend, complains of her betrayal and ill-usage by a gentleman (England), despite her loyalty, and his favouring of another

(Scotland), although that lady is ill-natured and fickle. The second paragraph makes clear the identity of the characters in this triangle:

> A gentleman in the Neighbourhood has two mistresses, another and myself; and he pretended honourable Love to us both. Our three houses stood pretty near one another; his was parted from mine by a River, and from my Rival's by an old broken Wall.[7]

After a far from partial description of her rival as ugly, lewd, immoral and vicious, the Lady gives a self-portrait which has many features in common with the image of Cathleen ni Houlihan which will predominate two centuries later:

> I was reckoned to be as handsome as any in our Neighbourhood, until I became pale and thin with Grief and ill Usage. I am still fair enough, and have, I think, no very ill feature about me. They that see me now will hardly allow me ever to have had any great Share of Beauty; for besides being so much altered, I go always mobbed and in an Undress, as well out of Neglect, as indeed for want of Cloaths to appear in. I might add to this that I was born to a good Estate, although it now turneth to little Account under the Oppressions I endure, and hath been the true Cause of all my Misfortunes.[8]

Swift's allegory goes on to detail those 'Oppressions' and the causes of Ireland's poverty: the seizing of lands, the trade acts forcing Ireland to sell in England, unfair taxes, absentee landlords, the replacement of Irish administrators by English ones, and the removal of power from the Irish to govern themselves. All the Lady asks now is:

> only to enjoy a little Quiet, to be free from the Persecutions of this unreasonable Man, and that he will let me manage my own little Fortune to my best Advantage; for which I will undertake to pay him a considerable Pension every Year, much more considerable than what he now gets by his Oppressions; for he must needs find himself a Loser at last, when he hath drained me and my Tenants so dry, that we shall not have a Penny for him or ourselves.[9]

In an Answer to the Lady from her Friend, who presumably speaks in part for Swift himself, she is advised to act with greater independence, and not allow herself to be governed by the economic laws or other whims of the Gentleman.

In the nineteenth century, following the Act of Union and the dissolution of the Irish Parliament in 1800, Irish nationalists agitated for reform on several fronts. With inadequate planning or French aid, Wolf Tone with the United Irishmen attempted a

1. 'The Mad Doctor': John Bull consoles Hibernia and offers protection from the Fenian Frankenstein (cartoon by John Tenniel from *Punch*, 8 June 1867).

rising in 1798. Robert Emmet was executed for his involvement in another abortive rising in 1803. Daniel O'Connell led the movement for repeal of anti-Catholic laws, including the denial of the vote and other privileges to Irish Catholics; the short-lived Young Ireland movement, headed by Thomas Davis, was put down in 1848. During the Great Famine of 1845–7, England's perceived indifference to the terrible suffering and diminution of the Irish population by starvation and emigration, increased the bitterly anti-English feeling, particularly among the peasantry, and brought support for the militant Fenian Brotherhood, the Land League and Parnell as leader of the Home Rule movement. English views of such events are vividly displayed not only in the political and private letters of such men as Disraeli and Kingsley quoted below, but also in illustrations and cartoons in newspapers and journals.

Cartoons in *Punch* (see Illustrations 1 and 2) depict Hibernia as a virginal maiden, threatened by Fenians and other Irish radicals and sorely in need of rescue by paternal John Bull. The depiction of an

THE FENIAN-PEST.

Hibernia. "O MY DEAR SISTER, WHAT *ARE* WE TO DO WITH THESE TROUBLESOME PEOPLE?"
Britannia. "TRY ISOLATION FIRST, MY DEAR, AND THEN———"

2. Britannia protects Hibernia from 'the Fenian-Pest' (cartoon from *Punch*, 3 March 1866).

abstract nation in female terms is not, of course, restricted to Ireland alone – witness Britannia and France – but what is peculiar to Hibernia's character in these cartoons is her helplessness and passivity. Britannia is most frequently depicted as a warrior woman, often wearing a helmet and armour, and linked to the figure of the charioted Boadicea.[10] France often becomes merged with the image of Liberty and so appears active and triumphant rather than passive and despondent. A cartoon in *Punch* (3 March 1866) of Hibernia seeking advice from a fierce and stern Britannia provides a particularly striking example of this contrast (see Illustration 2). The representation of Hibernia also differs markedly from that of Africa or India as Britain's other colonized entities, for whereas these are generally shown as exotic, stressing features of colour, hair and dress which stress their 'otherness', Hibernia's image is likely to stress racial similarity, as befits a desirable wife or daughter whose relationship with England is to be a domestic one.

What many representations of France, Britain and Ireland have in common is the striking disparity between the depiction of the nation in the abstract, and the portrayal of individual Irish, British or French women and men. Yet that disparity is even more marked in the case of Hibernia and her people: if Hibernia embodies the extreme of angelic femininity dreamed by Victorian Englishmen – beautiful, graceful, spiritualized and passive – Hibernians are her opposite – bestial, dirty, loutishly masculine, aggressive and ugly: the extreme of masculine bestiality feared by Victorian Englishmen, and in this aspect like representations of African and Indian men. It is a contrast which takes place within the Victorian response to Darwinism and the whole debate concerning the relationship of human beings in general, and then of different 'races', to 'apes and angels',[11] a response which strongly influences the discourses concerning imperial as well as religious and sexual politics. A letter from Benjamin Disraeli to *The Times* in 1868 epitomizes that mid-nineteenth-century view of the Irish as a people:

> [The Irish] hate our free and fertile isle. They hate our order, our civilization, our enterprising industry, our sustained courage, our decorous liberty, our pure religion. This wild, reckless, indolent, uncertain and superstitious race have no sympathy with the English character. Their fair ideal of human felicity is an alternation of clannish brawls amd coarse idolatry. Their history describes an unbroken circle of bigotry and blood.[12]

Although his rhetoric is less violent, a letter from Charles Kingsley to his wife nevertheless indicates comparable repulsion towards the Irish and a view of them as pitiably apelike in their looks and condition:

> But I am haunted by the human chimpanzees I saw along that hundred miles of horrible country. I don't believe they are our fault. I believe there are not only more of them than of old, but that they are happier, better, more comfortably fed and lodged under our rule than they ever were. But to see white chimpanzees is dreadful; if they were black, one would not feel it so much, but their skins, except where tanned by exposure, are as white as ours.[13]

The import of such imagery is clear. Ireland must be rescued from the Irish, who are quintessentially undeserving of this desirable prize, and all too easily manipulated by wily Roman Catholic clergy. Her salvation lies in her rescue and 'marriage' to her English father/husband, whose benevolent and patriarchal governance will allow her to fulfil her essential self and remain feminine and Celtic. Thus, Arnold's series of Oxford lectures advocating the establishment of a chair of Celtic Literature emphasizes the need for the marriage of what he terms the Anglo-Saxon or Germanic qualities of honesty, industry and moral stability with the gentler Celtic graces in order to produce a balanced culture, but it is a marriage in which the Germanic qualities are to form the solid basis, softened and embellished by the subordinate Celtic ones. It is not at all surprising that Arnold opposed Home Rule for the Irish in 1886 on the grounds that the Irish were not capable of ruling themselves and were generally 'insubordinate, idle and improvident'.

It was not only members of the governing English society who imagined Ireland as female, however; Irish nationalists and unionists even more frequently depict Ireland as a lady in distress. Some of the images in Irish journals bear considerable likeness to English portrayals of Hibernia, but on the whole there is greater variety. The greatest differences between English and Irish portrayals come, of course, in their perception of the nature of the enemy and would-be rescuers; and there is also much less disparity between nationalist images of Ireland and their representations of the Irish. For example, an illustration reprinted in Curtis's *Apes and Angels* of 'Disturbed Ireland: before the Magistrate', a sketch by the Irish illustrator Aloysius O'Kelly for *The Illustrated London News* (5 Feb. 1881) shows a handsome and well-dressed young man before court officials, anguished Irish maidens crowding the doorway and courtroom itself (with one old mother in a lace cap), while the men – more shadowy and slightly menacing – peer through the window in the background. Another sketch by the same artist for the same journal (21 May 1881) shows in the foreground a single 'Erin-like' maiden about to hurl a stone and leading an angry but fine-looking group of men in their defiance of an official trying to serve an eviction.[14]

In general, Irish portrayals of their country fall into two categories: those that depict Ireland as maiden, and those that

RESTITUTION.

MRS. BRITANNIA—'' Dear Mrs. Erin, I've just stepped round to return you the keys of your house, and I hope, now that there is no quarrel between us, we shall be good friends.''
MRS. ERIN—'' My dear Mrs. Britannia, I'm really thankful to you, and trust that we shall be excellent friends for the future and always ready to lend a hand to one another.''

3. Irish view of the British: 'Restitution' (cartoon from *The Leprecaun*, June 1914, at the time the Home Rule Bill was passed).

depict her as mother. The maidenly image is epitomized in Mangan's popular ballad, 'My Dark Rosaleen', and derives in part from the eighteenth-century Gaelic genre of the *aisling*; the motherly image occurs in the traditional and equally popular figure of 'the poor old woman', the Shan Van Vocht of Irish legend and ballad. Both these images derive from and incorporate aspects of much earlier Irish traditions which, as Patricia Lysaght has shown, date from at least the eighth century. Lysaght demonstrates the convergence of the tradition of the *bean si* (anglicized as 'banshee')

– the fairy woman whose appearance is an omen of death but who may also appear as a more benevolent guardian figure – and the tradition of the *badhb*, who appears to derive from the war-goddess, Badb. According to Lysaght, the two aspects come together in the sagas in the figure of Fedelm, as a personification of sovereignty and prophetess of death:

> Since the sovereignty of the land was perceived as a woman who espoused the rightful king and thus conferred on him entitlement to his land and dominion over it, the connection of the death messenger with families in modern folk tradition can be explained in terms of the survivals of the concept of sacral kingship into modern times.[15]

Fedelm combines the often contradictory attributes of the *bean si* and *badhb*: she is 'war-goddess and land-goddess, death, aggressiveness, ugliness, old age, youth, beauty, abundance and benignity'.[16] Much of the effectiveness of the nationalist play, *Cathleen ni Houlihan*, composed by Lady Gregory and Yeats, derived from its reliance upon the emotive power of the folk traditions which converge in the image of old woman who is also a beautiful queen.

Irish cartoonists share with English ones the convention of depicting Ireland as a maiden in need of protection and comfort. Between 1860 and 1914 Irish newspapers and magazines feature the figure of Erin, often in the company of Pat or some equivalent male companion such as Parnell – handsome, upright, and respectable. Erin is dark-haired (while Hibernia is often fair), stately and slightly more mature than the limper, girlish Hibernia. She symbolized not only the nation in the abstract, but also an ideal of Irish womanhood. As L.P. Curtis describes her:

> Erin was a stately as well as sad and wise woman, usually drawn wearing flowing robes, embroidered with shamrocks. Her hair was long and dark, falling well down her back; her eyes were round and melancholy, set in a face of flawless symmetry. Occasionally she wore a garland of shamrocks and appeared with a harp and an Irish wolfhound in the foreground. Erin suggested all that was feminine, courageous and chaste about Irish womanhood, and she made an ideal Andromeda waiting to be rescued by a suitable Perseus.[17]

The image of Erin described by Curtis is a product of hundreds of years of Irish history and cultural change, strands of which were focused upon and reinterpreted by both Anglo-Irish Protestant and Gaelic Catholic nationalists in the nineteenth and early twentieth

AN CRAOIBHIN'S MISSION.

4. 'An Craoibhin's Mission': Erin greets her warrior redeemer, Douglas Hyde, on his return from America (cartoon from *The Leprecaun*, September 1905).

centuries. Those strands include elements of ancient Irish mythology and legend, ballad and other oral folk traditions, including the Gaelic bardic traditions, the influence of the Catholic Church and the increasing stress in the nineteenth century on the worship of the Virgin Mary as Mother of God, the 'Celtic Twilight' school popularized in England as well as Ireland by Thomas Moore, and the influence of English and European literary and artistic traditions with their uses of medieval and classical motifs and images.

Richard Kearney, in his Field Day monograph, *Myth and Motherland*, maintains that although the existence of a Mother Goddess, Dana, is well documented, it is not until the eighteenth century that Ireland itself is mythologized as a motherland. According to Kearney, the term *an t-athardha* (Fatherland) was used to denote Ireland in much bardic poetry until the seventeenth century, and he speculates that the change from fatherland to motherland has much to do with dispossession: 'The more colonially oppressed the Irish became in historical reality the more spiritualized became the mythic ideal of the Motherland.'[18] It seems that Kearney here ignores the prevalence of the *bean si* tradition which precedes the *aisling* poems which form a significant genre after the English policy of plantation in the seventeenth century and the cruel massacres and repression of the Cromwellian occupations. The *aisling* typically envisages Ireland in a dream vision as a beautiful woman pleading for rescue from the invaders, or, less frequently, as a harlot collaborating with them. Perhaps the best-known *aisling* poet is Aogan O Rathaille (1675–1729), translated here by Thomas Kinsella:

> Brightness most bright I beheld on the way, forlorn.
> Crystal of crystal her eye, blue touched with green.
> Sweetness most sweet her voice, not stern with age.
> Colour and pallor appeared in her flushed cheeks.
>
> Curling and curling, each strand of her yellow hair
> as it took the dew from the grass in its ample sweep;
> a jewel more glittering than glass in her high bosom
> – created, when she was created, in a higher world.
>
> True tidings she revealed to me, most forlorn,
> tidings of one returning by royal right,
> tidings of the crew ruined who drove him out,
> and tidings I keep from my poem for sheer fear.
>
> Foolish past folly, I came to her very presence
> bound tightly, her prisoner (she likewise a prisoner . . .).
> I invoked Mary's Son for succour: she started from me
> and vanished like light to the fairy dwelling of Luachair.
>
> Heart pounding, I ran, with a frantic haste in my race,
> by the margins of marshes, through swamps, over bare moors.
> To a powerful place I came, by paths most strange,
> To that place of all places, erected by druid magic.
>
> All in derision they tittered – a gang of goblins
> and a bevy of slender maidens with twining tresses.
> They bound me in bonds, denying the slightest comfort,
> and a lumbering brute took hold of my girl by the breasts.
>
> I said to her then, in words that were full of truth,
> how improper it was to join with that drawn gaunt creature
> when a man the most fine, thrice over, of Scottish blood
> was waiting to take her for his tender bride.
>
> On hearing my voice she wept in high misery
> and flowing tears fell down from her flushed cheeks.
> She sent me a guard to guide me out of the palace
> – that brightness most bright I beheld on the way, forlorn.

The Knot

> Pain, disaster, downfall, sorrow and loss!
> Our mild, bright, delicate, loving, fresh-lipped girl
> with one of that black, horned, foreign, hate-crested crew
> and no remedy near till our lions return from the sea.[19]

Like other poems in the *aisling* genre, this poem has some elements
in common with medieval religious poems which transformed
courtly love conventions to descriptions of the Virgin Mary, poems
where the poet is visited by or comes across a beautiful and
idealized maiden. Here, however, the vision and the loss is clearly a
political rather than a religious one, despite the references to Christ
and to devilish and pagan creatures. Indeed, one of the odd things
about this poem is that the prison and the violators are at one and
the same time identified with the magically druid past and the real
contemporary oppression of the foreign, and that the invocation of
the 'Son of God' causes the maid to be whisked away to the realm
of Irish legend, 'the fairy dwelling of Luachair', which is also her
prison. Presumably, this serves partly to heighten the distinction
between the foreigners who have occupied Ireland, who have made
it their home, and those other foreigners from across the sea, the
Scots under James, who might rescue her (and restore catholicism).
The image of sexual debasement, violation and rape as opposed to
marriage with a rightful suitor who will treat her as a 'tender bride'
is one that is either implicit or explicit in both English and Irish
representations of Ireland, and is suggested in a number of
nineteenth-century cartoons from both countries.

This *aisling* shares with others of its genre remnants of older
Gaelic beliefs and social structures to which the image of a woman
who embodied the land and whose espousal conferred sovereignty
was essential. According to Maire Cruise O'Brien, pre-Christian
Irish kings were 'legitimized only by marriage with the goddess
who – by an extension of her function as Mother Earth – is at once
the tribe and its territory. In this manifestation she is known as the
Sovereignty – almost a technical term.'[20] The Irish sagas portray
Maeve, Queen of Connaught, as having many of the attributes of
'the Sovereignty', and the goddess appears in early literature and
legend under a number of other guises, including Eire, Banba,
Fodhla, Bridget (often subsumed into St Bridget), Macha and
Emer. Maire Cruise O'Brien also identifies the Hag of Beare as an
emanation of the goddess, in this case speaking through the voice
of a male poet who is her votary:

> The old woman speaks words almost certainly put into her mouth by
> a votary of the goddess, almost certainly a man, who sees with the
> conquest of Christianity his occupation gone. The ageless divinity,
> the lover and spouse of Kings, is made mortal on contact with the

new religion; as Oisin is in the Fenian cycle or the Children of Lir in the Tuatha De Danaan tales.[21]

Similarly, Cruise O'Brien sees the poems attributed to Gorm-fhlaith, whose name she translates as 'cerulean sovereignty', and who is remembered as the widow of the Cormac of Cashel, Carroll of Leinster and Niall Glundubh, as dramatizations of 'Ireland lamenting three great provincial Kings, each of whom aspired to paramountcy over his fellows and each of whom paid for the attempt with his life'.[22] O'Brien's interpretation of the tradition and her assumption that the 'Hag of Beare' was composed by a male poet have been questioned by a number of scholars. What is certain, however, is that the tradition she belongs to has often been appropriated by male poets, including Yeats and Pearse.

Probably the best-known nineteenth-century poem deriving from the *aisling* tradition, is James Clarence Mangan's ballad, 'Dark Rosaleen', which is in turn a reworking of an earlier folk song 'Roisin Dubh', or 'Little Black Rose', the black rose being an emblem of Ireland. The earlier folk version combines political allegory concerning the Catholic and anti-English allies from whom Ireland seeks aid, with frank sexual imagery and desire typical of the earlier poems which evoke the mother-goddess figure, as the first and fifth stanzas illustrate:

> Roisin, have no sorrow for all that has happened you:
> the Friars are out on the brine, they are travelling the sea,
> your pardon from the Pope will come, from Rome in the East,
> and we won't spare the Spanish wine for my Roisin Dubh.
> [. . .]
> If I had six horses I would plough against the hill –
> I'd make Roisin Dubh my Gospel in the middle of Mass –
> I'd kiss the young girl who would grant me her maidenhead
> and do deeds behind the *lios* with my Roisin Dubh.[23]

In Mangan's version, the political allegory remains and is elaborated, but the sexual imagery and desire is diluted and etherealized; the 'earthiness' of the Earth-goddess is suppressed. Mangan renders the fifth stanza of the folk song quoted above thus:

> I could scale the blue air,
>   I could plough the high hills,
> Oh, I could kneel all night in prayer,
>   To heal your many ills!
> And one . . . beamy smile from you
>   Would float like light between

My toils and me, my own, my true,
  My Dark Rosaleen!
  My fond Rosaleen!
Would give me life and soul anew,
A second life, a soul anew,
  My Dark Rosaleen![24]

Mangan also renders another *aisling* poem, from the Irish version by William Heffernan, 'Kathaleen Ny-Houlahan', which again links an idealized figure of a woman, embodying Ireland, with political allegory calling for salvation by a royal Stuart. Here the female figure of Ireland is even more spiritualized and etherealized than in 'Dark Rosaleen', although it has a closer resemblance to the Hag of Beare's lament with its metaphor of apparent ugly old age disguising hidden youth and royal status. The poem ends with a prayer which draws on what was to become a familiar comparison between the Irish and the Israelites. I quote here the second and the final stanzas:

Think her not a ghastly hag, too hideous to be seen,
Call her not unseemly names, our matchless Kathaleen;
Young she is, and fair she is, and would be crowned a queen,
  Were the king's son at home here with Kathaleen Ny-Houlahan!
                    [. . .]
He, who over sands and waves led Israel along –
He, who fed, with heavenly bread, that chosen tribe and throng –
He, who stood by Moses, when his foes were fierce and strong –
  May he show forth His might in saving Kathaleen Ny-Houlahan.

Mangan's versions of these *aislings* reveal the influence of nineteenth-century English literary conventions as well as the political fervour of the Young Ireland movement with which he is associated. However, in his works and in poems and illustrations by later artists the spiritualized ideal of Erin is also intensified by and linked to the increasingly puritanical and asexual ideal of women by the Irish Catholic Church in the nineteenth century. Richard Kearney speculates that:

Woman became as sexually intangible as the ideal of national independence became politically intangible. Both entered the unreality of myth. They became aspirations rather than actualities. Thus it might be argued that a sociological transposition of Irish women into desexualised and quasi-divine mothers corresponds somehow to an ideological transposition of Ireland from a Fatherland . . . into idioms connoting a Motherland. As psychoanalysis reminds us, the mother has always been a powerful unconscious symbol for one's forfeited or forbidden origins.[25]

As Maire Cruise O'Brien demonstrates, the influence also works in reverse; the attributes of the Irish Mother-goddess figure also blend in to the image of 'Mother Church', the Roman Catholic Church (as in earlier times and continuing folk legend, the identities of the Celtic goddess Bridget and St Bridget become merged).[26] Here, at a time when catholicism and nationalism were increasingly identified with one another by Irish Catholics, the mistress evoked in this poem by Thomas Moore might well have been Cathleen Ni Houlihan but is in fact the Roman Catholic Church, according to Thomas MacDonagh who reprinted it in *Literature in Ireland*, the influential study of Irish and Anglo-Irish literature which he completed just a few months before his execution as one of the leaders of the 1916 Easter Rising. MacDonagh included this poem as an example of 'Poems of the Irish Mode':

The Irish Peasant To His Mistress

Through grief and through danger thy smile hath cheered my way,
Till hope seemed to bud from each thorn that round me lay;
The darker our fortune, the brighter our pure love burned,
Till shame into glory, till fear into zeal was turned;
Yet, slave as I was, in thy arms my spirit felt free,
And blessed even the sorrows that made me more dear to thee.

Thy rival was honoured, while thou wert wronged and scorned,
Thy crown was of briars, while gold her brows adorned;
She wooed me to temples, whilst thou lay'st hid in caves,
Her friends were all masters while thine, alas! were slaves;
Yet cold in the earth at thy feet I would rather be,
Than wed where I loved not, or turn even in thought from thee.

They slander thee sorely who say thy vows are frail;
Hadst thou been a false one, thy cheek had looked less pale;
They say too, so long thou has worn those lingering chains,
That deep in thy heart they have printed their servile stains
Oh! I do not believe them, no chain could that soul subdue:
Where shineth thy spirit, there liberty shineth too.

MacDonagh's note to the poem reads: '*The Irish Peasant To His Mistress* is addressed to the Irish Catholic Church which suffered under the penal laws, not yet quite removed, persecution unparalleled.'[27] In the late nineteenth and early twentieth centuries, the identity between Erin/Cathleen Ni Houlihan and Mother Church and the Mother of Christ continues to merge in the rhetoric, drama and poetry of nationalists. It reaches its epitome in the speeches and writings of Padraic Pearse, Catholic Nationalist leader of the 1916 Easter Rising. Pearse's last poem, written on the

THE BIRTH OF THE IRISH REPUBLIC · 1916

5. 'The Birth of the Irish Republic, 1916': the image of Erin here draws on the iconography of the Assumption and transfiguration of the Blessed Virgin Mary after her death.

eve of his execution, and printed and reprinted in newspapers and broadsheets, was entitled 'A Mother Speaks', in which the Mother is primarily Mother Ireland, but identifies with the Mother of Christ and her faith in redemption through sacrifice: 'Dear Mary, I have shared thy sorrow and soon shall share thy Joy.' Posters soon after the executions of the 1916 leaders showed 'the martyred

Pearse reclining *pietà*-like on the bosom of a seraphic celestial woman brandishing a tri-colour: a mixture of Mother Ireland, the Virgin Mother of Christ and the Angel of Resurrection'.[28]

Another popular Pearse poem which explicitly identifies the speaker with Mother Ireland and with the Gaelic tradition signified by the 'Hag of Beare' is his 'I Am Ireland':

> I am Ireland:
> I am older than the Old Woman of Beare.
>
> Great my glory:
> I that bore Cuchulain the valiant.
>
> Great my shame:
> My children that sold their own mother.
>
> I am Ireland:
> I am older than the Old Woman of Beare.

CHAPTER TWO

Mother Culture and Mother Church

If we are to accept Maire Cruise O'Brien's hypothesis that poems such as the 'Hag (or Nun) of Beare' are part of the tradition out of which developed the *aisling*, and the demonstration by scholars such as Patricia Lysaght of the continuing survival of the woman sovereignty symbol in folklore, then Richard Kearney's speculation that the notion of motherland does not predate plantation and dispossession needs modification. What the evidence does seem to suggest is that the waning in the seventeenth and eighteenth centuries of the bardic tradition and the social, political and economic structures which supported it, a loss mourned in the *aislings* of O Rathaille and others writing in Gaelic, is, as Kearney suggests, accompanied by an intensification of the unreal and visionary imagining of Ireland, although it is an imagination and convention growing out of the tradition of 'sovereignty' conferred by the earth-goddess. Moreover, the *bean si* figure has always been associated with other-worldliness. The eighteenth and nineteenth centuries, however, see the development of a new concern with nationhood and national identity, now involving those members of the Anglo-Irish plantocracy which had long settled in Ireland and which increasingly, although sometimes ambivalently, identified itself as Irish. That concern with an Irish rather than English identity was focused by the formation of an independent Irish parliament in 1782, and perhaps even more by the Act of Union which dissolved that parliament in 1800. (The strictly political application of the term 'Union' quickly took on connotations of sexual and marital union, a connotation foregrounded in Seamus Heaney's 1975 poem 'Act of Union'.)

The dream vision of Ireland as maiden and mother, both betrayer and betrayed, is arguably made more intense and given further emphasis by dispossession. The poet of the *aisling*, whether O Rathaille or Mangan, can only watch from a distance and hope for the salvation of the motherland by foreigners. And if a commitment is to be declared, it is the motherland, or Erin, herself who must make the choice. As resistance increased in the late eighteenth century and continued throughout the nineteenth, from the Rising of 1798 led by Wolf Tone and the United Irishmen through the movements for Repeal of anti-Catholic laws, and for land reform, the members of the Anglo-Irish Ascendancy class saw themselves as *threatened* with dispossession, both in terms of political and economic power, and the related issue of land ownership. The threat of dispossession, and much of the resulting rhetoric, was based on the question of legitimacy – the right of possession, the claim to Irishness. Hence there was a need for a commitment to an Irish identity, the declaration of a relationship by birth and inheritance and passed from the motherland to her would-be children who needed to prove themselves her rightful heirs. It is in this context that questions of racial purity on the one hand and cultural tradition on the other become increasingly fraught. And there is a clear relationship between the cultural movement often referred to as the 'Celtic Twilight' and the political change which might be termed the Anglo-Irish Twilight. Certainly the Anglo-Irish literature of the nineteenth and early twentieth centuries shows a striking preoccupation with themes of legitimacy and pollution. In Yeats's earliest and latest plays, these issues are dramatized: *Cathleen ni Houlihan*, marks the demand for commitment by the sons of Ireland; *Purgatory* focuses on the issues of legitimacy and blood pollution, as well as the nightmare of recurring history. Similarly, the Somerville and Ross novel, *The Big House at Inver*, published in 1925, began with the vision of a ruined great house and portrays the tragic and futile struggle of an illegitimate daughter to preserve the fortunes and reputation of the Prendeville family. Here, as in Maria Edgeworth's seminal Anglo-Irish novel, *Castle Rackrent*, family history is doomed to repeat itself as the inheritance of arrogance, beauty and irresponsibility leads successive sons to waste their fortunes and mate with 'the natives'.[1]

One of the landmarks in the attempt to establish a legitimate Irish *cultural* tradition is Charlotte Brooke's *Reliques of Irish Poetry*. Published in 1789, it is a collection of translations (together with the originals) of Irish verse, including renderings of the Red Branch and Fenian sagas, which strongly influenced later writers. Brooke's work is in turn influenced by the interest in English, Celtic and Norse antiquities which marked eighteenth-century English literature – Bishop Percy's *Reliques of Ancient English Poetry*, for example, and James MacPherson's translations of Ancient Scottish poetry. The Royal Irish Academy was established in 1786 to encourage work on Irish literature; the Gaelic Society began in the early nineteenth century to publish translations of the Deirdre legend and other early Irish works; and as Sir Walter Scott's novels nourished and developed an interest in Scots culture and history, so in Ireland the fiction of writers like Lady Morgan, Charles Robert Maturin, and Samuel Lover fed and helped to encourage an appetite among Irish and English readers for Irish folk culture and history.

In Ireland as with other nations, the concern with cultural history and restoration is rarely divorced from political concern. Charlotte Brooke's *Reliques* and its claim for the existence of a long-established Irish civilization seeks to counteract the English denial that such a civilization existed or was worthy of consideration, and in her introduction to the collection she expresses the hope that the British and Irish muses may be 'sweet ambassadresses of cordial union between two countries that seem formed by nature to be joined by every bond of interest and amity'.[2] Brooke's collection is also related to the claim for Catholic redress and is responded to by Ledwich's *Antiquities of Ireland*. As Seamus Deane remarks:

> As in the seventeenth century, no research into the past could be innocent. The result was always going to be the formation of an official or semi-official myth which would give credence to the claims of one political or religious grouping.[3]

In Ireland literature in English which seeks to speak to the question of Irish identity (as so much of it does), is complicated not only by the difficulty of defining that identity and the political issues involved, but also by the problem of multiple audiences – Catholic or Protestant; Irish, Anglo-Irish, and English; male and female. It is almost impossible for Anglo-Irish writers to take for granted a common set of assumptions, religious, political or cultural, between themselves and their audiences, while the significance of the writers' subjects as well as the language they write in will be wrestled with and over by the varying communities to whom or for whom the writers speak. The result throughout the history of Anglo-Irish writing has been, as Deane says:

> time and again in Swift, in Joyce, in Standish O'Grady and many others . . . a critique of the idea of authority. Authority and its legitimacy and effectiveness was always a matter of concern in Ireland, since it has only seldom proved its claim to either.[4]

That questioning of authority frequently reveals itself in terms of the questioning of patriarchal authority, and in struggles between father figures and sons in the literature of both male and female writers.

The fiction of Lady Morgan, Charles Maturin, Samuel Lover, Sheridan LeFanu and Emily Lawless, the drama of Dion Boucicault, the poetry of William Allingham and Samuel Ferguson, and in different ways the works of Maria Edgeworth and William Carleton, spoke to both the Anglo-Irish desire for identity and belonging, and the English desire for the exotic, for self-definition in opposition to 'the other'. The problem of speaking to several audiences at once is one I shall take up in later discussions. It is one that the Young Irelanders sought to avoid by determining on an audience that would be solely Irish and solely committed to Irish liberation from English rule. Despite, or perhaps because of their differing backgrounds – Thomas Davis was a Protestant whose father had been a surgeon in the British army; John Dillon a Catholic from Mayo of tenant-farmer origins; Charles Duffy a northern middle-class Catholic; Smith O'Brien a Protestant landowner; and John Mitchel a Presbyterian from the North – and despite their growing differences with O'Connell whose movement for Repeal of the Union they had supported with greater fervour than O'Connell himself appeared to after 1845, the Young Irelanders, through the medium of the *Nation* newspaper, tried to forge an audience and a nation which would rise above sectarian and class differences and unite in the cause of Irish freedom. In this aim, two kinds of appeal to the past were central: one was the invocation of Wolf Tone and the United Irishmen, commemorated in Davis's

ballad, 'Who Fears to Speak of Ninety-eight', and the other was
the invocation of and revival of the Gaelic cultural tradition, which
the poetry of James Clarence Mangan was particularly potent in
recreating. Davis and Mangan and other poets with similar aims
were published in *The Nation* newspaper, and later reprinted in a
volume called *The Spirit of the Nation*. This volume went into
dozens of editions and was one of the most popular and best-known
anthologies in late nineteenth- and early twentieth-century Ireland.
The 1882 edition is described by Seamus Deane as bound in green
and gold 'with harp and shamrock motifs, a frontispiece containing
Celtic harpists, a Celtic warrior, female representations of Mother
Ireland and, in the centre, the eagle of freedom slaying the serpent
of despotism'.[5]

At this stage, however, the appeal to the Gaelic past is a cultural
rather than a political one, although, as I have noted above, such an
appeal does have political implications. The political model is
supplied by Wolf Tone, who was in turn influenced by the
American and French revolutions. But it was the *United* element in
his programme, rather than his revolutionary social agenda, which
was most invoked by later followers. The Gaelic past is cited in
order to establish Ireland's separate identity from England, and
thus to support the movement for Home Rule and an independent
parliament. In the early twentieth century, Gaelic social structures
would be invoked for political and military purposes by leaders like
Pearse and Connolly who sought a more radical solution to
Ireland's political and economic oppression. The influence of the
later forms of the Gaelic Revival is demonstrated by Donal
McCartney in a comparison of two popular and influential histories
of Ireland, *The Story of Ireland* (1867) and *The Making of Ireland
and Its Undoing* (1908). The first was written by A.M. Sullivan,
proprietor of *The Nation* after Charles Gavan Duffy's departure,
and its 'main political message might be said to have been that
Ireland reached its highest point of political development in the
independent parliament of Grattan's time'. This message, and its
consequent foregrounding of Henry Grattan as the patriot hero who
won Ireland legislative independence in 1782, contributed forcefully to the 'two great mass movements of the nineteenth century,
Repeal and Home Rule'.[6] The later history ignored the achievements of eighteenth-century Anglo-Irish culture and the establishment of an independent Irish parliament in 1782, concentrating

instead on the formation of Gaelic Ireland, its institutions and culture. For Alice Stopford Green, author of the 1908 volume, Ireland is by definition 'Gaelic Ireland' and it is 'undone' by the invasions of the Normans and Tudors, and the imposition of English institutions and culture.

But during the nineteenth century, the Gaelic culture which preceded the English settlements was invoked by Unionists, Home Rulers and Republicans alike as a means of establishing an Irish identity distinct from an English one and to legitimize all three political stances, whether they called for the maintaining of power or the attempt to obtain it. Many saw the appeal to a Gaelic tradition as a means of 'transcending' political interest, and believed that an identity which glossed over the various plantations and settlements, as well as the religious oppression of Catholics, might be a means of uniting all sections. Examples of the uses to which Gaelic culture were put in the nineteenth century are provided by three poets: Thomas Moore, William Allingham, and Samuel Ferguson.

Of these three, Thomas Moore was and continues to be the best known, though not necessarily the best poet. His ten volumes of *Irish Melodies*, published between 1807 and 1834, set his own lyrics to traditional music in the Irish mode, and were much appreciated both in England and Ireland for their languorous and sonorous nostalgia, evoking an Ireland distant and vague in time and place (although sometimes specific place names are given to link past and present). His 'Song of Fionnuala' remained in the twentieth century one of his most popular pieces (alluded to in several of Joyce's works). Moore's note to this lyric tells us that it is based on the legend that Fionnuala, the daughter of Lir, was transformed into a swan, and condemned to wander through Ireland until the coming of Christianity, when she would be released by the first mass-bell:[7]

> Silent, O Moyle! be the roar of thy water,
>   Break not, ye breezes, your chain of repose,
> While, murmuring mournfully, Lir's lonely daughter
>   Tells to the night-star her tale of woes.
> When shall the swan, her death-note singing,
>   Sleep, with wings in darkness furl'd?
> When will heaven, its sweet bell ringing,
>   Call my spirit from this stormy world?

> Sadly, O Moyle! to thy winter wave weeping,
>   Fate bids me languish long ages away!
> Yet still in her darkness doth Erin lie sleeping,
>   Still doth the pure light its dawning delay!
> When will that day-star, mildly springing,
>   Warm our isle with peace and love?
> When will heaven, its sweet bell ringing,
>   Call my spirit to the fields above?

The merging in the second stanza of the legendary heroine with Erin is by no means uncommon in the poetry of Moore and others. Nor is this lyric untypical in its passive longing for salvation from some external force, and in its fusion of redemption and death. In other poems, Erin herself is the primary heroine:

> Let Erin remember the days of old,
>   Ere her faithless sons betrayed her;
> When Malachi wore the collar of gold
>   Which he won from her proud invader.[8]

And:

> As vanquish'd Erin wept beside
> The Boyne's ill-fated river
> She saw where Discord, in the tide,
> Had dropp'd his loaded quiver.[9]

While Moore continually professed and made a profession of his Irishness, William Allingham was rather more divided in his allegiance and identity. His collected *Poems* include nineteen pieces entitled 'Irish Songs' gathered together, and separated from the main body of his work. His 'Irish' lyrics are suggestive of oral and folk traditions in form, and dwell on the image of the Irish as fey and childlike. His most frequently anthologized piece, 'The Fairies', is representative of his 'Irish Songs', and begins:

> Up the airy mountain,
>   Down the rushy glen,
> We daren't go a-hunting
>   For fear of little men.

The rest of the poems in the volume, however, are imitative of nineteenth-century English poets, particularly Wordsworth, Tennyson and Arnold, and generally exclude imagery or forms connotative of Ireland.

Despite the possible influence of Allingham in poems such as 'The Stolen Child', it is Samuel Ferguson, along with Thomas

Davis and James Clarence Mangan, whom Yeats cites as his predecessor. Born in Belfast in 1810, Ferguson was a Protestant and a Unionist who sought to reconcile Irishmen divided by culture and religion. He believed that:

> once Catholics could have revealed to them their true identity as Celts, and Protestants could discover their true role, which was to absorb into modern civil forms the fire and passion of that Celtic heritage, then the new Ireland could emerge.[10]

Ferguson did much to recover that Celtic heritage and to present it in a way that was likely to impress and appeal to his contemporaries in both Ireland and England, translating or rendering bardic lays as well as epic stories from the early sagas. His lifetime of dedication to the recovery of Gaelic culture includes a series of translations published in the *Dublin University Magazine* in 1834, his *Lays of the Western Gael* published in 1865, *Congal*, an epic poem published in 1872 and based on the bardic romance of the 'Battle of Moyra', and a one-act verse drama, *Deirdre*, published in 1880, four years before his death. A. Norman Jeffares comments thus on Ferguson's verse in terms that the poet himself might have approved:

> Ferguson differed greatly from Mangan, who tended to be swept along by the emotions of his verse. There is a controlled, vigorous, masculine, marching quality in Ferguson's lines, a certain lack of the sensuous, which meant that his translations, though more accurate and more effective than earlier work, such as that of James Hardiman, did not achieve popularity. Ferguson was not good at creating character; he may, as Padraic Colum suggested, have been unduly desirous of making his Celtic heroes dignified Victorians.[11]

Ferguson's importance derives not only from the work he did in recovering a considerable portion of the Celtic heritage and showing how it could be made part of contemporary literature, but also in his development of the Celtic hero and heroine types which would dominate the Irish Literary Revival for which he laid much of the groundwork. In particular, the figure of Deirdre would be dwelt upon again and again by subsequent writers, including George Russell (AE), Yeats and Synge. Between 1850 and 1950, she appeared as the central character in over thirty-five Irish plays. Why this obsession with Deirdre? And why are other legendary female figures, such as Maeve, Gormlaith, Grania and Dervorgilla given so much less attention (although they are not ignored altogether). Lorna Reynolds sees in the difference between Maeve and Deirdre an illustration of the change from one kind of society to another, in which the powerful and sovereign Mother-goddess figure of Maeve is supplanted by a romantic and tragic heroine in a society where women lose their rights and become chattels, where 'the true lover could be seen as a deliverer from and protector against other men who would use women and wrong them in the most fundamental way'.[12] The significance of the pre-Christian version of the Deirdre story as a fable teaching that kings must act fairly and justly, harmonizing culture and nature, has been explored by Maire Herbert, who also notes the revisions made in the early Christian context, and the emphasis made by the monks who transcribed the story on analogies with the story of Eve.[13] In the nineteenth and twentieth centuries, Deirdre's appeal may have something to do with her analogy in these later versions to the figure of Erin, a figure fought over and betrayed. Her situation as a possession to be contested, the focus of conflict between the sons of Usnach and a possessive old man, a patriarchal figure, perhaps catches up the father–son conflict which runs through so much nationalist or anti-colonial literature. Certainly as the maiden/queen who summons young men to fight and die for her in order to liberate her from an oppressive suitor, she has much in common with the image of Cathleen ni Houlihan, and no doubt the two images reinforce one another.

Unlike the warrior-queen Maeve, she also forms a contrast with the typical male hero favoured by Irish cultural nationalists, and who becomes focused on Cuchulain. Although both are wilful and, as depicted in the dramas of Yeats, Synge and others, act wilfully and imprudently, always ready to challenge 'the despotism of fact', as Matthew Arnold so memorably phrased it from his English perspective, once having made her fatal choice, Deirdre is passive and sorrowing, Cuchulain is active and aggressive. As emblematic characters they develop in the nineteenth-century versions of the narratives into embodiments of the dichotomy between masculine and feminine that Ashis Nandy explores in the context of a colonized India. Nandy argues that the discourse of colonialism and anti-colonialist nationalism helps to produce an extreme division between what are seen as male qualities of militarism, and female qualities of passivity and submission.[14] The preservation of this dichotomy is particularly strong in the journalism and rhetoric, as well as the poetry and drama, produced by adherents of the Gaelic

League; and, as Elin Ap Hywel suggests, the antagonism of Catholic nationalist critics to many of the productions of the Abbey Theatre may be attributed partly to the intermingling of these categories in the plays of Yeats, Lady Gregory and Synge.[15] For whereas the publications of the Gaelic League's followers, in the columns of *Sinn Fein* or Gaelic League pamphlets on the role of women in the Nationalist movement (such as Mary Butler's *Irishwomen and the Home Language*), exalted Irishwomen as emblematic mothers or desexualized spiritual maidens, the Anglo-Irish writers of Protestant background often acknowledged sexual desire and power as significant elements in the characters and roles of their female heroines.

Mother Church and the Blessed Virgin Mary

Ferguson's ideal of uniting – or rather diluting – Catholic Ireland with the Protestant class by an appeal to the Celtic heritage, was both a response to and an attempt to obviate the growing strength of Catholic Ireland, the authority of the Catholic clergy and the development of a Catholic middle class. From the sixteenth century on, the effects of the Reformation in England and Henry VIII's rejection of Papal authority, combined with the policy of plantation in Ireland, which dispossessed many 'native Irish' of their lands, helped to forge a strong link between Catholicism and anti-English nationalism. It was a link that was reinforced in later centuries by the invasions and massacres led by Cromwell, together with further widescale confiscation of land, the Battle of the Boyne in 1690 which was a defeat for the Irish allied with the cause of a Catholic monarchy, and the introduction of Penal Laws against Catholics in 1695, denying political and civil rights and imposing harsh economic restrictions. Although much of the opposition to alien domination was non-sectarian in nature during the eighteenth century, and the leadership was often Protestant or, as in the case of Wolf Tone, Deist, the identification of Catholic Ireland with Gaelic Ireland remained. However, those who dominated in government and the professions were of English origin and the English language and English writing were the discourses of power, while Gaelic remained the language of the powerless. Denied access to education and the professions, Catholics generally remained Gaelic speaking.

In 1829, Daniel O'Connell's mass movement to win emancipation for Catholics finally succeeded. To Irish Catholics he became known as 'The Liberator'. O'Connell believed firmly in the necessity for the teaching of English to all Irish children, arguing that Gaelic speakers would fail to have access to 'progress', and he supported the introduction of a national system of primary education in the 1830s, despite its aim of making every pupil 'a happy English child'.[16]

He both represented and encouraged the growing power of Catholic Ireland and the development, through education and political power, of a Catholic middle class. By the end of the century, the strength of that class, and the split between the new Catholic ascendancy and the older Anglo-Irish Protestant ascendancy would be dramatized in the fall of Parnell. Parnell's fall also illustrated the power and authority of the Catholic clergy in Irish politics.[17]

The conflict between a landed Anglo-Irish ruling class which had governed in terms of a more or less feudal system, and a new, increasingly urbanized catholic bourgeoisie dominates nineteenth- and early twentieth-century Irish history. This conflict, and the Irish sense of their own history, was compounded by the terrible famine of 1845–8, when the potato crop, the staple food of the Irish peasantry, failed. By 1851, over a million Irish poor had died of starvation and disease. Another million or so had emigrated to America, Canada and Australia.[18] One result of the famine was the rapid diminution of a Gaelic-speaking culture, already threatened by the educational system and the privileged status of the English-speaking community in Ireland, where English was the language of commerce, politics and law, newspapers and journals, and the medium for most writing. According to F.S.L. Lyons:

> In 1845 . . . about four million people, or half the population, still spoke Irish as their mother-tongue. Only six years later, in a population reduced to about six and a half million, no more than 23% spoke Irish and only 5% were monolingual in that language.[19]

Another long-range effect of the famine was the destruction of an Irish economy dependent upon a combination of grain crops grown for cash, and ever smaller holdings used for the growing of potatoes. The area under cultivation and the size of holdings began to increase rather than diminish. E.R.R. Green summarizes the long-term effects thus:

> The pattern of modern Irish agriculture was beginning to emerge from the ruin caused by the potato blight – a family farm engaged on mixed tillage and livestock production, with the stock rather than grain increasingly providing cash income. The halt to subdivision of necessity brought fundamental social changes in Ireland as well. Gone were the days of early marriage and a countryside thronged with young people and children. For many the price of holding together the family farm was to remain unmarried . . . The resentment in Ireland against English handling of the famine crisis was deep and slow to heal. Worse still was the bitter hostility between landlord and tenant which boiled over into a great agrarian conflict when falling farm prices caught the farmer in the late seventies.[20]

The slowly increasing political and economic strength of a Catholic middle class, together with the changing social and family structure of the mainly Catholic peasantry, was accompanied by the growth in numbers, power and authority of the Roman Catholic clergy in Ireland, and the particular ideology it fostered. From a ratio of 1 Catholic priest to approximately 3,500 lay people in 1840, the numbers of clergy increased to 1 for every 600 lay people in 1960. A very large number of the clergy came from the 'respectable and fairly comfortable class of the tenant farmers'.[21] J.J. Lee argues that there was a close connection between the changing agricultural system to larger family farms and the changing structure and authority of the Catholic Church:

> Economic circumstances therefore conspired to make Ireland an increasingly male dominated society after the famine. The churches, and particularly the Catholic Church, whose members were disproportionately affected, could not escape the implications. The rise of the strong farmer coincided with the growth of clerical power . . . The number of churches, the number of clergy, the number of devotions, the frequency of the sacraments, not least confession, increased spectacularly . . . The church was able to preach its doctrines in detail for perhaps the first time in Irish history to the mass of the people just at the moment when the new image of woman, and the new public obsession with sex, was gaining the ascendancy. In addition, the spread of literacy permitted a rapid growth in the number of publications, religious as well as general, and provided yet another means of effective indoctrination.[22]

The development of the Catholic school system is also particularly significant here. Originally it had been envisioned that the national primary system should be non-denominational, although religious instruction would be included in the curriculum. Suspicion that these schools would be used as a basis for Protestant evangelizing, however, led some bishops to encourage the creation of Catholic schools, nominally open to all, but in practice mainly attended by Catholic children. By about 1830, there were 350 day schools run by parish priests, 46 convent schools for girls, and 24 schools founded by the Christian Brothers for boys.[23] The numbers increased rapidly after 1830. So also did the number of secondary Catholic schools. According to Lyons, 10 were set up before 1829, 10 more by 1850, and another 27 by 1867. Nevertheless, by 1911, only 1 in 17 Catholics proceeded beyond primary school level.[24]

Catholic ideology in Ireland in the nineteenth century was strongly influenced by that of Rome, where many aspiring Irish priests received their training. During the nineteenth century two doctrines were promulgated as Articles Doctrine which all Catholics were bound to accept – the doctrines of the Immaculate Conception (1854) and of Papal Infallibility (1878). Marina Warner argues persuasively that there is a link between this assertion of patriarchal authority, on the one hand, and the apparent glorification of Mary, the Mother of God, on the other. For the doctrine of the Immaculate Conception confirms the image of the Blessed Virgin as uniquely asexual, denying all biological functions, except as Warner points out, 'lactation and weeping' (in Ireland, even the lactation disappeared), while at the same time proclaiming motherhood as the ideal role for women.[25] Marina Warner summarizes thus the significance of the cult of the Virgin:

> Christ the God-Man and Mary the Virgin-Mother blot out antinomy, absolve contradiction, and manifest that the impossible is possible with God. But unlike the myth of the incarnate God, the myth of the Virgin Mother is translated into moral exhortation. Mary establishes the child as the destiny of woman, but escapes the sexual intercourse necessary for all other women to fulfil this destiny. Thus the very purpose of women established by the myth with one hand is slighted with the other. . . The twin ideal the Virgin represents is of course unobtainable. Therefore the effect the myth has on the mind of a Catholic girl cannot but be disturbing, and if it does not provoke revolt (as it often does) it deepens the need for religion's consolation, for the screen of rushes against the perpetual frost of being carnal and female. . . The process is self-perpetuating: if the Virgin were not venerated, the dangers of sex, the fear of corruption, the sense of

sin would not be woven together in this particular misogynist web, but would be articulated in a different way.[26]

After the famine in Ireland, the departure of a larger proportion of younger men to work in North America or Australia, and the turn towards 'familism', and the passing on of land to the oldest son, rather than subdivision among members of the family, the expectation that the bride would bring a dowry, which often limited the option of marriage to one daughter in a family, reinforced the encouragement of chastity, renunciation and self-sacrifice among women in particular (although it applied to men as well). The gap in age between husband and wife also lengthened, so that by the early twentieth century, according to J.J. Lee, about 50 per cent of husbands were 10 or more years older than their wives.[27] This greater maturity (in years) increased the authority and control of the husband, which had formerly been modified by the fact that women made a considerable contribution, both paid and unpaid, to the economy of the household.[28] The dowry system also tended to give the bride's father greater power in vetoing or approving suitors.

Although the role of wife and mother was held up as the social ideal for women, the reality was that many women worked and contributed to family finances, and also that a very high proportion of Irish women remained single. The number of single women in the Irish population was 43.3 per cent in 1861; by 1911 the proportion had increased to 48.26 per cent.[29] In 1925, 25 per cent of all women in Ireland aged 45 remained unmarried, even though by this stage 50 per cent of all emigrants were women.[30] At the same time, opportunities for female employment and economic independence had rapidly diminished. Before the famine, agriculture had been labour intensive, calling on men and women alike to fulfil its demands. Domestic industry had also been severely hurt, and opportunities for female employment as spinners of wool, cotton and linen rapidly disappeared, except in Belfast, where linen factories began to prosper. The main employment open to women became domestic service. In 1841, 30 per cent of women employed outside agriculture were in domestic service; by 1926, the number had increased to 60 per cent.[31] For those many women who would have to remain single, or who perhaps chose to, the convent provided an alternative and respected social structure, where the nun could take the vows of chastity, poverty and obedience, and become symbolically the bride of Christ. (In most orders, nuns wear wedding rings to symbolize their mystical wedding.) The convents also took on the roles associated with mothering: education (especially of small children), the training of girls, nursing, and charity. Those who were most successful in the convent were promoted from 'Sister' to 'Mother' and took on greater authority and responsibility. Ultimately a nun could proceed to becoming the head of an order, the Mother Superior. Nevertheless, all nuns, including the Mother Superior, were subject to the authority of any Father, or priest.

The cult of the Virgin endorsed not merely chastity and motherhood as womanly ideals, but also humility, obedience and passive suffering. In 1879, a Catholic woman writer, Mary Cusack, justified the ways of God and man to woman as the retribution due for:

> the first act of disobedience . . . committed by the woman and she is therefore at once and specially punished. She who had refused to submit to her Creator, must bear the pain of an especial subjection to a creature.[32]

Paintings and statues of Mary popular in nineteenth- and early twentieth-century Ireland tended to be very different from Renaissance depictions of robust madonnas, sometimes seen suckling the infant Jesus. She is most frequently portrayed as fully covered from neck to foot, cloaked in blue, and either in the attitude of humble acceptance of her destiny at the Annunciation, or wearing a crown to represent her special status. The infant Jesus, in one of the most popular images, is rather precariously perched on her right arm, thus emphasizing her motherhood, while at the same time asserting the dominance of the child rather than the mother, and distancing it from reliance on the nurture of the breast. Another very frequent image is of the *pietà*, the sorrowing mother holding her dead son's body, or of the 'stabat mater', the mother standing by the crucified Christ. The cult of the rosary emphasizes these aspects, with their series of Joyful Mysteries, Sorrowful Mysteries and Glorious Mysteries, during which the Ave Maria is said repeatedly while the person praying (often as a form of penance given after confession) meditates on the Annunciation and birth of Christ, his crucifixion and death, and then his resurrection and the Assumption of Mary into Heaven.

The representations of the Virgin Mary as Queen Mother,

sometimes with the moon or the world and a serpent at her feet, also suggest her correspondence with Mother Church, who nurtures and cares for all who belong to her, her children, and of whom Christ is mystically the bridegroom. In this abstract or allegorical character, Mother Church resembles Mother Ireland, both of whom are dependent upon their children to make them whole and glorious, but who are also the instruments of their children's redemption.

While the proclaimed appearance of the Virgin to a young peasant girl at Lourdes (repeating in different form the image of Mary, humble maiden in the Annunciation), is the most famous and influential of European nineteenth-century visions, the cult of Mary, humble maiden in the Annunciation) is the most famous Knock in County Mayo in 1879. According to reports, her appearance on the wall of a parish church during a driving rainstorm was that of a queen, in medieval dress, with sash, veil and crown, just like the icons and images so popular at the time. Witnesses also declared that they recognized the various saints who appeared with her 'because they looked like their statues'.[33] The shrine at Knock remains in the twentieth century Ireland's most revered centre for the worship of Mary. A holy card which has proved to be one of the best sellers at the shrine illustrates that combination of idealization and promised reverence with uncomplaining acceptance of a mundane domestic role which the cult of Mary could be used to endorse. The card pictures a young mother in an apron cooking at a stove, and contains the following 'Kitchen Prayer':

> Lord of all pots and pans and things,
> Since I've not time to be a saint
> By doing lovely things
> Or watching late with Thee
> Or dreaming in the dawn light
> Or storming heaven's gates
> Make me a saint by getting
> Meals and washing up the plates.[34]

By the late nineteenth century, two female images had become potent social, political and moral forces in Catholic Ireland – the images of Mother Ireland or Erin, and the Mother of God, often linked through iconography to Mother Church. Both demanded the allegiance of men and women alike, but it was for women that they provided models of behaviour and ideals of identity. For Protestant Ireland the cult of the Virgin had relatively little significance, except perhaps as an example of Catholic idolatry and superstition, but the figure of Erin and Mother Ireland is one some seek to adopt. Thus Ferguson, in 'A Dialogue Between Head and Heart', argued that the 'native Irish' right to nationality through blood inheritance could be balanced by the Anglo-Irishman's love of the land and emotional attachment to it. Writers like Ferguson also sought to align themselves with a 'mother-culture', whose descendants could include Protestants and Catholics alike. The mother culture would provide noble images and models such as Cuchulain and Deirdre, heroes and heroines to unite Irishmen, as Yeats, Lady Gregory and Synge hoped in their manifesto for the Irish Literary Theatre. It would also provide a model of society which included warrior-chiefs and peasants, dreams of 'noble and beggarmen', an agrarian and feudal model which excluded the Catholic bourgeoisie.

CHAPTER THREE

Cultural Nationalism:

Anglo-Irish and Gaelic Ireland

In the two decades preceding the turn of the century, three influential cultural nationalist movements were founded in Ireland. In 1884, Michael Cusack organized the Gaelic Athletic Association, which had a mainly rural base and sought to revive traditional Irish sports and Irish manhood. The association's first patron was Archbishop Croke, a supporter of the Land League but opponent of Parnell, and an evangelist for temperance as well as Gaelic sports. The Gaelic League, founded in 1893, aimed at restoring Irish as the spoken language and developing writing in Irish; it was also associated with a campaign to 'buy Irish', revive Irish cottage industries, and encourage the wearing of clothing and jewelry which were considered traditionally Irish in style. Unlike the Celtic Literary Society, it welcomed women as members, and caused some consternation among the Catholic clergy because it held mixed (male and female) classes and dances. The Irish Literary Society held its first meeting in London in 1891, to be joined a year later in Dublin and then supplanted by the National Literary Society, which played a central part in the Anglo-Irish Literary Revival and the establishment of an Irish theatrical base and tradition. While the Gaelic League and Gaelic Athletic Association had a mainly Catholic constituency, the dominant figures in the Irish Literary Society tended to be of Anglo-Irish and Protestant ancestry, members of the ascendancy class, whose economic and political dominance was being challenged by the Catholic majority.

All three movements encouraged the emergence of 'the Cuchulain cult'. As Donal McCartney puts it, Cuchulain 'was held up as the model of his race, replacing the comparatively prosaic Grattan or O'Connell, the models of the Home Rulers'.[1] Cuchulain is the hero of Standish O'Grady's historical romances, is given considerable prominence in scholarly works by Douglas Hyde, Eleanor Hull, and P.W. Joyce, becomes the hero of Lady Gregory's reworking of the sagas in her *Cuchulain of Muirthemne*, and is the subject of one of Yeats's earliest poems, 'The Death of Cuchulain' (1892 – revised as 'Cuchulain's Fight with the Sea' in *The Rose*), and also one of his very last ones, 'Cuchulain Comforted' (January, 1939). Cuchulain is also the protagonist of five plays written by Yeats between 1903 and 1938.

But Cuchulain was not the only heroic figure chosen 'to engross the present and dominate memory'.[2] In Anglo-Irish literary texts and in Catholic popular culture, Parnell rapidly became another such figure after his downfall in 1891. As Seamus Deane points out, 'The literature of early modern Ireland is, in essence, a heroic literature, in which pride of place goes to the new idea of Ireland itself as a force variously embodied by outstanding individuals.'[3] For Standish O'Grady, acknowledged by Yeats as the writer who 'deserved the lion's share' because 'his books have affected one more powerfully than those of any other writer',[4] the mode was both heroic and tragic. His 'histories' and recreations of the Irish epics are idealized versions, representing a series of aristocratic pasts – Celtic, Catholic and Anglo-Irish – emblematized by a hero who is betrayed. O'Grady continues and reinforces the themes of Ferguson's verse dramas about Deirdre and Cuchulain, as well as his essays and translations about the literature of the past. As Seamus Deane comments:

> The essential ground-theme of all [O'Grady's] writings is that of a lonely heroism betrayed. That, branching into the accompanying threnody for the loss of a sublime moment in civilization, and its replacement by a squalid, money-counting society, completes the background of Yeats's social thought.[5]

Cathleen ni Houlihan, written by Lady Gregory and Yeats, and first performed to an ecstatic audience in 1902 with Maud Gonne in the title role, dramatizes that idea of a lost Ireland which can be redeemed only by a lonely heroism which sheds a 'squalid, money-counting' present. It is a play which is particularly interest-

6. Scene from the first production of *Cathleen ni Houlihan* with Maud Gonne in the title role.

ing, and was at the time particularly powerful in its impact, because it managed to bring and hold together, for the moment, a number of strands in what were actually diverse, and sometimes conflicting, nationalist movements. It was also a play which sought, in Walter Benjamin's terms, to make 'the political aesthetic'.[6]

We are told by Lady Gregory that the 'idea' or 'vision' of Cathleen came from Yeats; the actual writing (and creation of the social world into which the vision intrudes) was hers.[7] Yeats generally spoke of the play as if it were entirely his own creation, but while it is impossible to disentangle precisely the parts for which each author was responsible, the evidence of the notebook in which the first draft is written suggests that Lady Gregory played a major part in its composition. The pencilled notes for the play's outline, the whole of the first draft, together with lines crossed out and corrected, are entirely in Lady Gregory's hand. Almost the only additions in the final version to this first draft, and these seem to have been Yeats's additions, are the songs. It is Lady Gregory who, remembering the stories of her nurse, Mary Sheridan, about the French landing at Killala in 1798 and the cheering she had heard, sets the play at that time, and adds stage directions for the distant cheering to be heard throughout the play.[8]

Several emotive symbols gave *Cathleen ni Houlihan* its appeal to a nationalist audience, an appeal which continued for many years and earned Yeats the authority to reprimand restive nationalists when Synge's *Playboy of the Western World* provoked them to anger five years later. In addition to drawing on the Gaelic *aisling* tradition, with its topos of a visionary beautiful young woman representing Ireland, which had been popularized by Mangan's 'Dark Rosaleen', and on the older folk tradition of the 'Shan Van Vocht', the poor old woman who was Mother Ireland, the setting of the play in 1798 near Killala summoned the memory of Wolf Tone, whose centenary had been vigorously celebrated four years previously. (Maud Gonne and Yeats had been prominent among the organizers of the centenary commemorations.) Wolf Tone was not only one of the leaders of the 1798 rebellion, celebrated in one of the most popular nationalist songs of the late nineteenth and early twentieth century, 'Who Fears to Speak of '98', but also represented an attempt to reconcile the religious divisions which to this day disrupt Ireland and create conflicting political allegiances. The United Irishmen also embraced the republicanism of the American and French revolutionary movements, and came to stand for a radical anti-imperialism looking towards an enlightened and progressive future which would shed the 'superstitions' of Catholicism and Celticism. For patriots of Protestant and Ascendancy stock, like Lady Gregory and Yeats, Tone's concern with disconnecting the link between patriotism and religion (particularly Catholicism) was important; others were more attracted by his anti-imperialism and his concern with dismantling political structures which supported the continuing rule of an aristocratic class. For both groups he represented an Anglo-Irish nationalism, which was inherited and promoted by the Young Irelander movement of the 1840s, and which stood side by side with Gaelic Nationalism and its yearning for an idealized past.[9]

The play continues a theme which is typical of Yeats's poetry and drama in the 1890s, the conflict between the material and mundane on the one hand, and a spiritual or poetic ideal on the other. It is a conflict stated and restated in Yeats's first epic on an

Irish subject, *The Wanderings of Oisin*, in shorter poems such as 'The Stolen Child', 'The Rose', and 'The Song of Wandering Aengus', and in plays such as *The Land of Heart's Desire* and *The Countess Cathleen*. Of that period Yeats wrote self-mockingly at the end of his life:

> What can I but enumerate old themes?
> First that sea-rider Oisin led by the nose
> Through three enchanted islands, allegorical dreams,
> Vain gaiety, vain battle, vain repose,
> Themes of the embittered heart, or so it seems,
> That might adorn old songs or courtly shows;
> But what cared I that set him on to ride,
> I, starved for the bosom of his faery bride?
>
> And then a counter-truth filled out its play,
> *The Countess Cathleen* was the name I gave it;
> She, pity-crazed, had given her soul away,
> But masterful heaven had intervened to save it.
> I thought my dear must her own soul destroy,
> So did fanaticism and hate enslave it,
> And this brought forth a dream, and soon enough
> This dream itself had all my thought and love.[10]

'Starved for the bosom of his faery bride', Yeats had incorporated in *Cathleen ni Houlihan* his dream vision of the otherworldly Mother Ireland/queenly bride who will draw the young man, Michael, from the mundane world of dowries, gold, new suits, marriage, family and hearth, into a dream of glory, where, dead to this world, he 'will be remembered forever' for sacrificing his life to redeem Ireland. Although the symbols are pagan, the re-enactment of the sacrifice which so many have undergone for Ireland's sake – a sacrifice which redeems the idea only, as the audience is reminded by the futility of the already historically enacted and defeated rebellion of 1798 – alludes to the Christian myth of redemption through Christ's offering of himself as sacrificial victim, a myth also re-enacted daily in the ritual of the Catholic mass. It is this bringing together of the Christian myth of redemption by blood-sacrifice with the Gaelic nationalist myths of an Ireland who as Mother or bride awaits redemption, which made the play such a powerful invocation of nationalist sentiment and reinforced the rhetoric of martyrdom and blood-sacrifice which informed so many of Padraic Pearse's speeches.

Those who must act are the sons; the role of the female is either to inspire or to resist. As other-worldly visitant, she has affinities with the 'faery bride', the *femme fatale* who haunts so much nineteenth-century poetry; as Catholic peasant mother, she is shrewd and kindly enough, but limited and limiting in her vision, which is entirely pragmatic and domestic in its concerns. Michael's prospective bride, Delia, is given so little space that she remains merely a figure of the choice, linked to dowry, which Michael makes in disregarding his father's words so that he can devote himself to the idealized mother-figure who will become his young queen. As Joseph Chadwick argues, the nationalist allegory is also a resolution of the Oedipal struggle in which the authority of the political colonial father as well as that of the natural and Church fathers is rejected so that the son can devote himself to 'a highly idealized version of the mother who is also a lover'.[11] In a society as small as Dublin's, the fact that the role of Cathleen ni Houlihan was played by Maud Gonne, already poeticized by Yeats as his muse and daimon, and by nationalists as a figure of Erin,[12] must have added to this powerful fusion for the audience of nationalist allegory and idealized sexual romance.

The struggle for authority played out between father/son figures is one that recurs almost obsessively in Irish drama and fiction of this period, and I have argued at greater length elsewhere that such a conflict is typical of the literature of cultural nationalism.[13] It is found in Joyce's fiction and Synge's drama, as well as Yeats's poetry and drama. *On Baile's Strand*, written a year after *Cathleen ni Houlihan,* focuses on the struggle between Cuchulain, a younger and 'unsettled' warrior-king, and the older, pragmatic Conchubar, who wishes for reasons of state to impose his political authority. Cuchulain's acceptance of that authority results in his destruction of his own son. In this play, the allegorical sub-plot of the fool and the blind man emphasizes the analogy between imposed political authority and the pragmatic materialism so often in nationalist rhetoric ascribed to England, while the fool and Cuchulain are the wayward and poetic 'sons' who act in their own best spirit and interests when rejecting such pragmatism. The battle between Christy and his father in Synge's *The Playboy of the Western World* sets up a similar conflict between Old Mahon's concern with money and the dowry that his son can obtain through marriage to a widow whom Christy describes as 'a hag this day with a tongue on her has the crows and seabirds scattered, the way they wouldn't cast a shadow on her garden with the dread of her curse'.[14] The play repeatedly poses a choice between material benefit and aesthetic value: in favour of the lovely Pegeen (rivalling Helen of Troy), Christy rejects his father's choice and the Widow Quinn's offer of fine clothing and a cottage and land; while Pegeen herself rebels against both her father and Father Reilly in rejecting the relatively prosperous but unadventurous Shaun Keogh for the handsome and poetic daredevil she takes Christy to be. A similar choice between ugly material security in the person of her ageing living-dead husband and the brief but poetic respite offered by the tramp is offered Norah in *The Shadow of the Glen*.

Like Synge, Joyce treats the father/son conflict with irony, as action closer to farce than Yeatsian tragedy. Nevertheless it is a conflict that is significant in all of Joyce's work, and whether explicitly named Simon or not, fathers and father figures are recurringly presented as failing through 'simony', the degradation of spiritual ideals through materialism. In Joyce's fiction priests are aligned with natural fathers and with the English in their desire to be 'men of the world', in their suppression of rebellious thoughts, and in their distrust of the artist.

But what happens to the women figures who are so often the focus of this conflict? And how does the political analogy affect the portrayal of 'realistic' women figures in the drama and fiction of these male writers? The continuing influence of Cathleen ni Houlihan can be seen in the work of the authors with whom the Irish Literary Revival is most often identified, but it is an influence modified and complicated by a (generally) subtextual dialogue which takes place *between* those writers, the one frequently reacting to the other, sometimes in contexts which are analogous to another kind of father/son conflict, the reaction of a younger writer to his literary predecessors described by Harold Bloom as 'the anxiety of influence'.

Although only six years older than Synge, W.B. Yeats was well established as a writer in the forefront of the Irish Literary Revival when Synge began composing his first play, *When the Moon Sets*, in 1900. Synge's next two plays, *Riders to the Sea* and *The Shadow of the Glen*, were both written in the summer of 1902, a few months after *Cathleen ni Houlihan* was first staged, and like it were one-acters produced by Frank and Willie Fay. Critics have pointed out a number of correspondences between *Riders to the Sea* and

Cathleen ni Houlihan: both plays are set in a peasant cottage near the sea, with the main action introduced by the examination of clothing interrupted by an old woman at first off-stage. Both of the old women repeatedly name or describe the deaths of men linked to them, and both lose sons named Michael, whose fate and its consequences are at the heart of the drama. Other echoes include the offstage priest whose intervention in both plays is seen as out of harmony with the deeper instincts and knowledge of the Irish, and the name of the older daughter in Synge's play, Cathleen. The similarities make more evident a series of sharp contrasts, however: Yeats's Michael is preparing for a wedding, which he rejects for immortality, while Synge's Michael is being prepared for a funeral; Yeats's young heroes go down to the sea to join the French, Synge's go down to the sea to trade their horses. Maurya's final words, 'No man at all can be living for ever, and we must be satisfied', echo and refute the promise of Cathleen ni Houlihan:

> They shall be alive for ever,
> They shall be speaking for ever,
> The people shall hear them for ever.

These contrasts serve to focus the differing vision and concerns of the two dramatists with regard to Ireland and Irish women. Cathleen ni Houlihan celebrates death; Maurya, together with her two daughters, laments it. In Yeats's drama, the stage props – the clothes, the gold – are seen as unworthy and trivial distractions, merely material or mercenary concerns, which distract from the abstract ideal represented by the words and vision of Cathleen. Here, heroism is divorced from sensual or material gain; the nationalism of the play has little to do with the aims of the Land League, which implied the creation of a bourgeois peasantry. Cathleen summons men to die for an abstract notion of the four beautiful green fields and idealized concept of Ireland, not so that individual men and women might live in greater security, comfort, or even justice.

Synge rejects such abstract heroism, and hence abstract nationalism or mere patriotism, both directly and indirectly. Michael and Bartley, like their father and brothers before them, die in the cause of trade, a trade carried on to bring the bare necessities to their mother and sisters, and it is this which has destroyed all the men. Their deaths are mourned as individual sons and brothers, and also in terms of the hardship left to the women who must somehow carry on without them. Synge's stage props – the clothes, the nets, the bread, the spinning wheel, the pine boards – are things in themselves, but also objects which take on increasing significance and poetic power as the play progresses. Like much of Synge's drama, *Riders to the Sea* celebrates the ways in which the ordinary and the everyday is made poetic by human interaction, by words, and by love. Heroism consists not in great patriotic gestures, but in day-to-day living.

For Yeats there is a dichotomy between the mundane and the heroic. His characters must belong to one or the other, although for some there is a choice to be made – a choice which is dramatized again and again in his early works from *The Wanderings of Oisin* to 'Easter 1916'. True, the heroic may sometimes be deceptively clothed in the appearance of comic realism, as in the case of Michael and his family, the Old Woman who is Cathleen and the men who took part in the 1916 Rising, but their involvement in a moment of grandeur will allow them to appear in their fixed and lasting character, where 'They shall be alive for ever'. Synge's characters gradually take on nobility *through* their involvement in this world. Maurya compares with Cathleen ni Houlihan as a mother-figure; her age and grief give her dignity, but the loss of her menfolk makes her older rather than younger. She can expect no glorious transformation. And the play focuses less on the quietly practical and matter-of-fact heroism of the young men than on the suffering of the sisters and, above all, their mother. As the play progresses, so too Maurya progresses in stature, from a rather frail and uncertain figure offstage who must be protected from grief, to one who embodies all mothers, confronting grief and death fully and accepting both. Her strength gradually is equated with that of the sea, the natural force which takes her men from her. As Ann Saddlemyer describes her, 'Maurya is indeed an impressive figure – the rock within this island of rock, the surrounding sea threatening her identity as it does the very shores of Aran.'[15] Maurya becomes a figure of Aran, which has moulded its people, and so, for Synge, a figure of that which is essentially Irish and Ireland. She is a mother who must survive in spite of the loss of her men; she will not be transformed by them.

The Shadow of the Glen, written that same summer, also places a woman at the centre of the drama, a woman profoundly influenced by the Irish countryside, and choosing at the last to go out and become a part of it. The tone and style are very different however, although here too it is a young man, Michael, who is at first posited as her saviour. There is in this short play an interesting reversal of gender roles with *Cathleen ni Houlihan*, for the homeless wanderer who shatters the world of domestic security offered Nora Burke by both her elderly husband and his young would-be replacement is a male tramp, and it is Nora who makes the choice to follow him into a future which will lead to an early death, but a more poetic and adventurous one. Nora is the first of many Synge heroines who actively participate in the making of their destinies, rebelling against patriarchal control, and, to the outrage of Irish audiences, expressing their sexuality as they do so.

Like other Anglo-Irish writers of the Ascendancy class, including Yeats and Lady Gregory, Synge celebrated the peasantry as the location of true 'Irishness'. Unlike many of his co-writers, he did not confuse celebration with idealization. The distinction he draws in his famous Preface to *The Playboy of the Western World* between his drama and that of Ibsen or Mallarmé – 'One has, on the one side, Mallarmé and Huysmans producing this literature [rich and copious in its words]; and, on the other, Ibsen and Zola dealing with the reality of life in joyless and pallid works. On the stage, one must have reality, and one must have joy.'[16] – is valid for all the drama he wrote after 1900, and also reflects his rejection of Yeats's early drama, and the cult of Cuchulain, in what he described as an 'unmodern, ideal, breesy [sic], springdayish, Cuchulanoid National Theatre'.[17]

Synge's portrayal of Nora, like his portrayal of Pegeen four years later, reveals his consciousness of the actuality of the lives led by a large proportion of Irish women, especially in the rural areas. This actuality has been described in my previous chapter where it is pointed out that at the time Synge was writing, about 50 per cent of Irish husbands were 10 or more years older than their wives, and marriage for economic reasons rather than romance was the norm. The deprivation of rural areas in consequence of the famine, British policy with regard to Irish trade, and an outmoded and harsh feudal system sustained by the landlord class, is described in detail in the series of articles Synge wrote for *The Manchester Guardian* in 1905. In his plays he is less concerned with the causes of deprivation than the consequences, which are suffered more intensely by women. But whereas other writers were likely to show women as mere victims, helpless greyhaired Irish mothers or innocent and beautiful colleens awaiting rescue by an Irish hero or two, Synge's women rebel against their situation, which they experience not so much as victims of economic oppression as of sexual repression, and they ardently and actively seek their liberation. Nora speaks bitterly of the living death of her marriage with Dan Burke, 'an old man, and an odd man' for whom 'maybe cold would be no sign of death . . . for he was always cold, every day since I knew him . . . and every night, stranger . . .'.[18] It is suggested that Nora has sought escape with Patch Darcy from that living death, and she looks forward to a new marriage with the younger Michael Dara. The collaboration between men to exclude and suppress women whenever their own interests and security are in question is sharply satirized in the closing scenes where Dan Burke and Michael Dara settle down together to enjoy 'a quiet life'.[19] Nor can we see her departure with the Tramp as more than a bravely poetic gesture born of necessity, given her knowledge of the harsh reality of a tramp's life and his collaboration with Dan Burke in the plan to catch Nora betraying him with Michael Dara so that he can give her a sound beating.

This closing scene is echoed in the last lines of *The Playboy* when, as another pair of wanderers, Christy and his father, depart to 'go romancing through a romping lifetime', Michael Flaherty commands his daughter to draw drinks for himself and Shawn, her 'quiet' suitor. 'By the will of God', says Michael, 'we'll have peace now for our drinks.' Shawn invokes yet another patriarchal authority to endorse a return to the pallid future destined for Pegeen at the beginning of the play:

> It's a miracle Father Reilly can wed us in the end of all, and we'll have none to trouble us when this vicious bite is healed.

The comic and ironic tone which has dominated *The Playboy* is superseded and cut off in its closing tableau by an image and cry more tragic than comic:

> *Pegeen:* [Hitting him a box on his ear.] Quit my sight. [Putting her shawl over her head and breaking out into wild lamentations.] Oh, my grief, I've lost him surely. I've lost the only Playboy of the Western World.

That final tableau of a young Irish woman, shawl over her head, keening, evokes many an Irish political cartoon of Erin or Irish womanhood, and focuses the way in which *The Playboy* links the economic and sexual oppression *within* Irish rural communities as portrayed in *The Shadow of the Glen* to the psychology of the nationalist drama with its father/son conflict. The series of conflicts between Christy and his father is juxtaposed with the submission of Shawn to Father Reilly and the authority of another alien patriarch, the Pope. Only through defying and finally subduing his father can Christy become 'a likely man'. Pegeen becomes a figure of Irish womanhood and Ireland longing for defiant sons to cast off the authority of the fathers, including her own and Father Reilly's, and her name suggests the Pagan spirit which for Synge was the true Irish spirit covered by only a thin veneer of Catholicism.[20] But in the end, it is Christy who benefits; the situation of the peasant community and Pegeen are left unchanged. It is perhaps this suggestion, as well as Synge's recognition of women's sexuality and desire (expressed by all the women in the play, including the Widow Quinn), which provoked the dismay and outrage which erupted in the riots at the Abbey Theatre when *The Playboy* was first performed.

Synge's next and final play, *Deirdre of the Sorrows*, moves even closer to a linking of the plight of woman with the plight of Ireland. I have already indicated Deirdre's significance as an iconic figure in theatre of the literary revival, her story the subject of a multitude of plays. Like Nora she has been pledged to a possessive old man, Conchubar, but he has been able to keep her hidden not only from other men, but also from knowledge of her own identity and desire. She begins by being seen as part of nature, a nymph-like figure who identifies with the natural world around her; the intrusion of the Sons of Usna allows her to see herself not only as an object of desire, but to discover herself as desiring, a discovery which creates disaster for herself and for all around her. As Ann Saddlemyer points out, the use of the saga material, set in a pre-Christian and distant era, allowed Synge to set aside his comic theme of the conflict between natural instinct and Christian–Victorian convention: 'here naked passions war for possession of the same object – possession of Deirdre.'[21] The story and the play begin with Deirdre owned as the patriarch ruler Conchubar's chattel, defined by him as his bride-to-be. She is freed by the Sons of Usna, and it is significant that both in the saga material and

Synge's play their status as 'sons' is always part of their collective titling. In committing themselves to freeing Deirdre from Conchubar, however, they are also committing themselves to becoming part of the legend, in which like the men who fight for Cathleen ni Houlihan, they shall be 'young for ever', and part of 'a story will be told for ever'.[22] Like Cathleen, Deirdre as their queen and bride calls upon them to choose this fate.

It would, of course, go against the grain of Synge's writing to read any of his plays, including *Deirdre of the Sorrows*, as mere allegory. Indeed, much of the interest of his last play arises from his counterpointing of the legendary and the heroic with the realistic and anti-heroic, from the ambivalence of the characters towards playing out the roles assigned them, and their struggle for the power to define those roles, and imbue them with their own meaning. If Deirdre cannot resist being made into a Queen, she will clothe herself and invest herself with her own authority, not merely an authority given her by Conchubar. It is a play which also carries echoes of ritual seasonal drama; the struggle against Conchubar is also a struggle of youth against old age, of Spring against Winter, and of youthful, especially female desire, to seek its own expression, and of an individual woman to govern her own destiny. Nevertheless, the recurring literary use of the Deirdre story as part of the effort to recover an Irish national identity also means that this play cannot be entirely disassociated from the national conflict, and it does contain verbal, thematic and imagistic echoes of Yeats's *Cathleen ni Houlihan*.

Synge's dramatization of the Deirdre legend differs most strongly from Yeats's, performed at the Abbey Theatre two years earlier, in its emphasis on her dual character as child of nature and as Queen. The imagery and the idiom of the language she uses is, like that of all Synge's peasant characters, drawn from the natural landscape and speech of Irish rural life. And by staging Deirdre's first meetings with the Sons of Usna and their life in exile, Synge gives prominence to Deirdre's role in creating her own destiny and her rebellion against Conchubar's possessiveness, as well as the rebellion of the young men, the Sons, against the father-figure. Yeats's *Deirdre* concentrates all the action in the last hours of Deirdre's life, her entrapment by Conchubar, and her resolution to redeem some nobility within the narrow confines of the cage Conchubar has caught her in. Whereas Synge's Deirdre is a young country girl who takes on the role of a queen, and whose fears of old age and loss of love lead her and her lovers to face an early death, Yeats's Deirdre is a queen who plays the role of a young and wanton girl in order to deceive Conchubar, and who is led reluctantly to her fate by the insistence of Naoise and Fergus on the primacy of male trust and comradeship over womanly intuition and experience. Synge's Deirdre is portrayed as one who is most at home in and as having a kinship with Irish land and landscape, like Maurya and Nora and Pegeen, and like Christy Mahon. Yeats gives his queen fewer local affinities. She is 'of mysterious origin', and like Helen of Troy, 'she'd too much beauty for good luck'.[23] She becomes one of a series of beautiful women victims caught up unwittingly in the nightmare of a history seen as repetition, portrayed in Yeats's drama and poetry – Helen of Troy, Leda, and Maud Gonne. Whereas Synge's Deirdre weaves her own tapestry foretelling her meeting with the Sons of Usna, and goes to meet her destiny, Yeats's Deirdre plays out the roles assigned her by Naoise, who casts her in the role of Lugaidg Redstripe's wife and sets her to playing chess with him as they did while they awaited their betrayal.[24]

In both plays, however, the end is death and destruction for all but Conchubar. Ultimately, the ancient tragedies as well as the contemporary comedies suggest pessimism: the revolt of the sons will leave Ireland and Irishwomen doomed or unchanged, and the old men in charge. At best, the revolts are a poetic gesture, creating yet another story which 'will be told forever', benefiting artists and musicians rather than the characters involved. Yet, although these women are portrayed as victims, they are also represented as the cause, both witting and unwitting, of destruction. The dual character of helpless woman and *femme fatale* is seen not only in the two aspects of *Cathleen ni Houlihan* but also in the Deirdre figure, and in Yeats's characterization of Maud Gonne as a second Helen of Troy who is a helplessly destructive victim of her own beauty:

> 'No Second Troy'
> Why should I blame her that she filled my days
> With misery, or that she would of late
> Have taught to ignorant men most violent ways,
> Or hurled the little streets upon the great,
> Had they but courage equal to desire?
> What could have made her peaceful with a mind
> That nobleness made simple as a fire,

With beauty like a tightened bow, a kind
That is not natural in an age like this,
Being high and solitary and most stern?
Why, what could she have done, being what she is?
Was there another Troy for her to burn?[25]

Gaelic Ireland and Easter, 1916

Founded in 1893 by Eoin MacNeil, the Gaelic League attracted
writers involved in the National Literary Society and the Irish
Literary revival, including the League's founding and perennial
president, Douglas Hyde, but it also appealed to a much wider
constituency. Seamus O'Neill asserts: 'No other organization has
had as great an effect on the cultural and political history of Ireland
as the Gaelic League. From the first, it attracted a support that
none of the other language societies had enjoyed.'[26] Like the
Literary Society, it gained momentum from the energies displaced
by a general disillusion with political activity following Parnell's
death in 1891. Unlike the antiquarian societies which had preceded
it, with their emphasis on Irish language and civilization as things
of the past to be rediscovered with nostalgia, the Gaelic League
emphasized renewal. Irish customs, Irish crafts, and, above all, the
Irish language, should again become living, and the Gaelic League
encouraged new writing in Irish. Douglas Hyde himself wrote
poetry, prose and drama in Irish, and argued that the recovery of
Irish as a living language was necessary for the 'De-Anglicisation'
of Ireland and the creation of a separate and 'genuine' Irish identity
involving a resurrection of the 'Gaelic past which, though the Irish
race does not recognize it just at present, is really at the bottom of
the Irish heart . . . In order to de-Anglicise ourselves, we must at
once arrest the decay of our language.'[27] Among the many young
people who responded to this call was Patrick Pearse.

Padraic Pearse had begun to learn Irish while still at school, and
joined the Gaelic League in 1896. In the same year he was
co-founder and president of a group called The New Irish Literary
Society. (Whether in ignorance of, indifference to or as a challenge
to the National Literary Society founded by Yeats and Hyde is not
known. Certainly it differed somewhat from the National Literary
Society in its emphasis on Gaelic literature, and also in its
predominantly Catholic, rather than Protestant, leadership.) The

members also included Pearse's sisters, Margaret and Mary Bridget, who contributed to musical and recitation events, as well as to the size of Padraic's audience for recitations from Shakespeare (he played Hamlet and Mark Antony). Pearse also gave a series of three lectures in 1897 on Gaelic language and literature. In seconding a vote of thanks after his brother Willie had given a paper on Cuchulain and the Red Branch Cycle, Pearse declared that 'the noble personality of a Cuchulainn forms a true type of Gaelic nationality, full as it is of youthful life and vigour and hope'.[28]

In 1907, Pearse's sister Margaret founded a school for infants. The school was short-lived, but may have given Pearse the inspiration to develop his own project for an 'Irish-Ireland' school for Catholic boys the following year. The prospectus for St Enda's school stated that it would promote the Christian virtues of purity, temperance, fortitude, triumph and loving-kindness', as well as 'a manly self-reliance', and patriotism. The Irish prospectus elaborated on this last virtue, saying that the school would attempt 'to inculcate in [its pupils] the desire to spend their lives working hard and zealously for their fatherland and, if it should ever be necessary, to die for it'.[29] The motto of the school was taken from a saying ascribed to Cuchulain: 'I care not though I live but one day and one night, if only my fame and my deeds live after me.' Pearse wrote in the school paper that he and his pupils must 'seek to recreate and perpetuate in Eire . . . the high tradition of Cuchulainn, better is short life with honour than long life with dishonour'.[30] According to Pearse's pupil, Desmond Ryan, Cuchulainn became 'an important if invisible member of the staff' at St Enda's.[31] As McCartney points out: 'The image of Cuchulainn strapped to a post and shedding his life's blood in the defense of his people while a torpor hung over their minds did much to inspire the blood-sacrifice doctrine of the 1916 leaders.'[32] This doctrine, very evident in Pearse's writings, was also shared by Plunkett, MacDonagh, MacDermott and even Connolly. It was linked to the cult of a personified Mother Eire, and is seen in the language of the 1916 Proclamation. At St Enda's school, an allegorical painting by Beatrice Elvery (later Lady Glenavy) depicted Cathleen ni Houlihan as a hooded figure, with a child on her knee, 'presumably Young Ireland', and behind her a ghostly crowd of martyrs, patriots, saints and scholars. Maud Gonne had bought this picture and presented it to St Enda's College: 'I met one of the boys from the school and he told me that the picture had inspired him "to die for Ireland". I was shocked at the thought that my rather banal and sentimental picture might, like Helen's face, launch ships and burn towers.'[33] There were also paintings by Jack B. Yeats, AE, stained glass windows by Sarah Purser, and a sculpted panel by Edwin Morrow showing the boy Cuchulain taking arms, framed by the motto quoted above. Pearse's own poetry in Irish, discussed in Chapter One, combines invocations to the traditional imagery of 'Mother Ireland' with the iconography and phraseology of addresses to Mother Church and the Blessed Virgin Mary.

Like Yeats's Cathleen ni Houlihan, the female figures in Pearse's poetry are abstract and asexual. The linking of the virtues of purity and patriotism, common to the English Boy Scout movement and the Irish Fianna alike, was reinforced in Ireland by the ardent Catholicism of that majority of Irish nationalists for whom adherence to the Catholic Church and Irish identity were inseparable. The riots caused by the first production of *The Playboy of the Western World* illustrate the growing gap between the notion of a national theatre and literature held by Anglo-Irish leaders of the revival – Yeats, Synge and Lady Gregory – and the 'Gaelic Leaguers', so violently rejected by Synge in this 1907 letter as indulging in 'the hysteria of old women's talk':

> I believe the nation that has made a place in history by seventeen centuries of manhood, a nation that has begotten Grattan and Emmet and Parnell will not be brought to complete insanity in these last days by what is senile and slobbering in the doctrine of the Gaelic League. There was never till this time a movement in Ireland that was gushing, cowardly and maudlin, yet now we are passing England in the hysteria of old women's talk . . . there is more in heaven and earth than the weekly bellow of the Brazen Bull-calf and all his sweaty gobs, or the snivelling booklets that are going through Ireland like the scab on sheep.[34]

Synge's own almost hysterical affirmation of 'seventeen centuries of [Irish] manhood' now threatened by effeminacy and its extreme opposite, the bestial Bull-calf, echoes the racial categories and dichotomies established by English journalists and cartoonists, and will be echoed again in many of Yeats's later poems.

Outraged disapproval of *The Playboy* was voiced by many members of the Gaelic League, including Maud Gonne and Patrick

Pearse. The reactions it caused can be ascribed in part to the violence of its language and realistic action, unusual in any theatre in 1907, and also to the perceived contempt for Catholic sensibilities. That this outrage came to focus on what was claimed to be an 'insult to Irish womanhood' is not surprising, given the constant convergence between images of Ireland, images associated with the Catholic Church, and the ideal of Irish womanhood. All three were seen as the inspiration and touchstone of Irish manhood and identity; the violation of one was the violation of all, and a source of humiliation to the men whose duty was to protect and sustain them. Marx's comparison and comment are pertinent here:

> A nation and a woman are not forgiven the unguarded hour in which the first adventurer that came along could violate them. The riddle is not solved by such turns of speech, but merely formulated differently.[35]

While the 'cult of Cuchulain' particularly influenced the nationalist military movement, the Gaelic revival also coloured the socialist movement, and helped to link socialists like Connolly with the nationalists. Donal McCartney claims that Connolly 'accepted a glorified picture of early Irish society' from Alice Stopford Green 'who in her turn owed much that was scholarly in her work to MacNeil, described by many as the driving force behind the Gaelic League'.[36] Connolly saw capitalism as a foreign intrusion in a society which had been marked by independence, equality, democracy and communal ownership, and he looked forward to the 're-conversion of Ireland to the Gaelic principle of common ownership'.[37] Larkin sent his boys to St Enda's school, as also did W.P. Ryan. Both Connolly and Ryan dismissed Grattan's parliament as a model for the future nation. However, there were also important differences in the vision and rhetoric of Pearse and Connolly which bear on the role of women in their revolutionary movements and in their envisioned future Ireland. Pearse's vision sets up a clear division between an active male warrior Cuchulain who fights for his country, and dies for it, a Christlike redeemer and Messiah which is also by traditional iconography male, and the passive female figure of Mother Ireland who waits to be redeemed, or perhaps inspires, and then accepts the sacrifice of her sons. Pearse offered no role for women in either his educational or his military practice and philosophy. In contrast, women actively participated in Connolly's Irish Citizen Army (ICA). Countess

Markievicz was a member of the council of four which decided on its formation; she became its co-treasurer, wore the uniform, and was second-in-command of the group which occupied St Stephen's Green on Easter Monday. Dr Kathleen Lyn gave lessons on first aid, while Helena Moloney taught girls to drill and do rifle practice under the auspices of the ICA. Connolly also put much energy into the women's trade union movement, encouraging and speaking his strong support at meetings of the female mill workers and setting up a textile workers' section of the ITGWU. Connolly's rhetoric and iconography are not focused on a single male and single female figure; his discourse is in terms of a social *group*, a vision of 'an Ireland ruled by Irish men *and* women, sovereign and independent from the centre to the sea' (my emphasis).[38] Connolly wrote:

> In Ireland the women's cause is felt by all Labour men and women as their cause; the Labour cause has no more earnest and whole-hearted supporters than the militant women. . .
>
> The worker is the slave of capitalist society, the female worker is the slave of that slave. In Ireland that female worker has hitherto exhibited, in her martyrdom, an almost damnable patience. She has toiled on the farms from her earliest childhood, attaining usually to the age of ripe womanhood without ever being vouchsafed the right to claim as her own a single penny of the money earned by her labour, and knowing that all her toil and privation would not earn her the right to the farm which would go without question to the most worthless member of the family, if that member chanced to be the eldest son.[39]

Connolly goes on to lament the collusion between peasantry and the clergy in regarding women as mere tools 'with which to work the farm' and get money, and the influence of the clergy – of all denominations – in teaching women to accept a position of social inferiority through insistence on 'duty'. The laws of primogeniture and inheritance by the eldest son were in Connolly's view institutions linked to capitalism, and did not according to him exist in pre-colonial Erin. And he was particularly scathing about the contradiction between the official statements upholding the 'sacredness' of home and family, and the necessity of 'protecting' women, and the fact that an overwhelming number of young untrained women were forced to emigrate as their elder brothers took over the farms, or to seek work in the most arduous and unskilled workshops and factories of Belfast and Dublin in order to help support their families.[40]

The movements that came to be led and emblematized by Pearse and Connolly differed with regard to their ideologies concerning the ultimate direction of the nation and the roles of men and women in liberation and formation. Nevertheless, they were linked by constituencies which were mainly Catholic, and which scarcely questioned the interrelationship between Irish identity and Catholicism. Moreover, both were mainly urban, and neither had a base in the Anglo-Irish Protestant landowning class which had nurtured Yeats and the other founders of the Irish Literary Theatre and the Abbey Theatre.

CHAPTER FOUR

Urban Women and Catholic Ireland:

James Joyce

James Joyce was a product of that emergent Catholic bourgeoisie so much distrusted by Yeats and Synge. Worse still, he was a Dubliner born and bred, and hence written out of the cultural nationalist movement which defined the essential Ireland in terms of those who lived on the land, whether as landlords or peasants. Like Synge, he rejected the 'Cuchulanoid' notion of Irish literature, thus dismissing not only the heroic mode but also the Celtic saga as his chief source material. He replaced it not with the rural folk tradition but with the urban one, defiantly asserting the place of his own Dublin Catholic world in the definition of Irishness. The title of his first attempt at a novel, *Stephen Hero*, announces with its emphasis on a contemporary man like himself, a product of English, European and Irish cultures, his challenge to the cultural nationalist heroic mode espoused by Yeats. This challenge is elaborated with greater complexity and maturity in his choice of Leopold Bloom, an Irish Jew, as the everyday hero of *Ulysses*.

Joyce cut and rewrote the 900 or more pages of *Stephen Hero* as *A Portrait of the Artist as a Young Man*, the first page and a half of which serves as a kind of overture to the whole novel, introducing the leitmotifs, the themes and images which will be picked up and elaborated in later sections, and which will give the narrative as a whole a particular kind of cohesion and resonance. Three main leitmotifs involve the division between male and female associations. The book, as is appropriate for a narrative which is to show

Stephen's developing identity and self-discovery of himself as literary artist, begins with story-telling: 'Once upon a time and a very good time it was there was a moocow coming down the road and this moocow that was coming down along the road met a nicens little boy named baby tuckoo . . .'.

One might notice several things about this opening – its conventional formula adhering to the norms of oral storytelling in English fairy stories ('Once upon a time . . .'); its subversive playfulness with language and whimsy; and its adaptation to audience. But also one might note that it is a male narrative, told by the father, and it has a male hero, with whom the son can identify. Here, as elsewhere in Joyce's fiction, and as in Synge's drama, language is a means of creating identity; a sense of self is constructed through language. But throughout the novel, speech, especially the power of narrative speech, is the prerogative of men, and particularly of fathers, whether in the series of anecdotes told by Simon Dedalus to his son, or in the powerful hellfire sermons of the preacher which take up a good thirty pages right at the centre of the book. Authority is also vested in the Church Fathers such as Aquinas or philosophers such as Aristotle who form the foundation of his aesthetic creed, the betrayed nationalist father, Parnell, with whom both Stephen and his father identify. In the end, of course, Stephen discards all of these fathers in his desire to fly by the nets of family, religion and nationalism, and turns to another mythical one, Daedalus, to whom he prays in the very last lines of the novel: 'Old father, old artificer, stand me now and ever in good stead.'

In contrast, the women in this novel are virtually speechless, with the important exception of Dante. While the father in this opening section is associated with story-telling and with the eye's visual imaging (he is seen at a distance, looking through a glass; he had a hairy face), the mother is associated with music, smell and touch, and also with the self that is experienced, which is known through the senses and feelings, rather than constructed through language. Where women do appear significantly, they appear as silent images and symbols – the figure of Mercedes, of the girl on the beach, the peasant woman Davin tells him of, and even Emma Clery, whose 'substantial image' and its surroundings disappear completely in the two poems Stephen writes for her. Whereas for Stephen the fathers and sons he encounters are all too real and his choice of an imaginary father is a deliberate means of escaping them, the distinction between imaginary and real women, whether Virgin Mary or whore, is often blurred. Eileen Vance, Emma Clery, the Tower of Ivory, and Mercedes all merge. When Stephen is older, the image of the peasant woman in an anecdote recounted by Davin becomes for him a symbol of the Irish race:

> The figure of the woman in the story stood forth . . . as a type of her race and of his own, a bat-like soul waking to the consciousness of itself in darkness and secrecy and loneliness . . .[1]

Later Emma Clery is absorbed into this image (or vice versa): 'She was a figure of the womanhood of her country, waking to the consciousness of itself in darkness and secrecy and loneliness. . .' (*PA*, 220) and he envies the priest to whom she listens rather than him. Although the reader can deduce that the reference here is to Emma Clery, it is significant that here and elsewhere she most often remains nameless, although the male characters are always clearly named. Here, this woman, who stands for all Irish women, becomes an image of the male artist's audience, whom he would wake and stir and bring to consciousness – herself batlike, hence songless and blind. Stephen as artist must speak and see on her behalf. In the final pages of the novel, Stephen, having abandoned the actual Emma to Cranly, thinks in the terms Yeats ascribes to the romantic artist figure, Seanchan in *The King's Threshold* (1904). Imagining the trivial chatter of the landed ruling class, Stephen longs to:

> hit their conscience or . . . cast his shadow over the imagination of their daughters, before their squires begat upon them, that they might breed a race less ignoble than their own. And under the deepened dusk he felt the thoughts and desires of the race to which he belonged flitting like bats across the darkened country lanes . . .
> (*PA*, 238)[2]

Woman for the would-be artist becomes a symbol of his imagined audience, whose soul he must awake, and indeed forge; she is also the symbol of his inspiration, his muse. Emma inspires his first poem, which we are only told about, and which ends with Stephen gazing at himself in the mirror; she also inspires the poem we see, and it is interesting how once again the woman herself, the inspiration, disappears into a recounting of the process of creation – as 'the word is made flesh in the virgin womb of the imagination'. The girl on the beach is for Stephen a crucial image, one which

confirms his intuitive discovery of his vocation as artist and gives
him a moment of ecstatic delight. She is his inspiration, and also
the embodiment of the art he aspires to create, a bird-woman, a
symbol, who combines both spiritual birdlike and material/sensual
qualities, escaping the dichotomy of virgin and whore that has so
far restricted Stephen's perception of women.

The important exception to all that I have been saying about the
women in *A Portrait* is Dante. She is the one woman to be given a
significant and memorable voice, both in the opening section and in
the Christmas dinner scene, although after that she disappears
except for a brief appearance in Stephen's fevered dream. Like the
men in the novel, she has strongly held beliefs with regard to both
nationality and religion, and she expresses them forcefully,
although her voice is finally overwhelmed by those of Simon
Dedalus and John Casey – overwhelmed mainly by a series of
anecdotes and ridicule. I have always found Dante a difficult figure
to place in terms of the structure and movement of the book as a
whole, not least because of the strangeness of her name, which is
neither Irish nor female. She is both powerfully dominant in the
young Stephen's mind, and yet marginalized ('Father Arnall knew
more than Dante because he was a priest but both his father and
uncle Charles said that Dante was a clever woman and a well-read
woman' *PA*, 10–11). As an unmarried woman, and a 'clever'
woman, she has no defined place in the Irish society Stephen knows
– and yet she is there. Her masculine name suggests that she is not
seen as truly female; and she is associated not only with Italy's
great Christian poet, but also with the Church – perhaps as Mother
Church, and possibly with Erin, or Cathleen ni Houlihan, that old
woman with the walk of a queen envisioned by Lady Gregory and
Yeats. Dante appears in the young Stephen's dream vision about
the dead Parnell 'in a maroon velvet dress with a green velvet
mantle hanging from her shoulders walking proudly and silently
past the people who knelt by the water's edge' (*PA*, 27).

It is important not to confuse Joyce's view of women with
Stephen's. *A Portrait of the Artist* is concerned with the developing
consciousness of a young man, mainly in his adolescence, who is, as
he himself says, created by Ireland, which like most societies at the
turn of the century was very much dominated by men. It is also an
exploration and exposure of the late nineteenth-century romanti-
cism and symbolism which so much influenced Yeats's early work

and which both Synge and Joyce were to reject. Certainly Stephen is presented with some irony, although also with much sympathy. Certainly, also, Stephen develops away from the complacent assumptions and clichés which typify the speech of his father, the priests who instruct him and his fellow male students; the book is a powerful critique of Irish male consciousness caught in the nets of family, religion and nationality. But because the work is concerned with Stephen's world and consciousness, women *are* peripheral, except in so far as they are the object of his adolescent desires for sensual or spiritual satisfaction. Readers are given little chance to garner an alternative view of male–female relationships, or of women in any connection other than with men. Yet there are one or two glimpses of the strains inherent in those relationships: the troubling reference to the mad nun whose screeching disturbs Stephen on his way to college; the little scene in which the whole hierarchy of male and female positions in the Dedalus family is revealed. Stephen is speaking to his mother who has rebuked him for being late for his college lectures:

> – Fill out the place for me to wash, said Stephen.
> – Katey, fill out the place for Stephen to wash.
> – Boody, fill out the place for Stephen to wash.
> – I can't, I'm going for the blue. Fill it out, you, Maggie.
>   When the enamelled basin had been fitted into the well of the sink and the old washing glove flung on the side of it he allowed his mother to scrub his neck and root into the folds of his ears and into the interstices at the wings of his nose.
> – Well, it's a poor case, she said, when a university student is so dirty that his mother has to wash him.
> – But it gives you pleasure, said Stephen calmly.
>   An earsplitting whistle was heard from upstairs and his mother thrust a damp overall into his hands, saying:
> – Dry yourself and hurry out for the love of goodness.
>   A second shrill whistle, prolonged angrily, brought one of the girls to the foot of the staircase.
> – Yes, father?
> – Is your lazy bitch of a brother gone out yet?
> – Yes, father.
> – Sure?
> – Yes, father.
> – Hm!
>   The girl came back making signs to him to be quick and go out quietly by the back. Stephen laughed and said:
> – He has a curious idea of genders if he thinks a bitch is masculine.
>
> (*PA*, 174–5)

As Stephen leaves the house he hears 'a mad nun screeching in the nuns' madhouse beyond the wall – 'Jesus! O Jesus! Jesus!'. 'His father's whistle, his mother's mutterings, the screech of an unseen maniac' are all voices which offend him, and from which he escapes into a self-contained world of art, cut off from his social world through nature:

> The rainladen trees of the avenue evoked in him, as always, memories of the girls and women in the plays of Gerhart Hauptmann; and the memory of their pale sorrows and the fragrance falling from the wet branches mingled in a mood of quiet joy.
>
> (*PA*, 176)

Such moments bring us briefly out of Stephen's consciousness and quite close to the world and technique of *Dubliners* which Joyce was writing at the same time as *A Portrait* (*Dubliners* was written between 1903 and 1910; *A Portrait* between 1904 and 1914). They recall those scenes of family life portrayed between the aunt, inebriated uncle and nephew in 'Araby' or in the closing section of 'Counterparts', where the drunken father vents his anger on his son in the absence of his wife. There are a number of scenes in *Dubliners* where the perception of women is quite similar to Stephen's in *A Portrait*, notably the young boy's infatuation with Mangan's sister in 'Araby', and his disillusion at the end, or Gabriel Conroy's fond imagining of his wife as 'a symbol of something' in a picture he would title *Distant Music*.[3]

But unlike such scenes in *A Portrait* those in *Dubliners* are set against alternative voices and consciences from which there is no escape. The structure of *Dubliners* is a very carefully built one, and like a musical piece has a number of movements within movements. There is the overall movement outlined by Joyce himself of childhood, adolescence, maturity and public life; but within that progression there are a series of triptychs, each beginning with a story which apparently focuses on one or more women, and followed by two stories which are either all male or which concern men in relation to women. 'The Sisters' is the first of these and opens the whole sequence, suggesting the ways in which women's lives are doubly constrained in colonial Ireland (their house is in Great Britain Street) as the servants of two masters, England and the Church. The title also evokes for Catholic Dubliners those women almost completely absent from Irish literature – the nuns who serve the priests. The remaining four stories which focus on women are 'Eveline', 'The Boarding House', 'Clay' and 'The Mother'.

There are ways in which the 'women's stories' are set up as both comparisons and contrasts with the men's stories: the constriction of Eveline's life devoted to the service of her father and brothers is imaged in the dusty window and curtains and the iron railings against which she presses her face, and contrasts with the freedom, however mismanaged, allowed young Jimmy Doyle after the race, and imaged in the exhilaration of the race itself and the young men roaming the streets. The seduction into crime of the serving girl by the Two Gallants is compared with the entrapment of Bob Doran by mother and daughter in 'The Boarding House', the sterile celibacy of Maria in 'Clay' compares and contrasts with the celibate and monklike existence led by James Duffy of 'A Painful Case'. The all-male world of electoral politics in 'Ivy Day in the Committee Room' is contrasted in 'A Mother' with the cultural nationalist scene, where women are allowed a means of expressing political sympathies. In these stories, Joyce often displays considerable sympathy and understanding for women, particularly those trapped in menial and domestic tasks. And, as others have shown, his depiction of the lives led by women in Dublin is concerned with the typical rather than the eccentric. Thus Florence L. Walzl has documented the sociological base for Joyce's 'moral history'.[4] The effects of the 1845 famine and English rule on the Irish economy, the resulting mass emigration and its exacerbation of the stagnant economy made Ireland one of the poorest countries in the world at the turn of the century; and 'for over a century after 1841, Ireland had the lowest marriage and birth rates in the [West], and the highest rate of unmarried men and women in the world'.[5] Marriages were often at a late age. In 1911, 70 per cent of males between 25 and 35 were unmarried, and when they did marry turned to women 10 years or more younger than themselves.[6]

Thus *Dubliners* is full of unmarried men and women, and of marriages which are the consequences of late and unromantic courtships and desperation. When marriages did take place, families were large, averaging five or more children. All these conditions, and their consequences for women and men alike, are recorded in *Dubliners*. Joyce's vision of family life, incorporated into *Dubliners*, is conveyed in a letter he wrote to Nora on 29 August 1904:

> How could I like the idea of a home? . . . My mother was slowly
> killed, I think, by my father's ill-treatment, by years of trouble, and
> by my cynical frankness of conduct. When I looked on her face as
> she lay in the coffin . . . I understood that I was looking on the face
> of a victim and I cursed the system which had made her a victim.
> We were seventeen in family.[7]

The roles expected of lower- and middle-class women, the jobs
available to them, the lives they led, are depicted with close
attention to sociological accuracy by Joyce. The same can be said of
his depiction of men, and the relations between men and women in
the Ireland of his youth. However, there are some interesting
differences in the way they are presented. Arguably, the women are
presented with greater sympathy, as victims of a system, or at
worst collaborators with it, as in the case of the two mothers, Mrs
Mooney and Mrs Kearney. They are also likely to carry a greater
symbolic weight, both in the minds of male protagonists and also
implicitly in their presentation by the narrator. Some of this weight
is suggested by their names – Eveline, Maria, Lily, Kathleen (who
is associated with Mr Holohan), the Madam (as Mrs Mooney is
termed) and 'a Mother'. Like the women in *A Portrait*, they
become 'figures of their type and of their race' – and also of woman
– and often their names become grotesquely unsuitable. Eveline is
shut out of any possible paradise because she resists temptation;
Polly is described as looking like a 'perverse madonna'; Maria
becomes a parody of the Virgin Mother; Kathleen is disowned by
Holohan. In contrast, the men have more everyday names, except
that many of them have the initials J.D., or are called James or Joe,
suggesting that they are in some sense a manifestation of their
creator James Joyce (with a D for Dedalus, the name Joyce used
for his first published stories).

The women in *A Portrait* are generally without names and
without speech; they exist within the limits of Stephen's imagination and consciousness. Women in *Dubliners* are seen both as male
constructs (as in 'Araby'), and as victims of colonial and patriarchal
rule, but they *are* given significant moments of speech or action
which disrupt the assumptions, the framework through which they
have been perceived. It is the aunt in 'The Sisters' who insists on
interrupting Mr Cotter's series of clichés to ask what he means.
The demented and enigmatic cry in Gaelic of Eveline's mother
haunts the reader as well as her daughter; Mangan's sister's, 'It is

well for you', her only words, reveal a wealth of hidden desire and bitterness concerning what freedom is allowed boys as opposed to girls; the newspaper account of Mrs Sinico's death, the painful actuality of her story told in another voice, cuts through the complacent self-assurance of James Duffy. But it is in 'The Dead' that women's voices and stories, untold as well as told, are given their most important space. Here Gabriel's often patronizing assumptions are constantly overturned, from Lily's bitter response to his remarks about her 'young man', to Miss Ivor's teasing, to Kate's anger at the Pope, to the final scene in which Gretta tells her story. In allowing Gretta's story and its effect on Gabriel to end the book, Joyce foreshadows the role of Molly Bloom in *Ulysses* as final voice (although unheard) which sets in question the male hegemony which has ruled her society and Joyce's book until that last episode.

Through Stephen as a type of the young romantic artist, Joyce proposes and questions the creation of idealized female figures often linked with Ireland, women who are 'types of Ireland' whose souls or consciences are yet to be formed by male artists such as W.B. Yeats and himself. But unlike Pearse or Yeats, Joyce cannot admire or affirm warriors or 'violent and bitter men'. In *Ulysses*, especially those episodes completed after 1916, one can read parodic and satiric versions of the nationalist narratives and heroics to which Pearse and Yeats were inclined. Both Stephen and Bloom detest 'physical force'; both try to resist it with reason and affirmation of love. Despite the slightly ignominious results of their resistance (Bloom is hustled out of the pub as a biscuit tin is thrown after him; Stephen is knocked out by a British soldier), it seems likely that Joyce is on their side. His 'violent and bitter men' are not members of the Anglo-Irish ascendancy, but Irish nationalists who articulate the cultural nationalism invoked by Pearse and others. Identified as 'Narrative Masculine' in the schema Joyce gave Gilbert, Episode Twelve in *Ulysses* ('Cyclops') satirizes and parodies the 'one-eyed' chauvinism and aggressive masculinity of 'the citizen' with his 'Gaelic speaking' dog. For the citizen and his cronies, Bloom's national identity and his sexual identity are both suspect. Bloom's Jewishness and his 'softness' – his refusal to participate in male rituals of hard drinking, gambling, and talking about female bodies – become targets for snide and vehement vituperation. Joyce, however, rejects the heroes of the Irish pantheon, from Brian Boru to Robert Emmet and Parnell, as subjects for celebration; his protagonist is instead Bloom, 'a womanly man', whom we first see in a domestic role, preparing Molly's tea, cooking his breakfast, feeding the cat, and reading his daughter's letter.[8]

Joyce wrote the Cyclops episode some time after the Easter Rising, and parts of it may be read as an implicit comment on that event and the attitudes which fostered it. In particular, the story of Robert Emmet, the epitome of the Romantic hero in patriotic Irish narrative, is mercilessly parodied and subverted. Robert Emmet had become even more popular than Deirdre as a subject for Irish drama, both nationalist and unionist, and is the central character in some forty plays, as well as poems and ballads by Thomas Moore and others.[9] In Dion Boucicault's *Robert Emmet* the eponymous hero chooses to die rather than accept a pardon, and in so doing leaves his earthly bride-to-be, Sarah Curran, for a divine one, whose iconography incorporates Cathleen ni Houlihan and the Blessed Virgin Mary. At the moment of Emmet's execution, Boucicault's directions for staging read:

> The wall behind slowly opens. A vista of pale blue clouds appears. The figure of Ireland clothed in palest green and with a coronet of shamrocks in her hair descends slowly and bending forward when she reaches the spot behind Emmet, she kneels. Two children at her feet, R. and L., draw slowly back the body of Emmet until his head lies looking up into her face.[10]

Lennox Robinson's play about Emmet, *The Dreamers*, staged in Dublin in 1915, has its hero declare that it is better to fight for Ireland than to die for her. Nevertheless it also has him die because Ireland is 'more to him than life or love'.[11]

For many Irish men and women, Emmet was a role model, a martyr for Ireland whose pattern they wished to follow. Padraic Pearse became increasingly attached to him as a heroic figure, replacing even Cuchulain as his inspiration after St Enda's School moved to The Hermitage, where legend had it Robert Emmet used to court Sarah Curran. Pearse wrote:

> Whereas at Cullenswood house I spoke oftennest to our boys of Cuchulainn and his compeers of the Gaelic prime, I have been speaking to them here of Robert Emmet and the heroes of the last stand. Cuchulainn was our greatest inspiration at Cullenswood; Robert Emmet has been our greatest inspiration here. In truth it was the spirit of Robert Emmet that led me to these hillsides.[12]

Three years later, he again eulogized Emmet more for the manner of his death than for his ideas or activities on behalf of Ireland:

> Here at St. Enda's we have tried to keep before us the image of Fionn during his battles – careless and laughing, with that gesture of the head, that gallant smiling gesture, which has been an eternal gesture in Irish history; it was most memorably made by Emmet when he mounted the scaffold in Thomas Street, smiling, he who had left so much, and most recently by those three who died at Manchester. I know that Ireland will not be happy again until she recollects that old proud gesture of hers, and that laughing gesture of a young man that is going into battle or climbing to a gibbet.[13]

The example of Robert Emmet and Sarah Curran, wed on the eve of his execution, may also have inspired Joseph Mary Plunkett, one of the signatories to the Easter 1916 Proclamation, who married the artist Grace Gifford in Kilmainham Gaol the day before he was executed. And Joyce may have had both Emmet and Plunkett in mind when he has Leopold Bloom dispute with the Citizen about 'the point, the brothers Sheares and Wolf Tone beyond on Arbour Hill and Robert Emmet and die for your country, the Tommy Moore touch about Sarah Curran and she's far from the land'.[14] Joyce's attitude to such romanticizing of death is conveyed in his parodic account of his Emmet figure as all gallant smiling gesture, embracing his beloved on the scaffold as she swears 'she would never forget her hero boy who went to his death with a song on his lips as if he were but going to a hurling match in Clonturk park. . . Oblivious of the dreadful present, they both laughed heartily, all the audience, including the venerable pastor, joining in the general merriment.'[15] Sarah Curran's pathetic story and her later marriage to an Englishman are turned into farce, as Joyce has a handsome young Oxford graduate step forward and offer his pedigree and an engagement ring on the spot. Thus Emmet loses both his life and his love to the English.

Next to the 'masculine narrative' of the Cyclops episode is placed the 'feminine narrative' of Nausicaa, a pairing which illustrates in elaborate, subtle and tragi-comic detail Ashis Nandy's assertion that one of the effects of colonialism and the nationalist response to it is to dichotomize the masculine and the feminine, emphasizing their extreme differences rather than qualities that male and female may have in common. In contrast, Joyce pairs the 'womanly' male, Bloom, who 'mothers' Molly, Milly and Stephen, and the 'manly' female Molly, who imagines herself a man. As Suzette Henke remarks, 'The final chapters of Joyce's novel mock what Deleuze and Guatari identify as Oedipal imperialism by proposing an infinite regress of substitutability in the family's sex-stereotyped scripts.'[16] I would wish to give the word 'imperialism' here its full range of meanings and reiterate the connection between family and nationalist romance discussed in the previous chapter.

Like Synge, Joyce recognizes women as desiring, not merely desired subjects, imprisoned within domestic, social and economic strictures which intensify their longing and their fantasies, while making them the source and subject of male fantasies. Molly Bloom is presented as an artist whom we never see performing, a story-teller who does not herself voice or write her own story; her monologue remains unheard by Leopold Bloom. Yet this unheard, unliterate meditation is both the end of one fiction and the beginning of a new and more subversive one in which women may have a fuller voice.

CHAPTER FIVE

Shrill Voices:

Yeats's Response to the Easter Rising

The Easter Rising has been seen by a number of critics as the culmination of that particular phase of cultural nationalism epitomized by *Cathleen ni Houlihan* and the *Playboy* riots.[1] Towards the end of his life, Yeats was troubled lest that play of his sent 'out/ Certain men the English shot'. At the time, however, Yeats was taken by surprise, as indeed were many of his contemporaries who had believed 'Romantic Ireland dead and gone'. The Rising surprised the people of Ireland; the executions which followed it shocked and angered them, bringing a series of profound changes in Ireland's political life. The most immediate of these was the transformation of Sinn Fein into a party which unified, at least temporarily, a number of factions, and which became the receptacle of the newly intensified nationalist and anti-British feeling aroused by the aftermath of the Rising, by the British attempt to extend conscription to Ireland after 1918, and by the presence and actions of the Black and Tans in 1920 and 1921. The consolidation of support around Sinn Fein also consolidated the influence of the Catholic middle and working classes who had long been associated with it; the open conflict with the British in the years following 1918 hardened the divisions between those who actively supported the IRA and those who did not. Thus the fissures which had been papered over by the earlier phases of cultural nationalism through the appeal to a distant Celtic past and the dominance of figures such as Wolf Tone and Parnell as heroes for nationalists of all creeds and classes, became irretrievably apparent. Such fissures had begun to appear earlier, of course, during the early years of the Abbey Theatre and the conflicts over what the Gaelic League and Sinn Fein expected of a national theatre as opposed to the programme endorsed by Yeats, Lady Gregory and Synge as managers. Yeats's disillusion with the 'Celtic' phase of nationalism is expressed in a series of poems written between 1907 and 1914, many of which pour scorn upon the 'paudeens', his term for the Catholic middle classes whose supposed 'fumbling in a greasy till', and ethos of 'praying and saving', had, in Yeats's view, brought about the death of the 'Romantic Ireland' epitomized by O'Leary, Fitzgerald and Tone. The title poem for the volume *Responsibilities* and 'September 1913' both assert what Yeats termed 'an Irish phase', and a new definition of Irish identity and nationalism in terms of the Protestant ascendancy class which 'withstood James and his Irish' at the Boyne. The poem 'Responsibilities' also links the phase he has forsaken with the 'barren passion' (for Maud Gonne) that kept him from acknowledging his true ancestry and identity.

On hearing about the 1916 Rising, Yeats wrote to Lady Gregory:

> I had no idea any public event could so deeply move me – and I am very despondent about the future. At the moment I feel that all the work of years has been overturned, all the bringing together of classes, all the freeing of Irish literature and criticism from politics.[2]

As Cairns and Richards point out, Yeats's comments about 'the bringing together of classes' and 'the freeing of Irish literature and criticism from politics' is somewhat disingenuous,[3] since his most recent poetry has involved an explicit assertion of class identity and disowning of any middle-class 'taint', as well as outspoken comment on political values and decisions in such poems as 'September 1913', 'Upon a House Shaken by Land Agitation' or 'No Second Troy', where Maud Gonne *is* blamed because 'she would of late/ Have taught to ignorant men most violent ways,/ Or hurled the little streets upon the great'.

As Yeats claimed to 'free Irish literature and criticism from politics' he also sought to free beauty, especially female beauty, from politics. Behind the claim lay Yeats's own particular desire to create or restore a political order which could be rendered artistic – in Yeats's later poetry the desirable female body and the desirable body politic become analogous. Moreover, it is a body which does not speak about politics, which supports but does not contest. Thus, in 'Easter 1916', the shrillness of Constance Markievicz's arguing political voice is contrasted with its sweetness when, as a beautiful young member of the landed aristocracy, she rode in that most aristocratic of pursuits, the hunt:

> That woman's days were spent
> In ignorant good-will,
> Her nights in argument
> Until her voice grew shrill.
> What voice more sweet than hers
> When, young and beautiful,
> She rode to harriers?

And, in this same volume of poems, *Michael Robartes and the Dancer*, he prays that his daughter might be protected from the coming storm with its egalitarian and democratic impulse, a 'haystack- and roof-levelling wind, /Bred on the Atlantic', so that she may become:

> a flourishing hidden tree
> That all her thoughts may like the linnet be,
> And have no business but dispensing round,
> Their magnanimities of sound

Above all, he prays that she will not become like Maud Gonne, exchanging beauty for an 'opinionated mind' and angry voice:

> Have I not seen the loveliest woman born
> Out of the mouth of Plenty's horn,
> because of her opinionated mind
> Barter that horn and every good
> By quiet natures understood
> For an old bellows full of angry wind?

Published as a volume in 1921, five years after the Easter Rising, *Michael Robartes and the Dancer* seems more than many of Yeats's volumes a particularly strange assortment of poems which has, at first sight, no obvious rationale for its ordering. In looking at this particular volume as a *collection* one wonders why these fifteen poems are brought together and placed in this particular sequence. A number of the poems, such as the opening one and the Easter 1916 group were written much earlier and could have been included in the previous volume, *The Wild Swans at Coole*. Other poems, such as 'Nineteen Hundred and Nineteen', 'Owen Aherne and the Dancer', and 'All Souls Night' were composed prior to the publication of this volume in 1921, but were held over for inclusion in Yeats's next volume, *The Tower*, which was not published until 1928. Hence this is not a collection of the poems Yeats happened to have ready at the time, but a selection, placed in an order which is not chronological in terms of composition. One way of describing the contents of this volume would be that it begins with four poems concerning relationships between men and women, followed by four poems reflecting on the Easter Rising and those involved in it, followed by seven poems which alternate between meditations on politics and meditations on his wife and daughter. Thus questions about the nature of this volume as a collection also raise questions about the connection – or disconnection – Yeats was making between the personal and the political, between the role of women in relation to men, and the role of men and women in relation to society and politics as Yeats viewed them between 1916 and 1920.

Denis Donoghue has contrasted the volumes that precede and follow this one in the following way: '*The Wild Swans at Coole* is history consistent with symbolism; *The Tower* is symbolism, glancing ruefully at history.'[4] *Michael Robartes and the Dancer*, I would suggest, is largely concerned with questioning the relationship between the process of symbolizing, of myth-making, and history and biography, a questioning which begins with the opening and title poem, 'Michael Robartes and the Dancer', reaches its fullest poetic expression in 'Easter 1916', and seeks a tentative resolution in 'A Prayer for My Daughter'. This process of questioning is closely tied to the problem of interpretation, of how to *read* the myths, symbols and images which artists present us and which the world offers us. And the problem of how to read also involves the role of men and women as artists, narrators and readers.

John Unterecker has no doubts about the interpretation of the title poem, asserting that 'the dancer' of the title is 'determined – in spite of Michael Robartes' warnings – to educate herself in the most modern way', and that 'though incapable of understanding his ingenious explication of the allegory of the altar-piece (she reduces everything to simple-minded platitudes), she would nevertheless put herself "to college"'. He concludes that the strength of the poem lies in 'a beautifully balanced ironic tension: too stupid to realize that she does not need the sort of education she would have, the lady coyly rejects the only education that could possibly be of value to her', that is, to learn 'to think with the whole body rather than the mind'.[5] Although their tone may be less dogmatic and there may be less sympathy with the views of 'Michael Robartes', most other male critics and several female ones seem to read the poem more or less as Unterecker does. In so doing, they may, like the male speaker in 'Michael Robartes and the Dancer', bring forward 'texts to prove them right' such as Yeats's essays, letters and other poems, notably 'A Prayer for My Daughter'. Certainly Yeats repeatedly expressed the view that women should not go to college. In 1889, he wrote to Katharine Tynan:

> What poor delusiveness is all this 'higher education of women'. Men have set up a great mill called examinations, to destroy the imagination. Why should women go through it, circumstance does not drive *them*? They come out with no repose, no peacefulness, their minds no longer quiet gardens full of secluded paths and umbrage-circled nooks, but loud as chaffering market places.[6]

Forty-five years later, he wrote to Ernest Rhys concerning his daughter's education:

> I play croquet and am still able to beat my family; my domestic authority is therefore unshaken. My daughter is fifteen and has just discovered Shakespeare and at her own suggestion is writing an essay upon Hamlet. Her sole education is languages, the Academy Act school and my conversation. My son aged 12½ toils through the ordinary curriculum and will go to St. Columba's in a year or two and then to College.[7]

Before rushing to judgement, we should note the self-deprecating humour of the Yeats whose authority rests only in croquet playing, and remember Yeats's own unhappiness at and with school. In *Reveries Over Childhood and Youth*, he tells us:

> I was unfitted for school work, and though I would often work well for weeks together, I had to give the whole evening to one lesson if I was to know it. My thoughts were a great excitement, but when I tried to do anything with them, it was like trying to pack a balloon into a shed in a high wind. I was always near the bottom of my class, and always making excuses that but added to my timidity.[8]

Thus, the sympathy with Michael's 'toiling through the ordinary curriculum' and the suggestion that women are fortunate to escape the 'mill' since 'Circumstance does not drive *them*' is indeed heartfelt. And yet while noting that Anne is encouraged to read and write about Shakespeare, we might also notice the less conscious revelation in that sentence, 'Her sole education is languages, the Academy Act school, and *my* conversation' (my emphasis). Did she never converse with her mother, and did she learn nothing from her? We know that George Yeats was widely read, and that *A Vision* came from her mind in collaboration with Yeats's. Why then is she not mentioned as one of Anne's educators? Equally, one might ask why Michael is excluded from the kind of education Anne is given, and forced to submit to a process Yeats himself claimed not to believe in.

At first reading it may seem that the answer is suggested by the role of the woman in 'Michael Robartes and the Dancer': she is both audience and image for a work of art which fuses mind and body, subjective and objective being; she does not instruct or construct, but is instructed and constructed.

Identifying with the male speaker and assuming that Yeats and he are at one in doing so, John Unterecker sees the woman as 'too stupid' to value this, or any other instruction. But what if we identify with the woman speaker? What happens to the poem if we listen to the male speaker through her ears? At least we should remember that this poem is, after all, a dramatic dialogue, whose significance lies in its form and not just in the content of the male speaker's words. Viewed from outside, how do they come across?

In reading the poem there has always seemed to me a delightful paradox in that opening line, 'Opinion is not worth a rush;' for what statement could be more opinionated, and are not the series of declarations and assertions that follow mere opinions and 'half-dead thoughts'? And how can the speaker assert so positively that 'it's plain/ The half-dead dragon was her thought'? Bordone's painting of St George and the Dragon in the Dublin National Gallery shows a city, anxious citizens and a maiden in an attitude of fearful prayer in the background. In the foreground a knight on a white horse rides over a typically devilish and bestial dragon, as he thrusts his lance into its mouth. There is nothing in that picture to warrant such a confident symbolizing of the dragon as thought, to explain why it runs counter to traditional interpretations of this particular allegory, which is more often read as a vanquishing of the beast of desire. Throughout the poem, the male speaker's tone and rhetoric are bullying and dogmatic: 'But it's plain'; 'Bear in mind your lover's wage'; 'Go pluck Athene by the hair'; 'I have principles to prove me right'. The resort to an unnamed Latin text for his concluding argument seems rather lame after his rhetorical question and flourish earlier:

> For what mere book can grant a knowledge
> With an impassioned gravity
> Appropriate to that beating breast,
> That vigorous thigh, that dreaming eye?
> And may the Devil take the rest.

The woman speaker's responses to this barrage of words and 'proofs' drawn from a series of male artists and writers seem to me in their very terseness, subversive rather than submissive or stupid. Her 'You mean they argued', might be read not as showing her 'incapable of understanding his ingenious explication of the allegory of the altar-piece' but as all-too-clear an understanding both of the speaker's argument and the impetus behind it. Throughout the poem, her responses seem to me both incisive and deflationary, puncturing the inflated rhetoric not in kind, but with amusement and gentle irony. Ironic amusement not 'coyness' seems to me to characterize the tone of her 'My wretched dragon is perplexed' or 'They say such different things at school'.[9]

The fact that she has the last sentence, and one that is lightly interrogative in its implication, suggests that this poem which commences the volume introduces an open debate rather than a series of reiterated opinions. One may note that the next two poems are also dialogues, and that a number of others involve implicit dialogues either between two speakers or within the poet himself, as in 'Easter 1916'. A large part of the poem I have just discussed is concerned with interpreting works of art and texts; the question of interpretation, of how to read signs, sounds, symbols, is often significant in subsequent poems in this volume. I see the opening poem, 'Michael Robartes and the Dancer', as a poem which encourages the reader to be circumspect and wary not to take the individual poems at face value, but to read the volume as a whole as a continuing dialogue in which the status of signs and symbols, of words and rhetoric, must be carefully judged and balanced one against the other.

Even the title of this opening poem might encourage the reader to question, as does the woman listener and speaker, rather than simply accept. Why is it called 'Michael Robartes and the Dancer'? It alludes, of course, to the poem which closes the preceding volume, 'The Double Vision of Michael Robartes', which focuses mainly on the vision of a girl dancing between a Sphinx and a Buddha:

> O little did they care who danced between,
> And little she by whom her dance was seen
> So she had outdanced thought.
> Body perfection brought.

But there is nothing beyond the title of the poem I have been discussing to indicate that the woman speaker is or has been *a* dancer, let alone *the* dancer. Just as the woman speaker gently but effectively resists the submission and denial of thought that the male speaker seeks to impose upon her, so I would suggest the poem as a whole resists its title. The dialogue deploys a man and a woman, here in a particular historical moment (when this woman, and other Irish women are beginning to contemplate going to University), and in a specific place (the Dublin National Gallery which holds the Bordone painting of St George and the Dragon). The title refers to symbols which transcend time and space; Michael Robartes seeks to dictate the behaviour of women by reference to artistic images and allegories; the woman speaker and the poem as a whole, through its dialogue, question such impositions.

The three poems that intervene between the first and 'Easter 1916' are all concerned to some extent with the problem of interpretation, with reading the signs, and the interrelationship between imagination and reality. In 'Solomon and the Witch', Solomon interprets the cry heard by Sheba as the cry of the cockerel announcing the coming together of Chance and Choice, a moment when two lovers find that their idealized images of a loved one coincide with the real images they find. Even here there is a hint of subversion of the image of wise interpreter in that rather absurd list of sounds Solomon is able to fathom:

> Who understood
> Whatever has been said, sighed, sung,
> Howled, miau-d, barked, brayed, belled, yelled, cried, crowed,
> Thereon replied: 'A cockerel
> Crew . . .

Nevertheless, the images of Solomon and Sheba provide a model for lovers in the present. 'An Image From A Past Life' also involves a dialogue between two lovers, in which the woman fears the influence of the hovering image of 'A sweetheart from another life', described in the language of Yeats's earlier love poetry, with its imagery of flowing hair and pale hands:

> A sweetheart from another life floats there
> As though she had been forced to linger
> From vague distress
> Or arrogant loveliness,
> Merely to loosen out a tress
> Among the starry eddies of her hair
> Upon the paleness of a finger.

The man seeks to reassure her by declaring that these past images 'Even to eyes that beauty had driven mad', can only make him fonder.

'Under Saturn', the fourth and final poem in this sequence in which a man addresses a woman, is also concerned with interpretation, in this case an insistence that the woman has misunderstood the reasons for his sadness:

> Do not because this day I have grown saturnine
> Imagine that lost love, inseparable from my thought
> Because I have no other youth, can make me pine;
> For how should I forget the wisdom that you brought,
> The comfort that you made?

This eloquent tribute goes on to regret that it has taken the speaker so long to rediscover his true home in Sligo, and that his heart had swerved from its childhood purpose 'never to leave that valley his fathers called their home'. Yet, although the poem is addressed to a woman, and celebrates her wisdom, it is a monologue – the woman's voice is no longer heard in its own right, nor will it appear again in this volume. It is replaced by the voice of the 'labouring man who had served [his] people', acclaiming Yeats's return. Here private and political life, past and present, come into harmony, as Yeats the poet redeems the past and continues the social order and family life which belonged to his ancestors. Written in 1919, after the birth of his first child, 'Under Saturn' may be read in part as a counterstatement to the opening poem of his 1914 volume, *Responsibilities*, 'Pardon old fathers', where Yeats invokes his ancestors and laments his failure:

> Pardon that for a barren passion's sake,
> Although I have come close on forty-nine,
> I have no child, I have nothing but a book,
> Nothing but that to prove your blood and mine.

After this series of apparently personal poems, which celebrate the comfort and wisdom of a marriage partnership, and a return to the home and social order of his ancestors, the poem 'Easter 1916' at first sight seems out of place, with its political concerns and questions. This disruptive placing serves effectively to question the assumptions which underlie the preceding poems. That is, it questions the continuity of social order invoked in 'Under Saturn'; it questions the authority of the male interpreter who speaks in the preceding dialogues; and it questions the assumption that a personal relationship, and the relations between men and women, can be separate from what is happening in the external, public world. 'Easter 1916' can also be read in part as a response to another poem in the 1914 volume, 'September 1913'. Both poems are reactions to a specific political event, but 'Easter 1916' admits to a misinterpretation, a superficial reading of the political scene and of the men involved in it.

Written two weeks after the Easter Rising was put down, and during the executions of its leaders, the letter quoted above from Yeats to Lady Gregory mentioned that he was trying to write a poem on the theme, 'Terrible beauty has been born again'. Yeats's sense of despondency and failure, his claim that he had been engaged in an attempt to unify the classes and disengage art from politics has been commented on earlier in this chapter. The letter does, however, reflect a vision of social and aesthetic unity which 'Under Saturn' endorses, a state in which the private and the political are no longer at odds and where the present is rooted in the past. 'Easter 1916' – both the event itself and the poem commemorating it – comes as a disruption of that sense of continuity and homecoming expressed in the poem that precedes it. And here it is not his audience, the woman to whom he speaks, who has failed to read him correctly: it is Yeats, the poet, who has misread and misjudged those he spoke to and the time in which they lived:

> Being certain that they and I
> But lived where motley is worn:
> All changed, changed utterly:
> A terrible beauty is born.

Much criticism has been devoted to the analysis of this poem, demonstrating its complexity of imagery, moving from theatrical to natural to domestic, the expression of the interdependence between art and politics, the changing sense of the refrain, 'A terrible beauty is born'. What has received less comment is the question of why particular participants in the Rising are described and named rather than others. Fifteen men were executed. One of the first was Thomas Clarke, who was also the first signatory on the proclamation of Independence. Another of the men executed and also a signatory was Joseph Plunkett, a poet well known to Yeats. Yet neither of these men is mentioned. Connolly is named, along with MacDonagh, Pearse and MacBride in the closing lines, but not described with them in the second section of the poem. Perhaps the most persuasive reason for the choice of this particular group is given by David Cairns and Shaun Richards, who note that here Yeats acknowledges the now established place in the story of Ireland of the Catholic middle class: 'The group which, in "September 1913" Yeats had thought incapable of the romantic heroism of Tone, Fitzgerald or Emmet, had seized their tradition.'[10] Indeed, their urban and middle-class status is recognized in the opening lines of the poem, when he speaks of them 'coming/ From counter and desk among grey /Eighteenth century houses'. MacDonagh, Pearse, MacBride and Connolly all came from Catholic backgrounds, and made their living in the city. Connolly, of course, came from, spoke and wrote on behalf of the urban working classes and argued for a socialist Ireland.

One of Connolly's staunchest defenders, both before and after his death, was Constance Markievicz, who wrote a number of articles and pamphlets explaining and popularizing Connolly's particular brand of Marxism. This may account in part for the substitution of her description for Connolly's in the second section of the poem. But one might still wonder why she is given pride of place, particularly since she was not executed; she is the first to be described, and she is given seven lines, while Pearse receives only two, MacDonagh five, and MacBride four.

Yeats wrote this poem in September 1916, when he was staying with Maud Gonne MacBride. In her memorial essay on Yeats, she recalled the composition of that poem:

Standing by the seashore in Normandy in September 1916 he read me that poem; he had worked on it all the night before, and he implored me to forget the stone and its inner fire for the flashing, changing joy of life; but when he found my mind dull with the stone of the fixed idea of getting back to Ireland, kind and helpful as ever, he helped me to overcome political and passport difficulties and we travelled as far as London together. In London we parted; my road led to jail with Constance de Markievicz and Cathleen Clarke, but Willie's road was more difficult, a road of outer peace and inner confusion, discernible in his later work.[11]

In the letter to Lady Gregory I quoted earlier, Yeats referred to Maud Gonne's reaction to the Rising:

Her main thought seems to be 'tragic dignity has returned to Ireland'. She had been told by two members of the Irish Party that 'Home Rule was betrayed'. She thinks now that the sacrifice has made it safe.[12]

In the light of these quotations, it is possible, I think, to read the poem 'Easter 1916' in part as a dialogue with Maud Gonne, seeking both to express her thoughts, 'tragic dignity has returned to Ireland', and 'the sacrifice has made [Home Rule] safe', and to question them. So the poem first seems to endorse the change from a comic to a tragic vision of those involved, and then in the second half expresses ambivalence about the event, its necessity ('Was it needless death after all?'), and the consequences. If this is so, then Con Markievicz also becomes a surrogate figure for Maud Gonne, both of them women who are accused of betraying their beauty and their class (conveyed in the memory of Constance Gore-Booth riding to harriers) for commitment to a political cause and to the Catholic middle- and working-class leaders of that cause. The arguments of Michael Robartes have failed to silence their dragon thought, and it is interesting that the only voices referred to in the poem are those of the poet and the woman whose voice once sweet is now shrill.

The description of Constance Markievicz precedes those of the others for another reason suggested in a comment in his *Autobiographies*: 'The Nationalist abstractions were like the fixed ideas of some hysterical woman, a part of the mind turned into stone, the rest a seething and burning . . .'[13] As 'the dancer' is a symbol for the complete integration of thought and body, for the thought which has become body, and as she, like a beautiful woman, is a figure of the integration of life and art, so the 'shrill-voiced woman' is an image of all those, men and women, who have devoted themselves to abstractions and denied body, art and beauty. A further passage in Yeats's *Memoirs* suggests that he linked this kind of shrillness particularly with nationalists of the lower-middle class:

The root of it all is that the political class in Ireland – the lower-middle class from whom the patriotic associations have drawn their journalists and their leaders for the last ten years – have suffered through the cultivation of hatred as the one energy of their movement, a deprivation which is the intellectual equivalent to the removal of the genitals. Hence the shrillness of their voices.[14]

And in the *Autobiographies*, Yeats expresses his anxiety about the effects of political involvement on women:

Women, because the main event of their lives has been a giving of themselves and giving birth, give all to an opinion as if it were some terrible stone doll. . . We [men] still see the world, if we are of strong mind and body, with considerate eyes, but to women opinions become as their children or their sweethearts, and the greater their emotional capacity, the more do they forget all other things. They grow cruel, as if in defense of lover or child, and all this is done for 'something other than human life'. At last the opinion is so much identified with their nature that it seems a part of their flesh becomes stone and passes out of life. It was part of F——'s power in the past that though she made this surrender with her mind, she kept the sweetness of her voice and much humour, and yet I am afraid. Women should have their play with dolls finished in childish happiness, for if they play with them again it is amid hatred and malice.[15]

The passage is interesting and relevant to an understanding of 'Easter 1916' not only for its imagery of the stone as the abstraction in opposition to life, but also for its references to 'sweetness of voice' and to dolls and children. In 'Easter 1916', when the woman has ceased to be apolitical and has lost her sweet voice, then the male poet must take on the woman's role, murmuring,

> As a mother names her child
> When sleep at last has come
> On limbs that had run wild.

Having misread the signs, as the first two sections of the poem confess, Yeats retreats from his male role as interpreter. The third section is remarkable not merely for its complex and yet fluid interweaving of nature imagery contrasting with the urban imagery of the first section, but also for its resistance to detailed interpretation or symbolizing. Only the stone can be isolated as symbol, and this isolation is done in a perfunctory way:

> Too long a sacrifice
> Can make a stone of the heart.

That brief statement is all the interpreting we are given. As readers, we are left to deal with those twelve lines beginning with 'The horse that comes from the road' and ending with 'Minute by minute they live', lines surrounded by the symbolic stone, but in themselves irreducible to statement or allegory.

After that abrupt statement about the meaning of the stone, the poem moves to a series of questions: 'When may it suffice?', 'Was it needless death after all?', 'What if excess of love/ Bewildered them till they died?'. The poet cannot answer these questions, he can merely name the dead leaders and allow the popular and political symbols to take over, 'Wherever green is worn'. The two poems that follow, 'Sixteen Dead Men', and 'The Rose Tree', continue the process recognized in that closing section. Pearse and MacDonagh, poets and leaders of the Catholic middle class, have by their deaths made debate or converse between different groups impossible in the present because their deaths have so powerfully linked them to the past, making the emotive tradition of Lord Edward and Wolf Tone, both Protestant leaders, their own. 'The Rose Tree', an imaginary dialogue between Pearse and Connolly, draws on the populist rhetoric of Pearse in particular, and on popular symbols which are relatively uncomplex. I read this poem not as an endorsement of either the rhetoric or the martyrdom, but as a drama in which Yeats's own voice has been entirely silenced as poet and politician (or statesman) – an illustration of how 'the work of years has been overturned'. Nevertheless, it is a poem which both acknowledges the power of that populist tradition and refuses comment on it. Implicitly, the comment may come from contrast with Yeats's earlier poetry, where the Rose and the cross, or rood tree, are given much larger range of reference. Those references include the traditional Irish folk symbolizing of Ireland as a Rose, but also link it to Rosicrucian and other cultural symbols.

Explicit comment does follow, however, in the two poems which succeed these, 'On a Political Prisoner' and 'The Leaders of the Crowd'. When writing the first in 1919, Yeats wrote to his wife, 'I am writing one on Con to avoid writing one on Maud. All of them are in prison.'[16] This poem can be seen as an elaboration of the seven lines in 'Easter 1916' referring to Constance Markievicz, and responding to Maud Gonne, but here the attitude towards their politics and the politics of those with whom they associated becomes even more outspoken and venomous:

> Did she in touching that lone wing
> Recall the years before her mind
> Became a bitter, an abstract thing,
> Her thought some popular enmity:
> Blind and leader of the blind
> Drinking the foul ditch where they lie?

But here, as the poem itself is about to become a bitter and abstract thing, full of enmity, it recovers its balance in the memory of Constance Markievicz's past beauty and freedom of spirit imaged in the gull, 'Sea-borne, or balanced on the air', a beauty and spirit now imprisoned literally, but also figuratively in the prison of her politics. A similar movement is found in the next poem, whose scathing attack on the leaders of the crowd threatens to get carried away with its own fierce rhetoric:

> They must to keep their certainty accuse
> All that are different of a base intent;
> Pull down established honour, hawk for news
> Whatever their loose fantasy invent
> And murmur it with bated breath, as though
> The abounding gutter had been Helicon
> Or calumny a song.

Whether or not Yeats intended self-irony in those opening lines, the accusation he levels against those others seems equally applicable to his own attitude in this poem, accusing all who are different from *him* of base intent. But neither for him nor for those others can 'calumny be a song'. The headlong rhetoric is pulled short by a question, uttered not by the dancer of the opening poem, but by the poet himself:

> How can they know
> Truth flourishes where the student's lamp has shone,
> And there alone, that have no solitude?

The poet must not only seek truth in isolation, but also become his own audience.

The resolution of this poem marks also a turning from the past and from present disillusion to a concern with the future. 'The Second Coming' envisions how a masculine world, symbolized by 'A shape with lion body and the head of a man', will come into being, bringing an age which is merely objective, 'blank and pitiless as the sun'. It will be a world without either beauty or compassion – a world without dancers.

The image of the rocking cradle in Bethlehem catches up the imagery of mother and child in the last section of 'Easter 1916', and is in turn caught up in the opening lines of 'A Prayer for My Daughter':

> Once more the storm is howling, and half hid
> Under this cradle-hood and coverlid
> My child sleeps on.

Against the threats of 'roof-levelling winds' coming across the Atlantic from democratic America, against all the forces foreseen in the previous poems, Yeats seeks to protect his daughter, and in so doing to protect the feminine, or rather, to recreate and nurture it, so that the social order and the kind of art he desires can be maintained. For Yeats, the maintenance of that social order and the maintenance of a particular kind of femininity, and with it a particular understanding of art, are inseparable, and both the style and content of this poem are a monument to that art and that order. It is a poem which gathers up and reorders many of the references to sweetness, shrillness, and intellectual hatred, and the recurring images of wind, storm, and birds in this volume, and which reaches its focal point in the fifth and sixth stanzas, the two central stanzas in this ten-stanza poem:

> In courtesy I'd have her chiefly learned;
> Hearts are not had as a gift, but hearts are earned
> By those that are not entirely beautiful;
> Yet many, that have played the fool
> For beauty's very self, has charm made wise,
> And many a poor man that has roved,
> Loved and thought himself beloved,
> From a glad kindness cannot take his eyes.
>
> May she become a flourishing hidden tree
> That all her thoughts may like the linnet be,
> And have no business but dispensing round
> Their magnanimities of sound,
> Nor but in merriment begin a chase,
> Nor but in merriment a quarrel.
> O may she live like some green laurel
> Rooted in one dear perpetual place.

The first of these stanzas reiterates and celebrates the theme of those other poems in this volume which are a tribute to the wife who brought wisdom and comfort; the second takes up those images of bird and tree, sweetness and natural harmony, which surround earlier memories of the women who in Yeats's view have now bartered '. . . every good/ By quiet natures understood / For an old bellows full of angry wind', a metaphor which links those women to the roof-levelling and screaming sea winds of social change with which the poem begins. The image of the laurel tree and the elegant Jonsonian style, with its series of classical references to Helen, Aphrodite, and the Horn of Plenty, establish Yeats's wish to continue that European and English courtly tradition invoked in 'Michael Robartes and the Dancer'. It is set up in contrast to and defiance of the symbolic Rose Tree and the folk-song style, which belongs to the populist political and poetic tradition now taken over by Pearse and Connolly, and their successors.

'A Prayer for My Daughter', like the other more personal poems in this volume, moves away from the insistence of Michael Robartes that *all* a woman should strive for is beauty and that 'her lover's wage / Is what your looking-glass can show'. Indeed it warns against 'Considering beauty a sufficient end', or becoming misled by 'Beauty to make a stranger's eye distraught, / Or hers before a looking-glass. . .' It does endorse learning, though not in college, and certainly not in the thoroughfares, but in courtesy. Indeed, the imagery of the 'hidden laurel tree' contrasted with the 'wares / Peddled in the thoroughfares' brings back to mind that letter written to Katharine Tynan thirty years previously concerning women who go to college: 'They come out with no repose, no peacefulness, their minds no longer quiet gardens full of secluded paths and umbrage-circled nooks, but loud as chaffering market places.'

Nevertheless, 'A Prayer for My Daughter' does not represent a peaceful or comfortable resolution to the issues debated in 'Michael Robartes and the Dancer'. Rather, with its furious denunciations of 'the loveliest woman born' to which the poem returns again and again, even in the last two stanzas, it enacts that struggle between hatred and desire which Yeats's very isolation from the new social order forces him to recognize as the source of his poetry. Michael Robartes' vision of the dancer brought together a complete unity of mind and body, the artist and his art, male and female, nation and culture. For Yeats, Easter 1916 and its political con-sequences confirmed the disillusion and vision of disintegration and disorder he already harboured; it also brought a good deal of self-questioning. With that dream of national unity overturned, Yeats turned towards a slightly different concept of art, which acknowledged and contained that struggle and disunity. Henceforth his artistic symbols and images would be erected not as consistent with history, as Denis Donoghue described the earlier volumes, but in defiance of it. His poetry would recognize and embody a disjunction between beauty and wisdom; it would be written in isolation and adversity, learning at last 'that it is self-delighting, /Self-appeasing, self-affrighting'. When in the external world 'the ceremony of innocence is drowned', and 'All is ruin once again', only his poetry would remain as a memorial to the ceremony and custom which could allow his art a fitting home.

CHAPTER SIX

Unaccommodated Women:

Crazy Jane and Other Women in
The Winding Stair and Other Poems

Eight years after the publication of *Michael Robartes and the Dancer*, Yeats published another volume whose poems celebrated and questioned female desire, while regretting or dismissing the involvement of women in political activity. With reference to that second volume, *The Winding Stair and Other Poems*, and the poems included in the revised and expanded volume published by Macmillan in 1933, he wrote:

> 'A Dialogue of Self and Soul' was written in the spring of 1928 during a long illness, indeed finished the day before a Cannes doctor told me to stop writing. Then in the spring of 1929 life returned to me as an impression of the uncontrollable energy and daring of the great creators; it seemed that but for journalism and criticism, all that evasion and explanation, the world would be torn to pieces. I wrote 'Mad as the Mist and Snow', a mechanical little song, and after that almost all that group of poems called in memory of those exultant weeks 'Words for Music Perhaps'.[1]

In this last decade of his life, Yeats made a number of observations about women, including the feelings he believed that he shared with them. He exclaimed in a letter to Lady Dorothy Wellesley, written in December 1936:

> My dear, my dear – when you crossed the room with that boyish movement, it was no man who looked at you, it was the woman in me. It seems that I can make a woman express herself as never before. I have looked out of her eyes, I have shared her desire.[2]

And to his wife Yeats wrote: 'I want to exorcise that slut, Crazy Jane, whose language has become unbearable.'[3]

Together, these three quotations convey Yeats's excited recognition of the energy and vitality of the set of poems he had created in *Words for Music Perhaps*, but they also suggest some of the contradictions and ambivalences, the deliberate elisions and evasions which characterize the poems. At one stage he acknowledges the woman in him and rejoices in her presence, while at another he desires to cast out 'that slut' whose language, he claims, possesses him. And the energy of those songs is seen as destructive, capable of 'tearing the world to pieces' if it were not for journalism and criticism, which he describes as 'all that evasion and explanation'. These alternating attitudes and stances are found within the larger unit of the whole volume titled *The Winding Stair and Other Poems* in which the two sequences 'Words For Music Perhaps' and 'A Woman Young And Old' were published in 1933. This volume is in turn a response and complementary vision to the preceding volume, *The Tower*. Yeats told Olivia Shakespear that on rereading *The Tower* he was astonished at its bitterness, and sought in his next volume, *The Winding Stair*, to 'cast out remorse and affirm passion'.[4]

Within Yeats's system of metaphors and symbols, the tower is a masculine symbol, and it gives the title to a volume which contains a series of poems affirming, disputing or meditating upon 'violent and bitter men' and the fruits of male endeavour – the building of eighteenth-century houses, of towers, the imposition of authority, civil war, and political enmity. The opening poem of *The Tower*, 'Sailing to Byzantium', begins with a search for a place for old men ('That is no country for old men'), and suggests a tentative solution to the dilemma of the old man in the separation of body and soul, and the creation of a static, non-natural and stylized artefact, the golden nightingale. The volume ends with the sequence, 'A Man Young And Old', to which the final sequence of *The Winding Stair*, 'A Woman Young And Old', is placed as a response.

While the tower is a phallic symbol of masculine power and intellect, the winding stair is a symbol of female sexuality. This volume is mainly concerned with women, and with what Yeats perceived as the feminine in man, which he seems to identify with the desire to affirm and accept sensual life on earth rather than oppose and reject it. Thus, even though two of the major poems in this volume take the poet's own psychic history as their subjects, both 'A Dialogue of Self and Soul' and 'Vacillation' end not in the 'holy city of Byzantium' but in affirmation of 'this country' and this imperfect fleshly life, choosing self rather than soul.

The opening poem in the volume is the elegy 'In Memory of Eva Gore-Booth and Con Markiewicz', an elegy which counterposes an aesthetic vision of a past social and political order with rhetoric and imagery of anarchy and disorder. Yeats's assertions about the political activities of Constance and Eva Gore-Booth resemble in form and substance his dismissal of the 'shrill voices' and 'ugly bodies' who 'vex him to nightmare' in the earlier volume. No room is allowed for questioning either the description or the assumed causal relationship, an assumption which also trivializes the political ideology and activity. Nevertheless, the reader should be reminded that Constance Markievicz's involvement with James Connolly's socialist/nationalist movement, her writings in defence of his particular kind of socialism, her articles and lectures addressed to Irish women, her active support for the 1916 rebellion and subsequently for an Irish Republic rather than the Free State supported by Yeats, and her role as Minister for Labour in the Cabinet of De Valera *can* be described in terms other than merely 'conspiring among the ignorant'. Similarly, one could find terms other than 'some vague Utopia' to define the very concrete aims and activities of Eva Gore-Booth to improve the condition of women textile workers in Manchester, to gain women's suffrage, and to defend Roger Casement. But my main interest here is the nature and theme of the elegy, celebrating and lamenting beauty and innocence in face of the ravages of time and experience. Like 'Sailing to Byzantium', this poem is concerned with the contrast between youth and age, or rather between the beauty of youth and the ugliness of old age. If 'That is no country for old men', it is no country for old women either. The contrasting states of innocence and experience, youthful beauty and ugly old age will be dramatized again and again in this volume, and particularly in the sequences of poems in 'Words For Music Perhaps' and 'A Woman Young And Old'.

But in the opening elegy and in the other poems concerning women in the first half of *The Winding Stair* volume, innocence and beauty are given a political context. The beauty and order, the ceremony of innocence that surrounds that image of 'two girls in silk kimonos' which haunts Yeats, are very clearly placed within the context of 'that old Georgian mansion', and the political order with which it is associated. Here political order and aesthetic order are in harmony (as Yeats asserts that ugly politics and ugly bodies are also reflections of one another). The image evoked is a visual one, a 'picture of the mind', sketched deftly in a few strokes in the first four lines, a static picture (these four lines have no verbs), to which the poet returns as a focus for the poem and for his art at the end of the first section – an image and an order which he would maintain if only he could destroy time. As does Lady Gregory's house in the two Coole Park poems which occur later in this volume, Lissadell provides the artist with an order and a framework from which to view the outside world. Both feature windows (as well as Lissadell's gazebo) from which the poet can view the impending 'light of evening' and the 'darkening waters', so that he can order both the natural world before him and the social and political past which is evoked in the second half of 'Coole Park and Ballylee, 1931':

> A spot whereon the founders lived and died
> Seemed once more dear than life; ancestral trees,
> Or gardens rich in memory glorified
> Marriages, alliances and families
> And every bride's ambition satisfied.

Lady Gregory, like the Gore-Booth sisters in their youthful and ideal state, belongs *inside* the house, maintaining the decorum and social order within which artists and intellectuals could find their proper role:

> They came like swallows and like swallows went,
> And yet a woman's powerful character
> Could keep a swallow to its first intent;
> And half a dozen in formation there,
> That seemed to whirl upon a compass-point,
> Found certainty upon the dreaming air,
> The intellectual sweetness of those lines
> That cut through time or cross it withershins.[5]

Against these civilized, decorous and accommodated women, providing focal images of order and beauty in the first section of *The Winding Stair*, is set Crazy Jane, who initiates the sequence called 'Words For Music Perhaps'. If the Gore-Booths and the Gregorys are the nobles, Crazy Jane belongs to the wild and unaccommodated beggars, whom Yeats affirms in 'The Municipal Gallery Revisited':

> We three alone in modern times had brought
> Everything down to that sole test again,
> Dream of the noble and the beggar-man.

To the ordered and static visual images evoked in the elegiac poems, the intellectual sweetness which can 'cut through time or cross it withershins', Yeats counterposes the music and movement of the Crazy Jane songs, in which she also challenges time not with intellectual sweetness but with passion and energy. The Gore-Booth sisters and Lady Gregory are seen and admired *within* the houses which signify the social and aesthetic order to which they belong and which ideally they maintain, although Crazy Jane is perhaps foreshadowed in that imagined conflagration which ends that elegy for the sisters and Lissadell, and in the excitement in which Yeats is momentarily caught up. Herself an outlaw, Crazy Jane is never placed in or near any building. She inhabits nature and her songs defy classical and neo-classical order, and – above all – the representatives of Christian order. They are anti-social, anti-aesthetic; she and her songs are laws unto themselves. And while the earlier poems about women view them from a distance, these and the following sequence, 'A Woman Young And Old', give women a voice, speaking from and of their bodies and their desires. There are, however, significant ways in which those voices are controlled, and I shall come back to this point.

Like many of Yeats's later dramatis personae, Crazy Jane has her origin in early work and experience. The 1904 play, *A Pot of Broth*, which Yeats wrote together with Lady Gregory (it is in style and subject much more like her plays than his), includes two stanzas of a song addressed to Jack the Journeyman which Yeats said were taken down, words and music, from an old local woman known as 'Cracked Mary', 'who wanders about the plain of Aidhne, and who sometimes sees unearthly riders on white horses coming through stony fields to her hovel door in the night time'.[6] Almost thirty years later, in a letter to Olivia Shakespear, Yeats described 'Cracked Mary' as having 'an amazing power of audacious speech':

> One of her great performances is a description of how the meanness of a Gort shopkeeper's wife over the price of a glass of porter made her so despair of the human race that she got drunk. The incidents of the drunkenness are of epic significance. She is the local satirist and a really terrible one.[7]

As a number of critics have pointed out, the name Yeats gives his character was a commonly used and ironically abusive one. It was also the title of a poem by the nineteenth-century poet Monk Lewis. His is a sentimental piece, in which the speaker laments her plight as a woman who was seduced and then forsaken. Yeats may well have sought to reject such poetry and such attitudes – the passivity and self-pity of the woman, the sentimentality and neatness of style and form – in offering his alternative Crazy Jane with her fierce defiance.

The opening lines of the first poem, 'Crazy Jane and the Bishop', with startling effect introduce a new style and new persona to the volume:

> Bring me to the blasted oak
> That I, midnight upon the stroke,
> *(All find safety in the tomb.)*
> May call down curses on his head
> Because of my dear Jack that's dead.

After the elegiac and reflective mode, the dialogues and debates of the earlier poems, the rhetorical questions which are characteristic of the first half of the volume, a powerful contrast is set up with the strong beat, the commanding tones, the insistent and hard monosyllabic words and alliterative lines which characterize this group. (Compare, for example, the preceding poem, 'Stream and Sun at Glendalough'.) The opening lines associate Crazy Jane with witchcraft, the blasted oak, midnight and curses, all traditional features in the literature and folklore of witches. It is an association which is also picked up in the sixth poem of the series, 'Crazy Jane talks with the Bishop', where her lines allude to the lines of the witches in *Macbeth*, but with an important difference. For whereas the Shakespearian witches insist that there is no distinction between fair and foul, Crazy Jane argues that there is a distinction, but 'Fair and foul are near of kin,/ And fair needs foul'. Crazy Jane's argument in that sixth song is one that is verified by the experience explored and affirmed in the intervening lyrics, where she moves from being the 'terrible satirist' of the first song who pours contempt on the Bishop's appearance, with his skin 'wrinkled like the foot of a goose' and 'the heron's hunch upon his back', and the dismissal in the second song with a nonsense refrain, *'Fol de rol, fol de rol'*, of those who would reprove her for defying the careful design of heaven and following mere impulse in the form of 'a roaring, ranting journeyman'. Her third song elaborates in concrete terms the more abstract statement, her philosophy, stated in simple epigrammatic form, in the opening stanza of 'Crazy Jane on the Day of Judgement':

> 'Love is all
> Unsatisfied
> That cannot take the whole
> Body and Soul';
> *And that is what Jane said.*

Note that in this refrain, she is no longer qualified as Crazy. In contrast to the previous *Fol de rol* refrain which is merely and lightheartedly dismissive, this one calls for serious attention. The next two stanzas elaborate on and give concrete substance to the more abstract assertion of the first. In this poem also, the ironic, non-committal male refrain contrasts with the simple and direct series of assertions by Jane.

Thus from the bitter negation of the first poem and lighthearted dismissal of male myth and argument in the second, Crazy Jane moves in the third to positive assertion, in simple and direct language, of her wisdom. From there the sequence moves beyond the final 'day of judgement' statement to visionary experience, an understanding of the lasting effects of intense passion not merely on the body but also on the soul, which will continue to relive that experience, and to share in the visionary experience of others. In these songs too, the language and tone have moved far from the 'terrible satire' of the first to a more contemplative, though still simple, direct and finely attuned style:

> But were I left to lie alone
> In an empty bed,
> The skein so bound us ghost to ghost
> When he turned his head
> Passing on the road that night,
> Mine must walk when dead.[8]

Thus, when we come to the sixth song in the sequence, 'Crazy Jane talks with the Bishop', we are ready to grant her the right to talk with him, and to listen seriously to what she has to say. In the first confrontation, we may well have been inclined to see her as merely a witch, merely wild, merely bitter. Crazy Jane's language returns to the assertive and audacious style of the first poem, but now we can grant her the right to such assertion and boldness, particularly when answering the equally assertive and cruel language of the Bishop. In response to the Bishop's denial of the flesh and his insistence on separating the world of the body from the world of the soul, Crazy Jane pronounces forcefully from the authority of her own experience upon the inseparability of body and soul, fair and foul, and by implication in the first lines of the last stanza, of male and female sexuality and experience:

> 'A woman can be proud and stiff
> When on love intent;
> But Love has pitched his mansion in
> The place of excrement;
> For nothing can be sole or whole
> That has not been rent.'

In response to the Bishop's four lines, Crazy Jane is given two stanzas in which she more than matches his theological language and uses it against him. The last stanza echoes Blake's line in *Jerusalem*, 'For I will make their places of love and joy excrementitious', and also recalls the crucifixion on Golgotha, called the place of excrement; while the rending refers both to the rending of virginity and also to the rending of the veil of the temple which is associated with the death of Christ. The complex web of allusion, the puns on 'sole' and 'whole', force the Bishop to hear theological and sexual truth combined, and insists on a more complex theology.[9] This set of poems embodies a wisdom which is to be set beside that expressed in yet another sequence, 'Supernatural Songs', in which Ribh challenges Patrick – the set of songs which ends the next volume, *A Full Moon in March*. In both sequences, Yeats reaffirms his rejection of what he called 'an Irish Protestant point of view that suggested by its blank abstraction chloride of lime' in favour of the faith of the peasantry which 'associated eternity with field and road, not with buildings'.[10] As Jacques Berthoud has argued with reference to the 'Supernatural Songs':

> Yeats's so-called sexual metaphysics . . . is a means of bringing the natural and supernatural into unreductive balance. . . As a love poet, he had discerned the eternal within the temporal. As supernatural poet he celebrates the organic within the divine.[11]

'Crazy Jane talks with the Bishop' is the climactic poem of the sequence, the affirmation of wholeness, but it is not the final song. In 'Crazy Jane grown old looks at the Dancers', the bitterness of love, the dance of oppositions is reiterated in its refrain, '*Love is like the lion's tooth*'. The poem is founded on a dream Yeats had of such a dance, a dream whose significance he interpreted as 'Blake's old thought "sexual love is founded on spiritual hate"'.[12] Such knowledge, and Crazy Jane's envious but helpless witnessing of the dance, may be seen as the final stage in these songs of experience. For while the Crazy Jane songs can be seen as songs of experience, those that immediately follow them are songs of innocence, the voices of young romantic lovers who are encountering for the first time love and passion, and who dread the consequences of old age already experienced by Crazy Jane.

Why should Yeats follow a sequence spoken by Crazy Jane in old age with a sequence spoken by a girl and boy? One reason might be to emphasize, ironically, the gap between experience and innocence and their languages; another may be to offer these visions of love as two visions having almost equal weight, rather than a youthful one inevitably to be overcome by old age, as reversing the two sequences may have suggested. Their voices also are a means of ousting Crazy Jane, whose insistent voice had come to annoy Yeats, as he wrote in that letter to his wife I quoted at the beginning of this chapter: 'I want to exorcise that slut, Crazy Jane, whose language has become unbearable.'

With the exit of Crazy Jane, the voices of both man and woman, or rather girl and boy, intervene, not in argument, but in juxtaposition, both seeking an idealized love, a permanent beauty in the face of time. We have, in a sense, returned to the opening lines of the elegy to the Gore-Booth sisters, where the young have yet to encounter and to witness the changes wrought by a 'raving Autumn'. Now, however, the young and the beautiful are removed entirely from the social or political context implied by Lissadell and Coole Park. The dialogue between the girl and boy consists of seven songs, responding to the seven songs of Crazy Jane which precede them. These are in turn followed by a new movement, three retrospective lyrics, beginning with a woman's song of what are designated the three most profound and essential moments in her life – her child at her breast, the pleasure she gave to her lover, and her own fulfilment with her 'rightful man'. Then after the lovely lullaby, which elaborates the legendary moments when men such as Paris, Tristram and Zeus found contentment and protection in the arms of women, comes the more personal lyric, 'After

Long Silence', summarizing the 'supreme theme' of all those songs
which have preceded it:

> Bodily decrepitude is wisdom; young
> We loved each other and were ignorant.

With this lyric begins a series of songs, all in male voices, some
in the voice of a kind of male counterpart to Jane, Tom the
Lunatic, who also proclaims (in assertively phallic imagery) a
religion of the flesh:

> 'Whatever stands in field or flood,
> Bird, beast, fish or man,
> Mare or stallion, cock or hen,
> Stands in God's unchanging eye
> In all the vigour of its blood;
> In that faith I live or die.'

The first two lines of the stanza recall the opening stanza of 'Sailing
to Byzantium', but in that poem 'Fish, flesh, or fowl. . ./ Whatever
is begotten, born, and dies', are rejected rather than celebrated. In
the lyric preceding 'Tom the Lunatic', 'The Dancer at Cruachan
and Cro-Patrick', the dancer has also rejoiced in 'All that could run
or leap or swim/ Whether in wood, water or cloud'. Though Jane
and Tom share a similar vision, one important difference is that
Jane offers hers in opposition to an explicit or implicit male
audience; Tom speaks and dances in isolation. His poem is the
culmination of three which take the dance as their central theme
and symbol, the first maintaining that 'Those dancing days are
gone'; the next centring on the medieval lyric, 'I am of Ireland', in
which the singer pleads with 'one solitary man' who insists that the
time and the music are out of joint, to come dance with her in
Ireland. There are political implications in this female figure, like
Cathleen ni Houlihan, a representative of Ireland itself. Only out of
all political and social context, as a solitary man or woman in
nature, or caught up in the intensity of love between an individual
man and an individual woman, can dancing take place.

* * * * * *

The composition of 'A Woman Young And Old' was first begun
in 1926 together with the 'Man Young And Old' sequence.
However, the two sequences were not published together, but as

counterparts to one another at the end of *The Tower* volume in the
case of 'A Man Young And Old', and at the end of *The Winding
Stair* in the case of 'A Woman Young And Old'. In terms of dates
of composition, 'A Woman Young And Old' might be seen as a
revision and deconstruction of Yeats's earlier romantic love poetry.
In terms of its publication and placing in this volume after the
Crazy Jane poems, it can be read as a modulation in more decorous
and courtly tones of the drama played out by Crazy Jane as
projected witch – a modulation in which her energy and assertion
are toned down and partly tamed, and yet recognized as a *source* of
the sweeter lyricism of this second sequence.

The first poem in this sequence, 'Father and Child', begins not
with the woman's voice, but her father's:

> She hears me strike the board and say
> That she is under ban
> Of all good men and women,
> Being mentioned with a man
> That has the worst of all bad names;
> And thereupon replies
> That his hair is beautiful,
> Cold as the March wind his eyes.

This poem begins by dramatizing an attempt to assert patriarchal
authority, subtly linked to a wider religious concept of authority
through its allusion to Herbert's lyric of defiance and then childlike
submission to God the Father. (Herbert's 'The Collar' begins 'I
struck the board and cried, No more'.) The daughter's response to
her father's argument is as surprising to him as it is to the reader,
for it is a response which entirely disregards the framework, the
boundaries he has set up, in favour of an amoral and natural
aesthetic. Having freed herself from the boundaries defined by
male thought, the woman is able in the subsequent poems to speak
in her own voice, in a series which asserts and reasserts beauty and
pleasure, however idealized and however complex, as the ultimate
quest. As Gloria Kline argues in *The Last Courtly Lover: Yeats and
the Idea of Woman*, 'her images of sexual union are of the body in
cancellation of the mind'.[13] What the intellect knows, and the
terrible knowledge that Oedipus speaks at the end of the 'Man
Young And Old' sequence – 'Never to have lived is best, the
ancient writers say' – can be momentarily obliterated in sexual
enjoyment:

> O but there is wisdom
> In what the sages said;
> But stretch that body for a while
> And lay down that head
> Till I have told the sages
> Where man is comforted.
>
> How could passion run so deep
> Had I never thought
> That the crime of being born
> Blackens all our lot?
> But where the crime's committed
> The crime can be forgot.[14]

The woman's recognition of bodily pleasure, her acceptance of it as such without the necessity to pretend that sexual union must be intertwined with romantic sentiment, gives her an emotional freedom and autonomy that the male lover lacks. Thus in 'A Last Confession', she scornfully rejects his assumption that he has gained her soul as well as her body:

> Flinging from his arms I laughed
> To think his passion such
> He fancied that I gave a soul
> Did but our bodies touch,
> And laughed upon his breast to think
> Beast gave to beast as much.

Such attitudes, like those of the daughter in the first poem, were a strong antidote to the long-nourished view of women as sexually unresponsive, and indeed they reverse the usual view of male and female sensibilities in sexual relationships. In more decorous language, they endorse the sentiments of Crazy Jane. But unlike Crazy Jane, the speaker in this sequence seeks to go beyond bodily pleasure to find one who can master her 'dragon thought' and, like St George or Perseus, set her free from the rings of conventional thought and behaviour which entrap her. Michael Robartes is justified, and this young woman no longer resists his view, but speaks it for him. She triumphs when she leaves the rings of 'dragon thought' for the realm of the irrational and the miraculous:[15]

> And now we stare astonished at the sea,
> And a miraculous strange bird shrieks at us.

The romantic image evoked in that poem is continued and varied in other forms in two subsequent lyrics. 'Parting' is a variation on the aubade, a form associated with troubadour, courtly love poetry, but after a conventional development it is given a more unconventional ending in the woman's final words:

> I offer to love's play
> My dark declivities.

Then in the eighth poem, 'Her Vision in the Wood', the image of the *femme fatale*, the courtly lady who governs the troubadour's heart and to whom he devotes his life and art, is confronted and finally dismissed. Here the speaker sees herself as part of the throng of women imagined by 'a Quattrocento painter . . ./ A thoughtless image of Mantegna's thought', and realizes that Adonis is no external symbol, 'But my heart's victim and its torturer', as she is his. Freed from this obsessively romantic image, the woman is able to sing in simple language of 'mere bodily pleasure' and to mock men who cannot accept it as such. Yet ultimately she seeks a union of souls, and a union in which the man shall rule:

> But when this soul, its body off,
> Naked to naked goes,
> He it has found shall find therein
> What none other knows,
> And give his own and take his own
> And rule in his own right[16]

The sequence ends with the 'sweeter word' found when both man and woman can cast off 'this beggarly habiliment'[17] of old age, and join in that powerful and poignant chorus from the *Antigone*, which pleads that womanly love and compassion overcome man-created wars and enmities, a hope which is doomed as 'Oedipus' child / Descends into the loveless dust'.[18]

* * * * * *

In the letter to Dorothy Wellesley which I quoted at the beginning of this article, Yeats congratulated himself on his ability to 'make a woman express herself as never before', to look out of her eyes and to share her desire. One might ask, having looked again at those poems in which he uses the voices of women, how Yeats compares with other writers who have seemed to allow women to speak for themselves.

Crazy Jane belongs to a long tradition of writing in which women question male authority. She has much in common with Chaucer's Wife of Bath, who rejoices in her sexuality, laments the coming of age, and defies the book-learning of Christian clerics with her 'authority of experience' and 'audacious speech'. Yet, as in the final 'Woman Young And Old' lyrics, her subversiveness is undercut by the story she tells, in which the ugly old woman demands sovereignty only to be redeemed as a young woman who will return the mastery to her husband.[19]

In the Celtic tradition, one has the ninth-century lament of the Hag of Beare, seen by some as a predecessor of Cathleen ni Houlihan, an old woman and outcast, who declares:

> Nothing but narrow bones
> you will see when you look at my arms.
> But they did sweet business once
> round the bodies of mighty kings.

and

> If the Son of Mary knew
> He'd lie under my cellar-pole!
> There's nothing much for Him there
> but I never said no to a man.[20]

Closer to Yeats's time are a number of Irish women characters, most notably Synge's peasant women such as Nora Burke in *The Shadow of the Glen*, Sarah Casey and Mary Byrne in *The Tinker's Wedding*, and Pegeen Mike in *The Playboy*. All of these women are portrayed as more vital and defiant in speech and spirit than the men – aged husbands, fathers, and especially priests, who seek to keep them under control, and who represent the economic and moral structures which restrict their lives and deny their desires.

In particular, one might compare Crazy Jane, and to some extent Yeats's other women speakers, with Joyce's creation, Molly Bloom. She too affirms the flesh, even in the face of ageing, and speaks frankly of sexual experience. She too laughs to think that Blazes Boylan should think that he has possessed any more of her than her body. She also is dismissive of the priests, their book-learning, and challenges them with the authority of her own experience. And like the woman speakers in 'Words For Music Perhaps', she is associated with music and song. Molly is contrasted with Gertie McDowell, a would-be painter of pictures, who is viewed from a distance, and who is not herself able to question the economic and social system in which she lives.

But the reader *is* encouraged to question Gertie's world, her endorsement of it and her perceived role as a female who sustains and does not question that world as it exists. Moreover, the women created by Synge (and O'Casey) and indeed, Chaucer, are given a social and economic context which is seen to be restrictive, limiting and to give real cause for their subversion and defiance, whether of deed or word. All of these women characters are given a language which might approximate their voices as peasant or middle-class women. Molly Bloom's language, however one might question its credibility, is nevertheless marked as authentically her own, and notably different from the language of the men. And, of course, it is placed in such a way that its subversive force is left to make a lingering impact.

Yeats has so arranged and written *The Winding Stair* poems that the reader is not encouraged to link female subversion with social or economic systems. In the opening poem, the subversive behaviour of the Gore-Booth sisters is merely dismissed as unaesthetic; it is described in abstract terms, and overpowered for poet and reader by the twice-repeated vivid and idealized picture of beautiful women in harmony with their social world which encloses their vague rebellion. The picture is elaborated in the Coole Park poems, where Lady Gregory within the house with failing strength sustains a failing order. In none of these poems are the women allowed to speak for themselves. The subversive female is removed from all social context, so that her critique of male power becomes concerned with a sterile Christian morality which Yeats contrives to divorce from political or economic structures, and her fulfilment is sought in bodily and emotional pleasure which ignores the economic restrictions acknowledged by Synge and O'Casey, and also by Joyce. Elizabeth Butler Cullingford has argued convincingly that 'A Woman Young And Old' and 'Words For Music Perhaps' (especially the Crazy Jane sequence) take on added force and meaning if read as part of Yeats's response to the political hegemony of the clergy and their increasing influence in Irish government and law in the decade following 1925.[21] Granted their role in challenging that Catholic hegemony and the censorious attitudes and laws it bequeathed to Ireland, Yeats's women nevertheless lack voices which would authentically tie them to class or economic place – Crazy Jane's idiom is not that of the peasant, but is instead a stylized and decorous one. She inhabits Yeats's tongue and expresses his desire, not her own. It might be argued that Yeats is here adopting a genre and style which has a long tradition through Blake's *Songs of Innocence and Experience* to Shakespeare's fools, but it should be noted that Yeats also departs from the uses to which Blake and Shakespeare often put that tradition – the radical questioning of the economic and social system, as well as the moral one.

And so when Yeats wrote in his note to *The Winding Stair* that he wrote 'Words For Music Perhaps' at a time when 'life returned to him as an impression of uncontrollable energy and daring of the great creators; it seemed that but for journalism and criticism, all that evasion and explanation, the world would be torn to pieces', we should not be misled. The explanation itself is evasive. Yeats has in this volume taken care that the energy these songs celebrate *is* controlled, and carefully kept in its place, so that his idealized order cannot be torn to pieces – at least by his own creations. Yet as he himself partly recognized – particularly in 'The Circus Animals' Desertion' – his very attempt to control the energy, to subvert the subversion by displacing it from a political to an aesthetic and then a sexual context, serves only to intensify it. Ultimately he must return to and acknowledge 'that raving slut / Who keeps the till', in a metaphor which suggests his unwilling recognition that subversiveness, material conditions and female protest are linked to one another, and that his poetry had often obscured and domesticated such intuitive recognition.

PART II

A Voice in Directing the Affairs of Ireland

CHAPTER SEVEN

'Groups Rather Than Individuals':

Women in Politics and Education

In 1910, Anna Parnell, the sister of Charles Stewart Parnell, wrote a letter to Helena Moloney, editor of the journal *Bean na hEireann* (*The Woman of Ireland*) with reference to her manuscript account of the activities of the Land League, *The Tale of a Great Sham*:

> I avoided personalities as much as possible, as I consider the actions of particular individuals are unimportant in history, while the actions of groups, classes, etc. of persons are most important, because the former are not met with again, and the latter are – I do not mean, of course that the actions are unimportant, only that it does not matter what particular individual does them except in so far as he or she represents others.[1]

The difference which Anna Parnell here suggests between her understanding of history and of historiography and the implicit or explicit view of the majority of historians writing at that time that history is primarily about 'great men', also marks the difference between her understanding of effective political action and the activities centring around her brother, Charles Stewart Parnell. To a large extent the apparent absence of women as powerful political leaders of the stature of Henry Grattan, Wolf Tone, Daniel O'Connor, Charles Parnell or Patrick Pearse from the pages of official histories is a consequence of their exclusion from the Irish political arena. Their exclusion and sometimes contemptuous dismissal is discussed by Dana Hearne in her analysis of historical writing over the last 100 years about the Land League and Charles Stewart Parnell.[2] But Anna Parnell's comment also suggests that there was an element of choice, which was not solely determined by what was acceptable given the laws, conventions and attitudes of the time in which they lived, but was also positively reinforced by their belief in the greater importance of group actions. The activities of numerous Irish women's groups from 1880 until the present time bear this out – the Ladies' Land League, the Irish Women's Suffrage and Local Government Association, the Inghinidhe na h-Eireann (the Daughters of Erin), the Irish Women's Franchise League, the Cumann na mBan (Council of Women), the Women's Social and Political Union, the Women's Peace Movement, to cite just a few. All of these groups involved many 'strong' women, but rarely did any of them depend upon being identified with one or two charismatic leaders.

An organization called the Ladies' Land League was originally formed in the United States by Fanny Parnell to raise money to help evicted tenants in Ireland and to further the work of the Irish Land League. Fanny and Anna Parnell had been active members of the American Famine Relief Committee and had helped organize their brother's 1879 political and fund-raising tour of America with William Dillon. Fanny had already achieved considerable fame or notoriety as a poet in the vein of the Young Irelanders, or of Speranza (Lady Wilde), with whom she was sometimes compared, and whom Roy Foster refers to as 'the Muse of nationalism'.[3] Like Lady Wilde, she was also accused of extremism, fanaticism, and 'excess'. Her best-known poem, 'Hold the Harvest', was published in the *Nation* in the summer of 1880. Davitt described it as the 'Marseillaise of the Irish peasant', and when it was read out by the Attorney General as evidence during the State Trials of 1880, those present in the court broke into applause.[4] Like many of her poems, it draws upon apocalyptic imagery such as Yeats used in his early poetry, together with the rhetoric of martyrdom, of bloodshed as fertilizing the land for future revolution, the imagery which proved so effective in *Cathleen ni Houlihan* and Patrick Pearse's speeches and poetry:

> The yellow corn starts blithely up – beneath it lies a grave,
> Your father died in 'forty-eight; his life for yours he gave;
> He died that you, his son, might learn there is no helper nigh,
> Except for him who, save in fight, has sworn *he will not die*.

The hour has struck, Fate holds the dice, we stand with bated breath;
Now who shall have our harvest fair – 'tis Life that plays with Death;
Now who shall have our Motherland? 'Tis Right that plays with Might;
The peasants' arms were weak indeed in that unequal fight!

But God is on the peasants' side, the God that loves the poor;
His angels stand with flaming sword on every mount and moor.
They guard the poor man's flocks and herds, they guard his ripening
   grain;
The robber sinks beneath their curse beside his ill-got gain.

O pallid serfs! whose groans and prayers have wearied Heav'n full long,
Look up! there is a law above, beyond all legal wrong;
Rise up! the answer to your prayers shall come, tornado-borne,
And ye shall hold your homesteads dear, and ye shall reap the corn![5]

Despite her own involvement in organizing and fundraising in
America for the Land League, Fanny Parnell here inscribes herself
as the muse who inspires men to fight; she cannot envision herself
as part of that action – perhaps because her class as well as her
gender mark her difference from the 'pallid serfs' she appeals to.
Like Cathleen ni Houlihan and the *aisling* women, her role is to
remind men of all that is lost, and to shame them into protecting
and redeeming 'our Motherland', invoking as she does divine
sanction for breaking man-made laws.

Of the founding of the Ladies' Land League she wrote in 1882:

The funds of the Land League, which had increased so rapidly when
Mr Dillon and my brother were here in this country, had fallen off
to almost nothing, a few hundred dollars a week; and it occurred to
me that by setting the women at work much needed stimulus would
be given to the men. I mentioned the idea to Mr Davitt a few days
afterwards and he was delighted with it.[6]

In August 1880, she wrote to a number of newspapers calling for a
women's organization to assist the Irish cause, and held the first
meeting of the New York Ladies' Land League in October.
Branches were rapidly formed throughout America, and she
encouraged women in Ireland to organize a similar movement.

When the British Parliament passed Coercion Laws to clamp
down on the activities of the Land League and agrarian 'crime',
Michael Davitt, foreseeing the arrest of himself, Charles Stewart
Parnell and other leaders of the League in 1881, urged on his
reluctant fellow leaders the formation of a local Ladies' Land
League in order to keep some semblance of the Land League alive
and administer its accounts. Anna Parnell was named as organizing

secretary (without previous consultation with her, she claimed). Her skills and political acumen were commended by Davitt, one of the founders of the Land League, while Andrew Kettle, a local secretary of the League and a strong supporter of Charles Parnell, wrote thus of her:

> [She has] a better knowledge of the lights and shades of Irish peasant life, of the real economic conditions of the country, and of the social and political forces which had to be acted upon to work out the freedom of Ireland than any person, man or woman, that I have ever met. . . . Anna Parnell would have worked the Land League revolution to a much better conclusion than her great brother.[7]

In the absence of the men who had been imprisoned or disbanded, the women members of the League took full control, interpreted policy and decided upon appropriate action. Anna returned from the United States to take on the role she says was thrust upon her and addressed the first public meeting of the Ladies' Land League on 13 February 1881.

From its very inception, the Ladies' Land League was regarded with disapprobation and suspicion. Parnell and some of his lieutenants feared it would bring ridicule upon the men if they were seen to be 'sheltering behind' the women. Most supporters of Parnell and many later historians seem to share or at least fail to question his attitudes. St John Ervine's 1925 biography of Parnell refers to the Ladies' Land League as 'Miss Parnell's band of harridans',[8] 'infested with fanatics' and asserts that Anna Parnell herself was mad. Like Yeats, Ervine declares that 'Irish women, when they take to politics, have a capacity for fanaticism which is almost inhuman.'[9] A more thoroughly researched and distanced biography of Parnell written by F.S.L. Lyons over fifty years later and including some analysis of the effectiveness of the Ladies' Land League, nevertheless refers to Anna as 'masterful' and 'fanatical'.[10]

Contemporary opponents of Parnell and the Land League also castigated as unfeminine and unnatural the women who participated in the Land League. Archbishop McCabe told the clergy in his diocese:

> Do not tolerate in your sodalities the woman who so far disavows her birthright of modesty as to parade herself before the public gaze in a character so unworthy a child of Mary. This attempt at degrading the women of Ireland comes very appropriately from men who have drawn the country into her present terribly deplorable condition.[11]

Despite the suspicion or outright disapproval of most men of their own class, and some women, the members of the Ladies' Land League set about organizing and following through what they interpreted as the actual programme of the Land League. The account of their work, and their disillusion with the huge gap between the rhetoric and stated aims of the Land League as articulated by its male leaders and the reality of its activities, is spelled out in Anna Parnell's *The Tale of a Great Sham*.[12] The members of the Ladies' Land League took at face value the 'No Rent Policy' proclaimed by the Land League in 1879, and saw it as a means not just of reforming tenure, but of retrieving the land for Irish peasants, and achieving Home Rule. They therefore set about accumulating detailed records of all landlords and tenants in Ireland, organizing resistance to the payment of rent and arrears, encouraging boycotts of those who took over lands from which tenants had been evicted, and building cottages to house those who were evicted. After its editor, William O'Brien, was imprisoned, they were largely responsible for keeping the paper *United Ireland* in print and for distributing it, together with many other political pamphlets. As General Secretary, Anna Parnell encouraged the women who joined her to become confident, independent, and self-sufficient, and many women who were later to become active in feminist and nationalist movements received their first training and sense of their abilities as political organizers in the two years of the Ladies' Land League's existence. They included Katharine Tynan, Jenny Wyse Power, Ellen O'Leary, and Hannah Lynch. It was a movement which also provided a model and inspiration for later activists such as Maud Gonne and Constance Markievicz.

During the two years before the Ladies' Land League was disbanded (or rather strangled through the withholding of any financial or other resources by Charles Stewart Parnell and his lieutenants once Parnell was released from prison), Anna Parnell travelled endlessly throughout Ireland, England and Scotland, organizing branches, fundraising, and addressing public meetings. This last activity was one she felt uneasy about. Her disquiet was not because she shared the view of the editor of *The Belfast News-Letter* that 'at no time is woman further from her natural position than when she appears upon a political platform',[13] but more because of her distrust of the emotionalism public meetings inspired, and their association with a particular brand of male politics. This association was in part due to the fact that at public meetings women had in the past kept well in the background, and were discouraged from attending at all. Once women began to address such meetings, more women began to attend them, and, to the disapproval of the men, 'no longer kept a respectful distance, but thronged around the platform as if [they] had a right to be there'.[14] However, Anna Parnell disliked the emotional mode of these meetings, and what she regarded as 'a peculiarly male form of political demagoguery [which] incited crowds to frenzied cheers regardless of the content of the speech'.[15] She did not harangue and incite, but spoke slowly and quietly. Her preferred method of political education and organizing was to hold meetings at the scene of an eviction to dramatize the political point, and then to hold discussions which would lead to a common policy.[16]

Anna Parnell's distaste for mass meetings and demagoguery is particularly noteworthy, given the accusations of 'excess' and 'hysteria' which have dogged accounts of her and the Ladies' Land League. It was her firm belief that the cult of personality, the mode of the mass meeting, the reliance on rhetoric rather than effective action were distastefully emotional, were 'excessive', that they dissipated good intentions in compromise and dishonesty, and were a feature of male political styles. She sought effective action and solid organization based on accurate information and rational discussion, leading to logically worked out conclusions; and she believed in submerging personality and enhancing group or collective strength. These she saw as the strengths women brought to the Ladies' Land League.

The increasing influence of the Ladies' Land League led to its proscription by Parliament in December 1881. Whereas the National Land League had simply melted away under similar circumstances a year earlier following the imprisonment of its leaders, the women responded by increasing their activities. As numbers of women were arrested, imprisoned (under statutes designed to curb prostitution!), and placed in solitary confinement, hundreds more women came forward to take their places and continued to distribute information, hold meetings, and support evicted tenants. Despite their distrust of 'the politics of the individual', Anna Parnell and other members of the Ladies' Land League became folk heroines. A popular song called 'The Land League Ladies of Erin' included this chorus:

> Then shout, boys, hurrah, and raise your voices well,
> Long life to Miss Reynolds and also Miss Parnell,
> May every Irish woman help the ranks to swell
> The Ladies Land League of old Ireland.[17]

In England, Anna Parnell was elevated to the status of Public Enemy Number Two by some opponents. Kitty O'Shea told Charles Stewart Parnell that Anna's effigy was burned beside that of the Pope on Guy Fawkes Day in Eltham.[18] That a young woman from an Anglo-Irish Protestant landholding family should find herself placed on equal footing with that symbol of Catholic power and patriarchy, the Pope, is indeed ironic. It also reveals the tremendous difficulty the Land League Ladies faced in their attempt to create a new kind of politics which would reject the cult of the individual, encourage group action by those who had been marginalized, and restrain political emotionalism.

The refusal of members of the Ladies' Land League to be intimidated by the pronouncement that 'Where any females are assembled . . . such meeting is illegal', and their determination to continue their mass meetings and activities in spite of arrests and prison sentences, was, as Jenny Wyse Power later wrote, 'the first time when Britain's power to "proclaim" was not only questioned but defied'.[19] Their defiance alarmed the British government; it also dismayed Charles Stewart Parnell, whose order that the Ladies drop their no-rent policy had been ignored. The British government and Parnell agreed to the 'Kilmainham Treaty' of 2 May 1882, which promised the reform of the Land Act, the release of the prisoners, and remission of rent arrears in return for a cessation of agrarian agitation. The Ladies' Land League was dissolved, and the women were told that they must hand over the political and financial reins and return to 'charitable works'. In retrospect the new Land Act *may* be seen as a considerable advance which weakened the hold of the landowning classes, but to Anna Parnell it was a betrayal.[20] Writing her history of the movement some twenty-five years later, she pointed out that the tenant farmers and rural workers remained as poor as ever, that the real economic problems of Ireland had not been addressed, and that Ireland still did not have Home Rule. Moreover, women remained excluded from political power. She believed that the Land League should and could have achieved genuine redistribution of the land and independence from England, and she saw little hope of change as long as Ireland was governed solely or mainly by men. In the concluding chapter of *The Tale of a Great Sham* she writes despairingly of the future of Ireland:

> We know, for instance, that the character of Irishmen is at present incompatible with any great change for the better in Ireland, since it is one that would prevent them from turning any opportunity to account, however good it might be, for changing the position of Ireland. I say 'Irishmen' because, whatever the relative values of men and women may be, it is certain that the former cannot be done without, when it is a question of altering the status of a country. If the men of that country have made up their minds it shall not be done, the women cannot bring it about.[21]

So deeply felt was Anna Parnell's disillusion that she moved to Cornwall, where she lived in poverty, and never again communicated with her brother Charles. Nevertheless, she maintained her interest in the political activities of Irish women, and sometimes supported them as best she could. She sent a donation to Maud Gonne for the 'Patriotic Children's Treat' (see Chapter Eight, below) and supported the formation of Inghinidhe na hEireann. She drowned while swimming at Ilfracombe in 1911.

Despite Anna Parnell's despair about the possibility of real political change in a male-dominated Ireland, the Ladies' Land League set several important precedents. It brought many women into the political arena and showed that they were capable of carrying on all the activities normally taken on by men, and in this case more efficiently and consistently. It showed that women could challenge the British state, would not be cowed by threats or the actuality of imprisonment, and could force the government to capitulate. Perhaps most importantly of all, in terms of later involvement by women in Irish political movements, it widened the agenda for Irish women concerned with change. As Rosemary Cullen Owens points out in *Smashing Times*, middle-class Irish women in the nineteenth century had both challenged and shared the assumptions of the Victorian society and/or conservative Catholic society to which they belonged. In general, their concern for the poor was expressed through patronage and charitable deeds rather than action for radical economic change; their concern for the vote was limited to its extension to women of their own class, and they rarely questioned the property conditions to which male suffrage was attached. Nor did they adopt other than constitutional means of attempting to challenge the exclusion of women from the vote.[22] Thus the activities of the Dublin Women's Suffrage Association, founded by Anna Haslam in 1876 and actively supported by her husband, Thomas Haslam, and his publication, *The Women's Advocate*, were focused on lobbying members of parliament and gathering signatures for petitions which asked that women be included in parliamentary bills introduced to extend male suffrage within well-defined limits, and also that Irish women be allowed to serve, as English women could, on Local Government Associations. (The Dublin Suffrage Association, after several changes of name, became in 1901 the Irish Women's Suffrage and Local Government Association – henceforth referred to, in all its manifestations, as the IWSLGA.)

The Ladies' Land League, on the other hand, involved women in militant action, disobeying laws which neither as women nor as Irish citizens they had had any part in formulating or supporting. It showed that women were capable of organizing militant and mass action, that the participation of women could make such action all the more effective, and it encouraged middle-class women to engage in a much more radical analysis of the economic and political systems which fostered imperialism, deprived Ireland of self-government, and did nothing to change the dire poverty of millions of rural Irishmen and women. Despite their relatively comfortable family origins, many of the women involved in the Land League movement were aware of the analogies and the connection between the situation of the Irish poor and their own situation as women without political or economic rights.

However, the widening of the agenda for women's involvement in politics also created problems, and the debate as to which issue should be first on the agenda – Irish self-government or women's involvement in government – was to continue through the first two decades of the twentieth century and occupied many columns in Irish journals and newspapers where it was often defined as a debate between feminism and nationalism, a debate heightened by the fact that Irish suffragettes were seeking votes and the right to be elected to a *British* Parliament. Moreover, the IWSLGA membership was, according to Rosemary Cullen Owens, 'overwhelmingly non-Catholic and middle-class',[23] at a time when there was an increasing identification between Catholicism and nationalism. The journalistic debate is discussed in the next chapter. In terms of the perceived conflict between nationalist and feminist concerns and its effect on women's suffrage movements, it is symptomatic that for a whole decade, from 1886 until 1896, the IWSLGA held no public meetings 'owing to the present condition of political controversy in Ireland'.[24]

A series of bills, passed in 1896, 1898 and 1901, did extend to Irish women the right to participate in and vote for Local Government and District Councils. Eighty-five women were elected to such councils in 1899, and local politics became for women a valuable means of gaining experience and demonstrating their competence. After 1900, the IWSLGA saw a rapid rise in membership. At the same time increasing numbers of women were seeking and gaining access to higher education, although they still found themselves barred from many professions such as Law, Accountancy, and the Civil Service. Thus the last decade of the nineteenth and the early decades of the twentieth century produced many experienced and articulate Irish women who found themselves excluded from exercising their talents and achieving their potential in existing political, professional and cultural organizations.

'Putting themselves to college': women and education

During the nineteenth century and earlier, one of the limited choices offered to Catholic women otherwise excluded from status or any role other than the domestic one, was the convent. The nineteenth century saw a rapid growth in the numbers of orders established in Ireland and the numbers of women joining them. Unlike earlier congregations for women such as those founded in medieval times offering a sheltered and contemplative life, and like political organizations such as the Ladies' Land League and the IWSLGA, congregations set up in the nineteenth century were generally oriented towards groups of women who sought a more active role in the community. Thus the Presentation Sisters were founded in the 1770s by Honora Nagle to provide education and social services for the poor. The Irish Sisters of Charity, the Loreto Sisters, the Mercy Sisters and the Holy Faith Sisters were all founded by devout Catholic laywomen of middle- or upper middle-class background, who gathered together other women to work for the good of the poor. Like their male counterparts in Ireland and throughout the British empire, they regarded education, cleanliness, middle-class norms of respectability and constraint as essential components in the moral and spiritual uplifting of the lower classes. In an increasingly urbanized society, as Tony Fahy puts it, 'they linked themselves to the secular project of social organisation, integrating mass populations into orderly, well-disciplined societies and cohesive nation states.'[25] And although they met with some opposition from the Catholic male hierarchy at first, it was soon accepted that they could act as valuable missionaries and 'counterparts' in the roles that were traditionally not defined as male roles – education of small children and girls, nursing, family support, and charitable works. In addition to orders founded in Ireland itself, such as those mentioned above, many overseas orders founded houses in Ireland. From France alone, thirteen congregations came to Ireland between 1840 and 1900. Between 1800 and 1901, the number of nuns in Ireland rose from 120 to over 8,000, so that by the beginning of the twentieth century the proportion of female religious had changed from a tiny minority within an overwhelmingly male Catholic Church to a large majority, more than double the number of priests and seven times the number of men in religious brotherhoods.[26]

Given the importance of nuns in Irish society, both in terms of numbers and their influence as educators, their absence from either historical or literary accounts of the period is extraordinary. It is as if the self-effacement preached by the religious orders and symbolized by the giving up of both personal and family names to be replaced by Saints' names upon entry into the convent has encouraged scholars and writers to erase their presence. While priests retained their family names and their place in Joyce's fictions and Yeats's poetry, as well as academic and popular histories, nuns appear only momentarily and anonymously, distantly heard as 'the mad nun screeching' in *A Portrait of the Artist* or 'a kind old nun in a white hood' who replies to Yeats's questioning.

What little evidence that has been gathered suggests that the role of the convents was both conservative and progressive. Catriona Clear's research on the backgrounds of choir and lay sisters in two Mercy convents in nineteenth-century Limerick, demonstrates that class barriers were reinforced and maintained within the convents. Choir sisters generally came with quite large dowries and were from relatively well-to-do families; within the convents they took higher vows, were admitted to more elaborate forms of worship, could participate in the governing of the convent, and wore clothing which set them apart from the lay sisters, whose clothing and duties established them as members of the servant class. As Catriona Clear summarizes the situation:

> Choir nuns were trusted in positions of responsibility and respected in positions of authority, and lay sisters existed as auxiliaries making the formers' concentration on apostolic work possible by dint of unremitting life-maintenance work, the performance of which, while seen as essential and praised as spiritually uplifting, did not confer a high status upon the worker. Virtually prohibited by 'birth', or socio-economic background, from holding executive position, lacking franchise, keeping in the background, and featuring only marginally, if at all, in histories, biographies and other accounts both contemporary and retrospective, lay sisters' position in the convents of the period was roughly analogous to that of women as a group in the larger society.[27]

In terms of their influence on Irish society and definitions of gender roles within it, the nuns also played an ambivalent role. On the one hand the convents offered women a channel for activity outside the domestic sphere, as teachers, educators, and administrators; and the Mother Superior of a convent was often a powerful figure held in awe by those outside as well as inside the institution. As role models, they established a norm for women outside the convent to become teachers, and contributed to the feminization of the teaching profession, though at the same time contributing to the expectation that women needed little or no pay since they were perceived as working for God and 'charity' rather than to sustain themselves or their families. In this field of education, they set high standards, and achieved a considerable reputation. Moreover, the convents established education for the lower classes and for girls as a norm, not merely a special privilege for the sons of the middle and upper classes. Yet, at the same time, the convent schools developed a potent ethos of the value of subservience and unquestioning obedience for women, who were expected above all to be pure, innocent, demure and ladylike. Thus inspectors for the National Education Commission frequently praised the ladylike 'accomplishments' of the nuns, especially in music, needlework and French, and their fine moral influence. Their effect on their girl pupils was commended by one inspector quoted in the 1864 report of the Commissioners of National Education thus:

> When I visited the (convent) school shortly after its opening, the girls were in the rudest possible state, boisterous, disobedient, and impudent, the greater part of whose time had been spent running almost wild in the streets. I now find these girls quite amenable to discipline and order, somewhat attentive to neatness and propriety, and generally improved in moral training.[28]

The role of the convents and their approach to an education for girls which emphasized the domestic and the 'ladylike' was strongly endorsed by the Catholic hierarchy. In 1871, Dr Paul Cullen, Archbishop of Dublin, cited St Paul to support his view that girls' education should differ from that given to boys:

> Teach the young women to be wise, to love their husbands, to love their children; to be discreet, chaste, sober, having a care of the house, gentle, obedient to their husbands, that the word of God may not be blasphemed.[29]

The ethos and influence of the convents in education were further strengthened by the establishment of denominational teacher training institutes in the 1880s, and the Mercy convent set up teacher training for Catholic women, thus becoming their principal means of access to primary-level teaching. Here, as Tony Fahy points out, subjects were allocated to genders, so that 'technical subjects such as science and mathematics were taught by lay males, while the nuns confined themselves to the accomplishment subjects like singing, music and foreign languages'.[30]

This ethos, influenced by the traditions of French convent school education for girls, and supported by the Roman Catholic hierarchy in Ireland as well as Catholic women such as Margaret Cusack,[31] was challenged in the latter half of the nineteenth century by a number of Protestant schools for girls, influenced by English and American approaches to education. The challenge was articulated and led most forcefully by Margaret Byers, headmistress of the Ladies' Collegiate School (later Victoria College) in Belfast. While she and her husband had been at Princeton in the early 1850s, she had been impressed by the American insistence that education for girls should not differ substantially from that offered to boys.[32] Her school employed masters to teach subjects not normally taken by girls, and the pupils took examinations similar to those set for boys.

When examinations were first set for women by Queen's University in 1870, her students were entered for them and achieved good results. In the 1880s Margaret Byers organized public meetings which addressed the need for improved standards for girls' schools and the inclusion of mathematics and Latin in the curriculum, so that girls could and should compete with boys at the public examinations and for places in Higher Education. As a result, when the Intermediate Education Act made examinations open to all schools in 1878, and the Royal University of Ireland Act opened University examinations to women in 1879, the Protestant schools like Victoria College in Belfast and Alexandra College in Dublin were well placed to see their pupils achieve good results. The publication of such results in the Irish papers stimulated the convents to change and to begin to offer a wider curriculum and classes for women wishing to enter University. In 1885 University classes were established at the Dominican Convent in Eccles Street, and in 1893 St Mary's University College was founded at Merrion Square, Dublin. Other convents quickly followed by including Latin and mathematics in their curriculum for secondary pupils, and establishing University classes. By the turn of the century, the distinctions and prizes gained by Catholic girls were beginning to outnumber those awarded to the Protestant colleges. At the same time, convent schools were increasingly beginning to educate young women for employment rather than just marriage or a convent vocation, although vocational training was confined to the spheres of clerical and secretarial or teaching occupations.

Although women were now permitted to take University examinations, there was as yet no provision for their teaching, and they were at first excluded from attending classes at the Queen's University Colleges or Trinity College. As a result, the colleges which had prepared them for entrance began to offer University-level tutorials, lectures and classes. Additionally, some few Fellows were willing to give lectures a second time especially for the women students. Such arrangements were far from satisfactory, and women, led by early graduates such as Mary Hayden and Alice Oldham, continued to campaign for full admission to the Universities and the right to attend lectures with male students, a right finally recognized by Queen's College, Belfast in 1882, Cork in 1886, and Galway in 1888. Social opposition to women attending the same classes as men remained strong however, and the Bishop of Galway forbade Catholic girls to attend the College.[33] Despite a long and vigorous campaign by women, their right to attend Trinity College lectures was not granted until 1904. Thereafter, a further fierce debate continued over the advantages and disadvantages of maintaining the separate women's colleges. Agnes O'Farrelly, Mary Hayden and Hannah Sheehy-Skeffington, all leading members of the Irish Association of Women Graduates, declared that women did not want 'to be shut into women's colleges',[34] and that 'if women will not consent to eat at a common table provided for men and women alike, it will, we fear, be their fate to go hungry or to be obliged to content themselves with a few crumbs and husks flung to them in half contemptuous charity'.[35] In defence of the role of the Women's Colleges, Norah Meade organized the Irish Women's Education Association which submitted a petition with over 3,000 signatures rejecting co-education on the grounds that 'essential differences in the modes of thought and mental development of men and women demanded separate education'.[36] The Dominican and Loreto Convents and Victoria College also sought to maintain their independence and establish a status as separate but equal colleges, but by 1911 all three had been refused recognition.

The changes brought about in the provision of education for women in the last quarter of the ninetenth century produced in the 1890s and early twentieth century a small but growing group of articulate and professional women, who had often formed a closely knit group in the colleges and Universities, and who went on to take their part in the variety of political and cultural movements which characterized Ireland between 1890 and 1914. The arguments for their exclusion from the vote, from the professions, from the cultural nationalist societies, all appeared increasingly hollow, as women demonstrated their ability to compete with men in intellectual and academic achievements. Where women were excluded from societies such as the Celtic Literary Society they proceeded, as did the Women's colleges, to create their own organizations and formulate their own aims, and refused to be seen, as Anna Parnell and the Ladies' Land League had refused to be seen, as mere auxiliaries to the 'Master' organization. Thus, the aims of the 'Inghinidhe na hEireann' founded by Maud Gonne eschew all mention of male nationalist groups or the offer of assistance to them. The organization's primary object is stated baldly as 'The re-establishment of the independence of Ireland'. Nevertheless, later literature produced by the Inghinidhe betrays that a certain ambivalence existed as to the desirability of separatist women's and nationalist organizations, and the relation between them.

All art is collaboration

An approach to history and to political change as the work of groups rather than individual personalities, articulated by Anna Parnell, also typifies much literary and cultural activity carried on by women with a commitment to Irish nationalism. Here too, the merging of individual identities, or rather the lack of concern about personal acclaim, is noteworthy. The women who founded and wrote for the journals discussed in the next chapter more often than not did so under pseudonyms or anonymously. For many years, Lady Gregory's role in collaborating with Yeats on a number of the plays ascribed to him as sole author remained unknown, and she consistently spoke or wrote of herself as merely working in the service of the Abbey Theatre, writing to keep it going, rather than as an author in her own right. The merging of identities in the collaboration between Edith Somerville and Violet Martin was so complete that it seems impossible to disentangle who wrote what, and even after Violet Martin's death in 1915, she was listed as co-author for subsequent novels. Yeats's letters and memoirs attest to the tremendous importance of women such as his sisters, Elizabeth and 'Lilly', Katharine Tynan, Olivia Shakespear, Ethel Mannin, Dorothy Wellesley, and Lady Gregory in his literary development and the maintenance of his physical well-being and literary stature. Then, of course, there is Georgie Hyde-Lees, whom he married in 1917 and who was a major contributor to *A Vision*, although Yeats alone is named as the author. Among other things, Elizabeth ('Lolly') and Lily Yeats ran the Cuala Press and saw most of their brother, William's, volumes through the whole process from manuscript to print. Katharine Tynan shared with Yeats an admiration for John O'Leary and Parnell, and they encouraged each other to take up Irish themes. She was the first to suggest that Yeats write a play on an Irish subject, and she supplied Yeats copiously with books, editorial help, criticisms and

sympathetic responses to his work and his aspirations in his earliest
years as an author. In those early years she also reviewed all of
Yeats's works, sometimes more than once, bringing him to the
attention of Irish and English audiences.[37] Yeats often recipro-
cated, it should be added, as a critical and sympathetic reader and
reviewer, and frequently helped Tynan and others by encouraging
anthologists and editors to include their work. Frequently, also,
however, he took and rewrote as his own work fragments or whole
poems sent to him by Tynan, Wellesley and others. Perhaps the
best-known example of such reworking is his use of a ballad by
Dorothy Wellesley to construct 'The Three Bushes'.[38] A reading of
Tynan's poetry evokes echoes of some of Yeats's best-known lines,
although a check reveals that it was Tynan who wrote the lines
first, and it is Yeats who echoes her. Her early ballad, 'Waiting',
which was published in *Louise de la Vallière and Other Poems* in
1885,[39] and takes as its subject the legend of Finn McCool
remembering past glories and awaiting the hour when he and his
warriors shall be called upon to fight again, may have suggested
Yeats's *Wanderings of Oisin*, which he began writing in 1886. Some
of the poems in *The Rose* and *The Wind among the Reeds* also bear
traces of the apocalyptic imagery which runs through Tynan's
poem and brings it to a close with these lines:

> Some day a voice will ring adown the glooms,
> 'Arise, ye Princes, for the hour is come!'
> [. . .]
> That hour shall sound the clash of sword and spear,
>   The steeds shall neigh to hear their master's call,
> And the hounds' cry shall echo shrill and clear.[40]

Yeats particularly praised Tynan's 'Catholic' religious poems,
which he liked for their simplicity of style and diction. These may
well have provided a model for Yeats's own early poems which take
on the voice of a Catholic priest or a young mother, as in 'The
Ballad of Father Gilligan', or 'Cradle Song'. But perhaps a more
striking echo comes in Yeats's famous 'In Memory of Robert
Gregory', where the terms in which Robert Gregory is praised
sound much more elaborately some of the notes sounded in
Tynan's elegy to George Wyndham, written in 1913:

> Soldier, poet, courtier,
>   He was these and more than these.
> He must go to find his peer,

Over mountains, over seas,
To some starry road afar
Where the constellations are.
Traveller from the realms of gold,
Sidney's brother, Raleigh's twin[41]

From the time they both began writing and publishing poetry, Katharine Tynan and William Butler Yeats acted as sympathetic readers and critics of each other's work. They encouraged, and in many ways nurtured, each other. Katharine Tynan acknowledges her debt to Yeats publicly in one of her most accomplished poems, 'Gorse', which is dedicated 'To W.B. Yeats, who taught me'.[42]

Although Yeats often drew upon the advice, encouragement and criticism of others, and although he frequently made women, such as Maud Gonne, Olivia Shakespear, Dorothy Wellesley, Margot Ruddock, and his wife the *subjects* of his poems, he publicly acknowledges a debt to only one woman, Lady Gregory. But the debt he acknowledges is to her patronage, her character, and her house, not to her artistry and creative collaboration.

The chapters on women journalists and on Lady Gregory which follow will explore the work of women for whom artistic collaboration was something they valued and insisted upon. Writing was for them part of a group enterprise, not a means of attaining personal glory and renown. Too often critics have taken the self-effacement of such women writers as an excuse for ignoring them.

CHAPTER EIGHT

'A Voice in Directing the Affairs of Ireland':

L'Irlande Libre, *The Shan Van Vocht*, *Bean na h-Eireann*, and Maud Gonne

In an early number of *Bean na h-Eireann*, the journal of the Inghinidhe na h-Eireann (Daughters of Erin), the editorial proclaims:

> Our desire to have a voice in directing the affairs of Ireland is not based on the **failure of men** to do so properly, but is the inherent right of women as loyal citizens and intelligent human souls. [Their emphasis][1]

Published monthly, though not always regularly, between 1908 and 1912, the *Bean*, edited by Helena Moloney, proudly declared itself in a later issue (no. 18), 'the first and only Nationalist Woman's paper'. It had, however, been preceded and in part made possible by two journals which, although not declaring themselves to be 'Nationalist Women's papers', were edited by nationalist women. These were *L'Irlande Libre*, edited, and often largely written, by Maud Gonne in France between 1896 and 1897, and *The Shan Van Vocht* (The Poor Old Woman), edited by Alice Milligan and Anna Johnson in Belfast between 1896 and 1898. All three journals were products of the desire of Irish women 'to have a voice in directing the affairs of Ireland', at a time when women were excluded from the vote and hence from parliamentary debate, and also from most of the nationalist organizations, both political and cultural, which sought to subvert English dominance. In varying degrees, all three carry the double-edged implication of that *Bean* editorial which

Vol. I, No. 4.   Feabra — FEBRUARY, 1909.   Price—One Penny.

MADE IN IRELAND.

THE KILKENNY WOODWORKERS

MANUFACTURERS OF

Bedroom Suites,
Diningroom Chairs,
Chesterfield Couches,
Comfortable Easy Chairs,
In many shapes and sizes.
Writing Tables,
Roll Top Desks,
Bookcases,
AND
Cabinet Making in all Departments

NEW DEPARTMENT—
BASKET AND WICKER WORK,
PERAMBULATORS.

SHOWROOMS—
6, 7 & 8 as sau St.,
DUBLIN.

DRIPSEY!

The "Kathleen Ni Houlihan" are Lovelier than Ever!
The Prices Lower than Ever!

By wearing Dripsey Dress Cloths the sensible women of Ireland have DOUBLED the Dripsey Mills in two years.

Editorial Notes.

ALAS, our statements on Women's Suffrage have got us into serious trouble. We carelessly stated in our December issue that there was nothing illegal in electing a woman to the Civic Chair of Dublin. This, it seems, is not so. Mrs. Sheehy-Skeffington has kindly written to us pointing out our mistake. Such an election would be against the English Law, and so we cry *peccavi* to those more learned in it than ourselves. We ought to have remembered that when England happens to pass a really good law, it seldom applies to Ireland. We still maintain that it would be an excellent propagandist policy for a woman to stand for election to the Municipal Council. If the Town Clerk could be induced to accept her nomination, and the Corporation and the ratepayers were prepared to stand by him, we fail to see how the illegality would matter. When a law is obviously unjust and iniquitous it should be unhesitatingly broken or ignored by all right-thinking people. The task of winning over the Irish public and the members of our elected bodies to the cause of Woman Suffrage does not appear to be so colossal one. We feel sure that if the case were put logically and forcibly before our countrymen their love of freedom and sense of justice would compel them to give to women a voice and a place in the government of their common country. A vote may be the hall-mark of equality, but it is in our daily lives—in matters of education, in commerce, on local administrative boards, and in the labour market, that we need real liberty and equality. It is from Irishmen that this must be won. The English Parliamentary vote is but a shadow of power.

Let us consider carefully whether the Parliamentary vote has been such an effective weapon in the hands of our countrymen, and whether it is really worth while agitating for. During the past century the trade, agriculture, and population of Ireland have gone steadily backwards, while the

they are not agitating for the Parliamentary vote because it is a desirable thing to have, but simply because men have it. We respectfully submit to the Irish Women's Franchise League that this is an unworthy and humiliating position for them to take up. If the English Parliamentary vote is not, in itself, a source of power, then we should not stultify ourselves by wasting time and energy agitating for it. It is disappointing to find women simply wanting to follow blindly in men's footsteps, instead of profiting by their experience and avoiding their mistakes. Bean na h-Eireann is, and will always be, as keen and enthusiastic an advocate for the Cause of Women as the most extreme "Suffragette" could wish. It is not a question of putting Nationality before sex, or sex before Nationality. The two questions do not clash at all, although at first sight they appear to. The Feminist Cause in Ireland is best served by ignoring England and English politicians, just as it is best served in England by keeping aloof from Party politics. At all events, women should first set their own house in order. Women are denied a place in some of the most important political organisations in Ireland. The United Irish League (with the exception of one branch, we believe), the Loyal Orange Association, the Liberal Home Rule Association, are exclusively masculine bodies. The Gaelic League and the Sinn Féin Organisation are the only ones in existence at present where women are on an equal footing with men. For that reason they are worthy of the support of every Irish woman Suffragist.

In taking this stand against any suffrage agitation in Ireland, let it not be thought that we are antagonistic to English Suffragists, or that we disapprove of their forcible methods. On the contrary, we commend them to Irishwomen and Irishmen, but let us fight for something worth the trouble and the risk. More than one hundred years ago, a great Irishman said that "the only argument that appeals to an Englishman's sense of

7. Front page of *Bean na h-Eireann* with the masthead drawn by Constance Markievicz.

both denies distrust of men and asserts it in bold type which brings their **failure** into prominence.

Maud Gonne is not usually thought of as either an exile or a journalist, so powerfully did Yeats's writings succeed in intertwining her image, as an image of beauty, with that of the Ireland which inspired his poetry and failed to respond to his aspirations for it. Yet she spent more than half of her time during the years 1890 and 1916, years in which nationalist activity was at its most intense, as not so much a political but a social exile in France. Her affair with Lucien Millevoye, and more particularly the birth of their two children out of wedlock,[2] could not be countenanced in Catholic *or* Protestant Ireland, and so she pretended that her daughter, Iseult, was an adopted relative and kept her in France, spending as much time as possible with her there. After 1906, following her separation from John MacBride (on grounds of his drunkenness and brutality), she was booed when she visited the Abbey Theatre. Thereafter, fearing that their son Sean might be abducted by his father if she brought him to Ireland, she kept Sean in France and made only brief trips to Ireland until after John MacBride's execution in 1916.

On her visits to Ireland, Maud Gonne was intensely involved in a number of political struggles and demonstrations: against evictions in rural Ireland; against the tours of Queen Victoria and King Edward VII; in support of the Boers against the English; against conscription or recruitment into the British Armed Forces; and on behalf of political prisoners, whether held by the British government or the Irish Free State. She also founded the Inghinidhe na h-Eireann in order to provide an organization for women who sought to involve themselves in the struggle for Irish independence, both cultural and political, but were excluded from political parties, the National League (successor to the Land League), and the Celtic Literary Society – as Maud Gonne found when she tried to join them.[3] In addition to mobilizing Irish feeling and action against British hegemony, the Inghinidhe na h-Eireann gave many Irish women an opportunity to discover their talents as speakers, teachers, organizers, leaders, and journalists. The organization also played a major role in developing an Irish theatre which drew on Irish actors and directors and which later formed the core of the Abbey Theatre Company.

Contemporary Irish observers commented on Maud Gonne's startling beauty and her electrifying effect on the political platform and on stage. In Ireland, she rapidly became a figurehead, a symbol of Cathleen ni Houlihan, of Ireland itself, of the beauty and dignity which would return to Ireland when 'the Stranger' had been repelled. Trained as an actress in her teens, Maud Gonne was well aware of the effect she could produce, and put it to good political use. As Margaret Ward has shown, Maud Gonne was particularly skilful at creating moments of symbolic political action – whether through the Patriotic Children's Treat which countered that provided in honour of Queen Victoria's visit to Dublin in 1900, or through hanging out her black petticoat as an alternative symbol of personal mourning (Pope Leo XIII had just died) beside the Union Jacks hung to honour the visit of King Edward in 1903. For many, including Arthur Griffith who affectionately called her 'Queen' or 'Queenie', she was not the 'servant of the Queen' (Cathleen ni Houlihan) as she designated herself in her autobiography, but the Queen herself, and Maud Gonne's chosen mode of appearance, habitually dressed in long, flowing robes, often accompanied by one of her enormous dogs, did much to enhance that image.[4]

When she was in Ireland, Maud Gonne *lived* her image. Away from Ireland, she was able to write. Most of her journalism was published in or sent from France, and these writings, although passionate and far from impersonal, often eschew the image. In many cases they are signed with a pseudonym or with her initials only, and sometimes not at all. Many of her early writings are written in French for *L'Irlande Libre: Organe de la Colonie Irlandaise à Paris* (which she herself edited with the assistance of Miss M. Barry Delaney), and *Journal des Voyages*, a fortnightly featuring tales of travel and adventure in Africa, Bengal, and other 'exotic' places, with stories and pictures catering to a taste for the sensational and the lurid. (See Illustration 8.) In this latter journal her series of six articles titled 'Le Martyre de l'Irlande' found a not altogether comfortable place in occasional issues between 1891 and 1894. Each article in the series took an example of British and/or landlord oppression, and recounted it dramatically and vividly, endowing it with the kind of local colour which was likely to appeal to the readers of such a magazine. 'L'affaire de Gweedore', the sixth in the series, provides a representative example of her technique and of the assumptions she appeals to:

> Dans le Nord-Ouest de l'Irlande près de cette côte, tourmentée et coupée par les vagues de l'Atlantique, dans un pays de montagnes, de marais, de pierres, se trouve le petit village de Gweedore.
> L'esprit du rare voyageur qui s'aventure dans ce pays où il n'y a pas de chemins de fer et où les auberges sont rares et assez primitives, est frappé par la sauvage mélancolie de la scène.
> Là, on voit les représentants de la race celtique la plus pure.
> Ils ont étés refoulés par les Anglais dans cette terre inculte. Derrière leurs montagnes, ils sont vécu pendant des siècles conservant leurs traditions, leurs coutumes et leur langue.

Journal des Voyages

ET DES AVENTURES DE TERRE & DE MER

JOURNAL HEBDOMADAIRE. — Dimanche 28 Octobre 1894. — *PARIS, 12, RUE SAINT-JOSEPH*

ABONNEMENTS. — UN AN : PARIS & SEINE, 8 fr. — DÉPARTEMENTS, 10 fr. — UNION POSTALE, 12 fr.

SOMMAIRE

MISS MAUD GONNE : Le Martyre de l'Irlande. — A. PILGRIM : Mme Hiawaczek. — H. LEVURQUE : L'Indien Blanc. — E. TOUCY : Volentum. — W. DE FONVIELLE : Le Tour de France en Ballon. — A. CHEVALIER : L'Héritier du Rajah. — R. JOLLY : Les Missions Françaises. — F. D'ESTRÉE : La Chasse à la Chouette.

— CH. LEROY : AUX PAYS des Timbres. — CAPITAINE MAYNE-REID : L'Ile du Diable. — F. DILLAYE : Considérations générales sur le 8e Concours Photographique. — J. HOCHÉ : Le Mont Thabor. — Chronique des Voyages. — Récréations Géographiques et Historique. — Variétés.

PRIX 15 C.

LE MARTYRE DE L'IRLANDE

PAR MISS MAUD GONNE

8. Cover of *Journal des Voyages*, 28 October 1894, featuring Maud Gonne's article, 'Le Martyre de l'Irlande'.

Travailleurs, doux, sobres, ces paysans sont exploités toujours par les landlords étrangers qui les ont réduits à une misère profonde. Est-elle sans espérance?[5]

The article then goes on to recount how hope was provided by a Catholic priest, Father Fadden, who took the side of the peasants against their landlords, joining forces with the Land League. The British and the landlords sent troops and police to arrest the priest while he was celebrating mass. Shocked at this sacrilege, and believing that Father Fadden had been murdered, the congregation turned upon the officers of the English law and killed one of them, for which Father Fadden was arrested and tried for murder and the whole village raided and burnt to the ground.[6]

Other articles in the series tell of evictions, famine, and the efforts of the Land League to help the rural poor in Ireland. There are also some later reports, including one on the 1897 demonstrations in Dublin at the time of Queen Victoria's Jubilee, when 'more than ten thousand people' followed a coffin and funeral parade symbolizing the death of the British Empire, and police charged the crowd causing the death of an elderly woman. Another takes the occasion of the 1899 unveiling of a memorial in Manchester to three Fenians hanged in 1867 ('the Manchester Martyrs'), to recount the story of their arrest and trial in the context of violently anti-Irish feeling and action. She includes a possibly apocryphal story of a schoolgirl murdered by her English schoolfellows for wearing a green rosette on the first anniversary of the hanging.

In May 1897, Maud Gonne and her editorial staff launched in Paris (the address was 6, rue des Martyrs!) *L'Irlande Libre: Organe de la Colonie Irlandaise à Paris*, a monthly paper usually consisting of four pages and selling for ten centimes, devoted to informing French readers, and Irish readers in France, about Irish affairs. The first issue declares its purpose – implicit in the title – of publicizing the Irish cause in France:

> Dans ce titre, expression de notre espérance, nous plaçons tout le programme de nos revendications nationales; est c'est à la France, pays si cher aux opprimés, que nous venons jeter ce cri de liberté. D'ailleurs ne sommes nous pas Celtes aussi, fils de la même race, et notre sang n'a-t-il pas coulé maintes fois sur les mêmes champs de batailles, sous nos drapeaux alliés?[7]

This first editorial goes on to cite the battles and history of Franco-Irish alliances against the British, emphasizing especially the 1798 rebellion, before going on to link Ireland's fate with that of other nations colonized by the British – Australia, India, Egypt and Africa:

> Vingt-cinq millions de marchands avides et déloyaux gouvernent déjà 400 millions d'hommes et revent de l'empire du monde, ou plutôt son exploitation.[8]

Reference is also made to the political significance of the Irish diaspora, and in particular to that of the 'seven million Irish in America', who have 'more than once blocked English diplomatic moves'.

L'Irlande Libre regularly reported news of Irish prisoners and prison conditions in England, political activities in Ireland itself, and fund-raising efforts in the United States and elsewhere. It also sought to expose the iniquities of British rule and exploitation throughout the empire, and reported on conditions in Ireland. There was a series of articles, signed 'Erin', on 'L'Irlande Sous Victoria', and Maud Gonne signed her own name to articles on the Jubilee, on famine at Belmullet, and on English atrocities in Ireland. The paper also commissioned and printed articles by James Connolly (at that time little known to French or Irish readers) on evictions and famine in Kerry; by W.B. Yeats on the Celtic Movement featuring Fiona McLeod and John O'Leary; by M. Barry Delaney on the Irish heroine Betsy Gray; by Michael Davitt on 'Anglo-Saxon Alliances'. The August issue in 1898 contained a number of articles on the Wolf Tone centenary, together with an article by James Connolly on the necessity for socialism in Ireland (vol. 2, no. 8). The main emphasis of *L'Irlande Libre* was nationalist, and it reiterated the political and economic consequences of British colonialism. Cultural–nationalist contributions, such as Yeats's articles on the Celtic Movement, were comparatively rare; so too were feminist pieces (however implicit), like Barry Delaney's account of Betsy Gray's heroism. Other short biographies in her series on Irish martyrs focused on figures from the male pantheon, such as Edward FitzGerald and Henry John McCracken.

In contrast, *The Shan Van Vocht* was firmly cultural–nationalist in orientation, and often implicitly feminist. Edited from Belfast by two Irish poets, Alice Milligan and Anna Johnson (who wrote under the name of Ethna Carberry), this literary magazine was published from 1896 until 1899. The magazine sought to avoid

9. Maud Gonne in 1897 when she was on a fund-raising tour of the United States.

party or factional politics, and in consequence suffered financially through the lack of any particular group to fund it. A relatively large proportion of the contributors were women, but male contributors included AE (George Russell), Yeats, and James Connolly, although the editors took pains to disassociate themselves from Connolly's socialism. The editors were also not averse to commenting wryly on the exclusion of women from public and cultural affairs. Thus, contrasting the harmonious work of the Irishwomen's Centenary Union with the wrangling which typified the men's organization, an editorial remarked: 'Is it not a fortunate thing that the better half (numerically, of course I mean) of the population of Ireland is not involved in these differences of the polling booths.'[9]

Most pages of *The Shan Van Vocht* belong very much to the Celtic Revivalist mode, with poems drawing upon Irish myth and legend; retellings of episodes from the Irish sagas and romances; articles on past writers such as James Clarence Mangan; instructions on how best to teach and restore Gaelic as the language of Ireland. There were also serializations of historical romances by Katharine Tynan. Poems such as Ethna Carberry's 'The Kisses of Angus', or Nora Hopper's 'To Sheila ni Gara' (Ireland), are barely distinguishable from similar lyrics by male poets of the Celtic Revival – they assume a male voice and speak from the viewpoint of a male lover, and, as in Yeats's early poems, the desired woman is a symbol of a lost or unattainable ideal, or an allegorical figure of Ireland – in both cases an unchanging essence whose physicality is at first subsumed into a stylized series of epithets:

> The first bird sings of my lady's eyes,
> The second her lips where the laughter lies,
> The third her beauty of white and red,
> The last the *cool* of her radiant head.

It is then safely buried beneath ogham stones and melancholy:

> *Mo bhron, mo bhron*, my lady's sleep
> Under the bracken is cold and deep;
> At head and foot stands an ogham-stone
> With my carved lament on each pillar stone.[10]

Within this prevailing mode, an early number of *The Shan Van Vocht* published a poem which is a kind of hymn to Maud Gonne, written by her associate editor for *L'Irlande Libre*, M. Barry Delaney. It reads:

Maud Gonne

Uncrowned, save by a nation's love, our island's maiden queen,
By spell of her young voice alone, unfurls the standard green,
Where in the days of gallant Hoche, the sword of Tone fell keen!

[. . .]

Alone our Maid of Erin pleads, as once the Orleans Maid
Before whose mystic banner fled the Saxon host afraid
As now when, by a maiden's words, are Erin's foes dismayed!

Oh, fairest flower of womanhood, her weakness is her strength:
Proud hearts unto her passionate plea a willing ear have lent,
And knees to her, the Uncrowned, bowed, that ne'er before had bent!

Not nobler the soldier who his sword in combat draws,
Or patriot who frames at home his country's code of laws,
Than she who pleads in stranger tongue her island's sacred cause.[11]

While this poem has all the sincerity and banality of others written at the time, for example those in the popular *The Spirit of the Nation* anthology, and parodied in Joyce's 'Ivy Day in the Committee Room', nevertheless, there are interesting ways in which it counters both the nationalist song tradition and poetry about women (including those love poems by Yeats relating to Maud Gonne). In the first place, it firmly asserts a woman as hero and as leader, in an allusion which would be quickly recognized by an Irish readership who habitually heard the title 'Our Uncrowned King' applied to Parnell. Moreover, it asserts that her heroism as speaker is just as noble as that of the male warriors celebrated in nationalist song. Secondly, it emphasizes, above all, voice rather than appearance or body, and actions rather than essence; as Joan of Arc was the Maid of Orleans (where 'of' signifies both 'from' and 'belonging to'), Maud is the maid *of* Erin, although, at times in the poem, she also gains the attributes of the unchanging fair maiden Erin herself. In response to those press reports and love poems which spoke mainly, or only, of Maud Gonne's physical beauty, the first stanza makes the assertion that it is 'By spell of her young voice *alone*' that she wins admiration and causes change [my emphasis]. For Barry Delaney (she signs the poem with this masculine version of her name), Maud Gonne is not to be compared to the passively beautiful and fateful Helen of Troy, but to actively crusading nationalists: Joan of Arc, Wolf Tone and, implicitly, Charles Stewart Parnell. The poem goes on to remind readers of Maud Gonne's activities – as Francophone journalist and lecturer 'Who pleads in stranger tongue her island's sacred cause', as helper to the evicted, and as a visitor to prisoners, 'The living-dead who pine within dark Portland's cruel walls'.

Maud Gonne and the editors of *The Shan Van Vocht* would not have dissented seriously from the import of Barry Delaney's poem that whatever activities women undertook in the cause of nationalism, among which activities speaking and writing might be pre-eminent, armed combat should pertain to male rather than female heroes. It is a view endorsed by Maud Gonne's patriotic play, *The Dawn* (1904), in which, as in *Cathleen ni Houlihan*, the men are inspired or shamed into fighting on behalf of their womenfolk, whose role is one of passive resistance. (One important difference between the two plays, however, is that between the abstract idealism of the one written by Lady Gregory and W.B. Yeats, where Michael leaves wealth and comfort to fight for the glory of Ireland and himself, and Maud Gonne's dramatization of the concrete sufferings – famine, forced labour, and evictions – which anger and stir to action the men who are to bring about 'the Dawn'.) This view that women should not be soldiers would not be endorsed by Constance Markievicz who, together with Maud Gonne, was a steady contributor to *Bean na h-Eireann*.

Founded at a meeting initiated by Helena Moloney, writer, actress, and secretary of Inghinidhe na h-Eireann, and attended by Constance Markievicz, Ella Young, and Sydney Gifford, the *Bean* was proudly advertised as the first Irish women's paper, and declared itself to stand for 'Freedom for Our Nation and the complete removal of all disabilities to our sex'. An article called 'Free Women in a Free Nation', signed 'Maca', one of the pseudonyms used by Constance Markievicz, typifies the line taken by the paper on feminism and nationalism. Arguing that 'no one should place sex before nationality or nationality before sex', the article acknowledges the importance of the vote and the ways in which its denial to women has been used to make them even more powerless. Nevertheless, Maca argues against affiliation of Irish women's groups with English suffragist societies, or their joining in demonstrations for the parliamentary vote at Westminster, since this would contravene Sinn Fein policy and would implicitly recognize English parliamentary rule over Ireland. Rather, Maca declares:

> We will teach our men to look upon us as fellow-Irelanders and fellow-workers, willing to strive as they have striven, to die as they have died, of whose usefulness there can be no question, and on whose right to citizenship no doubt can be thrown.

She urges women to trust in Irishmen's commitment to liberty as a total commitment, and assures them that: 'The day that Ireland stands free before the world shall see our emancipation too.'[12]

This article by Constance Markievicz is in line with an editorial in the same issue:

> The Feminist cause in Ireland is best served by ignoring England and English politicians. . . . At all events, women should first set their own house in order. Women are denied a place in some of the most important political organizations in Ireland. The United Irish

League (with the exception of one branch, we believe), the Loyal
Orange Association, the Liberal Home Rule Association are exclusively masculine bodies. The Gaelic League and the Sinn Fein
Organization are the only ones in existence at present where women
are on an equal footing with men. For that reason they are worthy of
the support of every Irish Suffragist.[13]

Both the article and the editorial were in part responding to a letter
from Hannah Sheehy-Skeffington, co-founder of the Irishwomen's
Franchise League, advocating that women press for the parliamentary vote. The November 1909 issue of the *Bean* published a much
longer statement of her position by Sheehy-Skeffington. In 'Sinn
Fein and Irishwomen', she argued that the recognition of women's
past glories and rights in pre-colonial Celtic society was 'barren
comfort for us Irishwomen' in 'the abject present', and went on to
ask rhetorically:

> Is the degradation of the average Irishwoman the less real, her
> education sacrificed to give her brothers ampler opportunities of
> having a good time loitering through their examination in the
> capital, her marriage a matter of sordid bargaining, broken maybe
> because an over-insistent prospective father-in-law demands a cow or
> a pig too much, her 'fortune' (the word is significant and the
> fortuneless had better never been born) instead of being, in French
> fashion, sensibly settled on her and her children, handed over to her
> husband to dispose of as he may think fit, it may be to pay his racing
> debts, or, if he is a generous brother, to endow a sister for the
> matrimonial market, or equip an aspiring brother for the
> priesthood.[14]

The situation of women in Ireland could only partly be blamed on
Anglicization, Sheehy-Skeffington argued, for they had even fewer
rights than Englishwomen did. Even within those organizations,
such as the Gaelic League and Sinn Fein, which had been forced to
admit women to their ranks, women were limited to traditional
roles related to mothering and housekeeping. She concluded:

> Until the Parliamentarian and the Sinn Fein women alike possess the
> vote, the keystone of citizenship, she will count but little with either
> party, for it is through the medium of the vote alone that either
> party can achieve a measure of success. This is a fact which we
> Parliamentarians have long been aware of to our cost, but which
> Sinn Fein women have yet to learn.

Hannah Sheehy-Skeffington's article was followed by a storm of
letters from women members of the Sinn Fein party, as well as
further comments from the editors and Constance Markievicz. One

When she gets it, what will she do with it?

10. 'When she gets it, what will she do with it?': one of many anti-feminist cartoons featured in *The Leprecaun*. This one is from the May 1913 issue.

correspondent accused her of 'scrambling for her mess of pottage', and urged her to regard the situation from the 'broader standpoint' of an Irish nationalist, not from the 'standpoint of a woman . . . willing to join with her country's conquerors and worst enemies to gain her end'. Sheehy-Skeffington was given ample space to reply to her critics in a two-page article in the January 1910 issue, in which she pointed out the inconsistency of those who paid British taxes, accepted British pensions, used the British postal service, and yet declared that it was a betrayal of nationalist ideals to seek the vote for women, since, anyway, the vote was not in and of itself a British institution and it was 'a mistaken piece of generosity on the part of "Sinn Feiner" to ascribe its invention to Englishmen'.

The debate continued over many numbers of the *Bean*, and although the priorities of nationalism and feminism were repeatedly argued by each side, neither really came to grips with the chief points made by its opponents. Hannah Sheehy-Skeffington was also involved more indirectly in another debate which occupied many pages, particularly in later issues of the *Bean*, and that was over the advocacy of physical force. She and her husband Francis were firm pacifists, and their pursuit of a parliamentary or constitutional resolution of both the national and the sexual conflict was consistent with their pacifism. Maud Gonne, Con Markievicz and the editorial columns of the *Bean* generally asserted both the necessity and desirability of physical force as a means of liberating Ireland. An unsigned three-page essay in the September 1909 issue dismisses Arthur Griffith's advocacy of 'Moral Force' stopping short of bloodshed as unrealistic in face of the actuality of British armed oppression in Ireland and elsewhere. Like a number of other editorials and articles in subsequent numbers of the *Bean*, it calls upon 'our boys' to stop enlisting in British forces and exercise their 'manhood' in the cause of Ireland, quoting John O'Leary's remark:

> Fighting, or any talk about fighting, has gone quite out of fashion in Ireland of late, but I must be excused for still thinking that a people who are not prepared to fight in the last resort rather than remain slaves will never be made free by any sort of Parliamentary legerdemain whatsoever.[15]

The following number included another editorial article along these lines and also began, as a regular feature, reports on the activities of the Fianna Eireann from their founder and leader Constance Markievicz, signing herself 'the Druid of the Fianna'. At the same time, she began contributing a regular column on gardening under the signature 'Armith'. The second year of the *Bean* added regular contributions on women and the labour movement, which exposed the terrible conditions under which many women worked, and denounced the failure of the Dublin United Trade and Labour Council to organize women workers. (Many members of the Inghinidhe, including Helena Moloney and Constance Markievicz, would later become very actively involved with James Connolly and the labour movement.) Maud Gonne contributed an effective plea for the provision of free school meals

11. Irish women unload guns from the *Asgard*, the ship which smuggled arms into Howth for the Irish Volunteers in July 1914.

for the poorer children of Dublin (the Inghinidhe set about organizing for their provision). Other regular items included a column called 'The Woman *with* a House', articles on fashion and cookery, and extracts from Constance Markievicz's lecture (reprinted as a pamphlet by the Inghinidhe na h-Eireann), 'Women, Ideals and the Nation' side by side with advertisements for 'Dripsey Dress Cloths' guaranteeing to make 'the "Kathleen Ni Houlihan" lovelier than ever! The Prices Lower than Ever!'. In short, the *Bean*, throughout its short life, contained all the circumscribed variety and inconsistency that one can find today on the Women's page of the liberal newspapers, although its debates were conducted with rather more urgency and intensity. A note from Constance Markievicz's gardening column, telling how to deal with slugs, combines, in a rather startling way, nationalist discourses of warriorhood and stereotyped feminization, and suggests

12. Constance Markievicz in the uniform of the Irish Citizen Army.

that although she herself did not accept the polarization of roles (she fought in the Irish Citizen Army and became the first elected woman member of Parliament and first Woman Minister, for Labour), she was still caught within the *terms* of those discourses:

> A good nationalist should look upon slugs in a garden much in the same way as she looks upon the English in Ireland, and only regret that she cannot crush the Nation's enemies as she can the garden's, with one tread of her dainty foot.[16]

CHAPTER NINE

'Working for What We Believed Would Help Ireland':

Lady Gregory

July 18, 1927. Poor Mme Markievicz also gone. Her funeral on Sunday was made a Republican demonstration. I knew her in her Castle days when she was rather a jealous meddler in the Abbey and Hugh's Gallery. But her energy found a better scope when she took up the Labour movement, and then a more violent outlet in 1916 when she fought with the Boy Scouts she had trained, against the English troops, and was imprisoned. I remember one evening when I was coming from some hard hours' work at the Abbey I felt tired and jaded on the tram. And then she got in, tired and jaded also from some drilling of her 'Fianna', and I felt drawn to her. There was something gallant about her. We were each working for what we believed would help Ireland, and we talked together.[1]

Lady Gregory's brief recollections of Constance Markievicz tell us more about herself than about her ostensible subject. They reveal her own fiercely protective attitude towards the Abbey Theatre and the Hugh Lane collection, her dedication and toil to both in 'working for what we believed would help Ireland'; her generosity towards those who differed with her about the best way to further that cause, her sympathy towards the Labour movement, and her dismayed reaction to the more violent outlet of physical force espoused by Maud Gonne and Con Markievicz. In these matters she differed from W.B. Yeats, and it is ironic that for Lennox Robinson, introducing the above extract, Constance Markievicz's lasting obituary is contained in Yeats's poems 'On a Political Prisoner' and 'In Memory of Constance and Eva Gore-Booth'

13. Lady Gregory, 1911.

rather than the words of Lady Gregory which comment on what the Countess did and felt, not what she looked like.

Yeats identifies the Gore-Booths in their youthful beauty with Lissadell and the social order epitomized by the Big House. Lady Gregory is identified by him as an even more powerful representative of that order, and as a patron of culture and the arts:

> I meditate upon a swallow's flight,
> Upon an aged woman and her house,
>
> [. . .]
>
> They came like swallows and like swallows went,
> And yet a woman's powerful character
> Could keep a swallow to its first intent;
> And half a dozen in formation there,
> That seemed to whirl upon a compass-point,
> Found certainty upon the dreaming air,
> The intellectual sweetness of those lines
> That cut through time or cross it withershins.[2]

'The Municipal Gallery Revisited' reiterates Yeats's equation of her house with the person of Lady Gregory:

> But in that woman, in that household where
> Honour had lived so long, all lacking found

but also praises 'All that pride and all that humility', and hymns shared ideals and work:

> John Synge, I and Augusta Gregory, thought
> All that we did, all that we said or sang
> Must come from contact with the soil, from that
> Contact everything Antaeus-like grew strong.
> We three alone in modern times had brought
> Everything down to that sole test again,
> Dream of the noble and the beggar-man.

These lines are among the more memorable in Yeats's *oeuvre* and are often quoted as summarizing not only Yeats's programme but also that of the friends he names. Few have stopped to ask how much they obscure Lady Gregory's own dream – and Synge's. Here, what is ostensibly praise of Lady Gregory in her own right – and at last a mention of what she said, rather than what she enabled others to say – is in fact a conscription of her work and Synge's into Yeats's own project. John Synge wrote of peasants and beggarmen but not of nobles, except in his very first and last plays. The first play about Mary Queen of Scots he rejected; the last turns Deirdre into a peasant girl. Yeats's Deirdre, by contrast, *is* a noble, and both she and Naoise determine to act their part as nobles in the same pattern as their royal predecessors, Lugaidh Redstripe and his wife. And although Lady Gregory wrote about Dervorgilla, Grania, and other 'nobles', it was not so much their 'nobility' that concerned her as their humanity. Similarly, her peasants, like Synge's and like O'Casey's Dubliners, exist not so much as essential oppositions to the nobles, but as poor people, caught in a particular way of life whose poverty of material and aesthetic conditions they often wish to escape.

In *Our Irish Theatre*, Lady Gregory wrote that she 'was the first to use the Irish idiom as it is spoken, with intention and belief in it'.[3] She refers here to her use and development of what she called 'Kiltartan' Irish for the language of her renderings of the Irish legendary cycles (*Cuchulain of Muirthemne*, 1902 and *Gods and Fighting Men*, 1904) and also for the language of *Cathleen ni*

Houlihan and *A Pot of Broth*, both written in collaboration with Yeats in 1902. In that same year she also wrote two comedies on her own, *The Jackdaw* and *A Losing Game*. Lady Gregory's phrase concerning her use of the Irish idiom 'with intention and belief in it' does indeed distinguish her from her predecessors who used the Irish idiom as a language which could evoke only humour or pathos, a language associated with the stage Irishman, and the butt of many an English (and Irish) joke. Like Synge she spoke and understood Irish well, and like him she found the language and the characters she wished to celebrate inseparable.[4]

Elizabeth Coxhead, in her seminal biography of Lady Gregory,[5] laments that after her death and a series of glowing obituaries in 1932, Lady Gregory has been almost forgotten in Ireland except as Yeats's friend. The surviving image of her as most importantly Yeats's patron and friend, and as an emblem with Coole Park of an aristocratic Anglo-Irish tradition to which he could appeal, Elizabeth Coxhead sees as resulting from Yeats's own disloyalty to her memory:

> In *Dramatis Personae* he belittled her personality and made no mention of her plays, and . . . he allowed Oliver St. John Gogarty to publish, and took no steps to contradict, insinuations that he, Yeats, had written the best of her plays himself.[6]

Sean O'Casey writing some years before Coxhead, in the fourth volume of his autobiography, *Inishfallen, Fare Thee Well*, had seen that friendship with Yeats as more fortunate for Yeats than for Lady Gregory. Referring to the writing of *Kincora*, which Yeats had advised Lady Gregory to 'give up', O'Casey comments:

> Why didn't Yeats mind his own business! A pity the woman was so near to Yeats while she was writing the play: he had a bad effect on her confidence in her own creation. She was concerned with him and her play; he concerned only with himself. He had no right to tell her to give up writing her play; but she served so frequently in so many common ways that Yeats easily dismissed from his mind her natural vigour in the creation of imaginative drama.[7]

From other comments, it appears that O'Casey nevertheless accepted Lady Gregory's own diffident assessment of her plays as 'work-a-day' pieces that kept the theatre going, but not comparable in importance with the drama of her better-known contemporaries – Yeats, Synge, Shaw, and O'Casey himself. For O'Casey, Lady Gregory's major achievement was to give the Abbey Theatre 'enduring life', given not by Yeats, not Martyn, not Miss Horniman but:

> By this woman only, who in the midst of venomous opposition, served as a general run-about in sensible pride and lofty humility, crushing time out of odd moments to write play after play that kept life passing to and fro on the Abbey stage.[8]

O'Casey's assessment is shared by Una Ellis-Fermor, who also seems to accept Yeats's view of a woman's role:

> Her contribution to the movement was, even as a writer, still characteristically feminine; it provided the means or the medium by which men of genius could realize themselves.[9]

Yeats was to use yet another metaphor to describe Lady Gregory's usefulness to him as well as the strength he admired in her; he wrote of her as 'an anvil on which he hammered out his thoughts'![10]

Elizabeth Coxhead argues the worth of Lady Gregory's plays in their own right as 'a source of pleasure and enrichment', forming 'the natural complement to those of Synge'.[11] In a later passage, Coxhead elaborates on this comparison:

> The ear which can catch the charm of her gentle notes is all the better fitted to appreciate the thunder of his. So, after a week of listening to the sea's surge and the gull's crying along the cliffs of Inishmaan, does one return in contentment to the blackbirds and thrushes of the Coole lakeside, and even to the homely cackle of the poultry yard.[12]

Coxhead's observation about Lady Gregory's work as comparable and complementary to Synge's is a valid one, but the terms she uses, suggesting 'nature' as their common element, are misleading, and the comparison of Lady Gregory's work to 'the homely cackle of the poultry yard' seems, to say the least, unfortunate! It is a comparison which suggests that even Coxhead's thinking is caught in categories which allot different contexts and expectations to works by male and female authors, the one forceful, vital and truly part of nature, the other gentle, domesticated, and rather sentimental. What Synge and Lady Gregory do share, in addition to a good ear for the spoken language and the ability to construct a plausible and effective Irish literary idiom from it, is the influence of French classical drama, and a sense of structure which is comparable to musical structures. Lady Gregory wrote in 1925:

When Birrell said he had seen De Valera, a young man, playing the
piano at school where he was at some ceremony, and I told him he
had been a mathematical master, he said, 'Yes, music and mathematics always go together,' and that seemed strange to me. But
thinking on *Quixote* yesterday, I thought that might also apply to a
play, the balance of weight, the minute calculating of it in advance,
(as they say, the dome of St. Paul's was built on a sheet of paper)
comes into the building of a play, as does 'music' – the balanced
delight of sentences – of words.[13]

Like Synge, Lady Gregory wrote drama, both comic and tragic,
based on Irish legend, folk tale and anecdote, for a national theatre.
Unlike Synge, but like Yeats, she also wrote some 'nationalist'
drama, which commented on and encouraged nationalist sentiment.
Cathleen ni Houlihan was the first of these; the setting was her
idea, but its ending and thus the force and direction of its
sentiment came from Yeats. Between 1905 and 1907, she wrote
three more nationalist plays, each of which in different ways can be
seen as endorsing an understanding of nationalism and nationalist
feeling which is distinctively different from that endorsed by Yeats.

The first of these, *The Gaol Gate*, which Lady Gregory later said
she 'liked better than any in the volume',[14] provides an interesting
contrast to *Cathleen ni Houlihan*. Mary Lou Kohfeldt describes the
play as one where 'a man gives his life for the ideals of his country
and his class'.[15] This seems to me a curious reading of the play.
For its reiterated message is not that Dennis Cahel has given his life
for an abstract ideal of country or class (indeed it is significant that
any mention of the ideals for which he and his friends thought they
may have been fighting is absent), but for his *neighbour*. And those
who are most affected by his death are not symbolic female figures,
who summon the hero to fight on their behalf, but his realistically
portrayed wife and mother. In *Cathleen ni Houlihan*, family and
social ties are seen as an obstruction to greater glory, and the
opinion of the father, mother and sweetheart are seen as 'not worth
a rush', being 'merely' materialistic and mundane; in *The Gaol
Gate*, the opinion of others, the 'good name' of the family, and
concern for one's neighbour, are the primary values.

In its focus on the women who take centre stage, while the son
dies off stage, in its intensity of feeling, aroused especially through
the powerfully lyrical *caoines* uttered first by Mary Cushin, the
wife, and last by Mary Cahel, the mother, *The Gaol Gate* is
comparable to Synge's *Riders to the Sea*. It even shares with *Riders*

the pathos of the dead man's clothing being all that is left to the two women, and their sadness at his being denied a proper burial. But in its ending it contrasts with *Riders to the Sea* as well as with *Cathleen ni Houlihan*, for Mary Cahel acknowledges the triumph of social feeling and Christian love, while Maurya accepts the power of nature. The stage setting of *Riders to the Sea* and its language is dominated by the presence of the sea, which will take all Maurya's menfolk from her; *The Gaol Gate*, as its title indicates, is dominated by the prison, constructed and guarded by men to protect a certain kind of society. It is a society which imprisons men who attack it, and excludes women both through the law and the letter. The women are prevented from intervening in the workings of those in power not only by their distance, but also by language and illiteracy, for they cannot read the letter which tells them Dennis is to be executed. The knowledge they think they have is based on rumour, and proves to be false, and it is significant that Dennis triumphs through silence. By refusing to speak, he saves the lives of his friends, and so saves his reputation but loses his life. The nationalism endorsed by this play involves neither violent confrontation with the enemy nor sacrifice for an abstract Ireland, but non-cooperation, and insistence on a self-contained Irish community which gives and sustains its own values. What the magistrates, judges, and other representatives of English order think is of minor significance, and indeed scarcely reaches the women in the play because it is couched in language which is foreign to them.

Whereas for both Yeats and Synge, Christianity, and especially Catholicism, represents part of an alien and imposed ideology which must also be cast off, for Lady Gregory Christianity forms an integral part of those communal Irish values. Not only do the two Marys, mother and wife, waiting by the prison gate, recall the traditional Christian iconography of the two Marys standing beneath the cross and waiting to receive the body of Christ, but the final triumphant words of the play directly allude to the New Testament declaration, 'Greater love hath no man than this, that a man lay down his life for his friends' (John, 15:13). In *Cathleen ni Houlihan*, *Riders to the Sea*, and *Playboy*, Christianity is linked with bourgeois and materialist values, which are thrown off when true Irishness makes its appeal; in *The Gaol Gate* traditional Irish and Christian values are shown to be closely related, and Mary Cahel rejoices because the family's good name has been redeemed *because* her son was truly Christlike. The Christian iconography of the staging, the resonance of the final lines embrace representative members of a community which in its language, politics, and culture, particularly demonstrated in the two *caoines*, is distinctively Celtic, and the two merge in the lines which begin and end Mary Cahel's traditional *caoine*.

The Rising of the Moon also takes up the theme of conflict between patriotic sentiment, identified with folk and childhood memory, and the law, but in comic rather than tragic mode. Like *The Gaol Gate*, it rejoices in the triumph of humane fellow feeling over self-interest and obedience to the law, and also merges such fellow feeling with patriotism. The play was at first viewed with some ambivalence by both sides:

> The play was considered offensive to some extreme Nationalists before it was acted because it showed the police in too favourable a light, and a Unionist paper attacked it after it was acted because the policeman was represented as 'a coward and a traitor'.[16]

It soon became one of Lady Gregory's, and the Abbey Theatre's, most popular plays, however, and is still frequently performed. *The Rising of the Moon* demonstrates her comic wit and imagination, together with her talent for dramatic construction, at its best. The image of the two men sitting back to back on a barrel on which is pasted the poster of the wanted rebel they are both ostensibly seeking, while the stranger gradually elicits the possibility that the two of them once might have been as one, is indeed a brilliant conceit. Here, as in *Cathleen ni Houlihan*, it is patriotic songs which can gradually subvert loyalty to the life of the law, uncovering buried memories, but it is typical of Lady Gregory's vision and desire, that this appeal to patriotism, and to the memory and love of Ireland, this time in the figure of 'Granuaile', should unite rather than divide the two main characters in the play, the rebel and the upholder of English law.

Such a resolution, together with the comedy of the play, masks a conflict which Lady Gregory, like Yeats and Synge, found less easy to resolve, the conflict between 'the small and the big', voiced in Yeats's 'Upon a House Shaken by Land Agitation'. The recognition of class conflict appears twice in Lady Gregory's play, the first time when the Sergeant tells his colleague, 'Haven't we the whole country depending on us to keep law and order? It's those that are down would be up and those that are up would be down, if it wasn't for us.'[17] At the close of the play, the interests of the nationalists and the interests of the poor are linked when the Man tells the Sergeant who has not betrayed him, 'maybe I'll be able to do as much for you when the small rise up and the big fall down . . . when we all change places at the Rising . . . of the Moon'.

Based in part on Lady Gregory's recollections of the story told her by her childhood nurse, Mary Sheridan, of the escape by boat of the rebel Hamilton Rowan, the play itself is, like so much of Lady Gregory's work, an attempt to merge her imagination with that of the Gaelic/Irish underclass which served members of the Anglo-Irish ascendancy. At the same time she strove to maintain Coole Park as a legacy for her son Robert, and then for his children. The conflict between her loyalty to her family and her sympathy for nationalist aspirations which also involved a vision of a time 'when the small would rise up and the big fall down', is one that she recognized, implicitly and explicitly, in her plays and journals. In 1930, two years before she died, she wrote in her journal on the eve of her grandson, Richard's, twenty-first birthday:

> But it is a contrast to Robert's coming-of-age, with the gathering of cousins and the big feast and dance for the tenants – Coole no longer ours. But the days of landed property have passed. It is better so. Yet I wish some one of our blood would after my death care enough for what has been a home for so long, to keep it open.[18]

Much of the humour and tension in *The Rising of the Moon* arises from the disguise worn by the rebel escapee, who pretends to be a wandering beggar and ballad singer. Disguise of one kind or another is a common device in Lady Gregory's plays, as it is in Synge's, and in her next play, *Dervorgilla*, produced at the Abbey in 1907 a few months after *The Rising of the Moon*, it is also significant, for Dervorgilla has attempted to conceal her identity as the woman who deserted O'Rourke for Diarmiud, and thus helped bring about the conflict which resulted in the first incursions of the English. In this play also, a ballad singer is responsible for revealing the buried feelings and memories which Dervorgilla seeks to have forgiven and forgotten. The play itself is also a thin mask or disguise for contemporary events, for Lady Gregory declares in *Our Irish Theatre*:

> *Dervorgilla* I wrote at a time when circumstances had forced us to accept an English stage-manager for the Abbey. I was very strongly against this. I felt as if I should be spoken of some day as one who had betrayed her country's trust.[19]

Lady Gregory's concern and anxiety over this specific event in turn partially conceals anxiety over her own identity as a member of the Anglo-Irish ruling class, which had prospered through the long history of English colonialism. The question which haunts Dervorgilla and the play is whether a historical wrong can ever be undone. Dervorgilla has hidden herself in the Abbey of Mellifont, and devoted herself to good works, giving most of her wealth and her attention to encouraging the young at their sports and crafts, all of which are distinctively Irish. Likewise, Lady Gregory had devoted herself to the Abbey Theatre, and used it as the base for furthering Irish plays and culture, and like some other members of her class, she had sought to be a generous and charitable landlady to her tenants. The play also simultaneously re-enacts and disguises a more carefully concealed guilt – Lady Gregory's infidelity to William Gregory in 1882/83 when she had a passionate affair with Wilfred Scawen Blunt, and one of the most intense passages in the play comes when Dervorgilla laments the wrong she did her first husband:

> Was it not I brought the curse upon O'Rourke, King of Breffny, the husband I left and betrayed? The head I made bow with shame was struck off and sent to the English King. The body I forsook was hung on the walls shamefully, by the feet, like a calf after slaughter. It is certain there is a curse on all that have to do with me. What I have done can never be undone. How can I be certain of the forgiveness of God?[20]

When her loyal servants, Flann and Mona, seek to comfort her by saying that she was merely caught up (like Yeats's Leda) in historical destiny beyond her control, Dervorgilla insists on not shirking the responsibility for what she has done. Her hope that the English may prove beneficial to Ireland after all, 'a rich powerful country to be joined to' and, in Flann's words 'the same as a girl of the ducks and the ashes that would be married to a great lord's son',[21] is shattered when the English soldiers shoot Flann, her supporter and theirs, as he tries to silence the troublesome ballad singer. The attempt to silence his truth has the opposite effect, for Dervorgilla's identity is revealed and she is exposed to 'the

merciless judgement of the young'. Given the context of the Abbey
Theatre and the suspicion of many nationalists concerning the
allegiances and intentions of its management following the *Playboy*
riots earlier that same year, given the increasing tension between
the second generation of nationalists, most of whom were ardent
Catholics and Gaelic Leaguers, and the older generation, founders
of the Literary Societies, Dervorgilla's final speech must also be
seen as a particularly brave and unflinching acknowledgement by
Lady Gregory of her own position. Dervorgilla at first seeks
forgiveness and understanding from the younger generation, but as
one by one they return their gifts and walk away, she accepts their
reproach:

> For there is little of my life but is spent, and there has come upon
> me this day all the pain of the world and its anguish, seeing and
> knowing that a deed once done has no undoing, and the lasting
> trouble my unfaithfulness has brought upon you and your children
> forever . . . There is kindness in your unkindness, not leaving me to
> go and face Michael and the Scales of Judgement wrapped in
> comfortable words, and the praises of the poor, and the lulling of
> psalms, but from the swift, unflinching, terrible judgement of the
> young!

One of the young, Frank O'Connor, wrote that this last speech was
'as noble as anything in Irish literature'.[22]

In a typescript essay titled 'Irish Literature' and dated 24
January 1907, Lady Gregory wrote of her discovery of Irish
literature as the fourth and greatest of the four great intellectual
excitements in her life. After reading Shakespeare for the first time
(for plays and poetry were not considered good for girls), after
learning German 'rather painfully by myself for only French was
thought necessary for a girl' and managing to read a ballad by
Heine, after learning Italian and discovering Dante, she then
learned Irish and 'read in her own language Deirdre's wonderful
lament'.[23] What particularly delighted her about Irish literature
was not only that it still lived and was retold by the peasantry, but
its women heroines. She comments that whereas women were
almost completely absent from the Roland cycle, and in contrast to
the austere women of the Norse and Germanic sagas, Emer and
Deirdre 'have the charm, the power of inspiring and *returning*
romantic love that belonged to the ladies whose lords were knights
of the Round Table' (my italics). Dervorgilla acknowledges the

passion she felt for Diarmiud, her willing acquiescence in their affair, and she remembers him with love and pride. She will not be seen as mere prey 'like the Connacht hag's basket, or the Munster hag's speckled cow. Does the marten that is torn from the woods lull itself in its master's arms?' And part of the terrible judgement she suffers is the misogyny of the young ballad singer, who like Joyce's citizen and Deasey, blames Ireland's problems on a woman. Like Eve, Dervorgilla is to be denounced as the ultimate cause of Ireland's ills:

> He cares little for life, puts trust in a wife,
> It is long it is known they go with the wind;
> A queer thing a woman was joined with O'Rourke
> To show herself kind to a pet from Leinster
>
> The rat in the larder, the fire in the thatch,
> The guest to be fattening, the children famished;
> It was Diarmiud's call that brought in the Gall,
> Let the weight of it fall upon Dervorgilla!

A double insistence on the responsibility of her class and the responsibility of women to reject the view of themselves as mere victims of history, as Ledas taken against their will, informs Lady Gregory's life and writing. Of her three-act play, *Grania*, composed in 1910/11, she wrote:

> I think I turned to Grania because so many have written about sad, lovely Deirdre, who when overtaken by sorrow made no good battle at the last. Grania had more power of will, and for good or evil twice took the shaping of her life into her own hands. The riddle she asks us through the ages is, 'Why did I, having left great grey-haired Finn for comely Diarmiud, turn back to Finn in the end, when he had consented to Diarmiud's death?' And a question tempts one more than the beaten path of history.[24]

Because this play was even closer to her own secret history and her own riddle, Lady Gregory never allowed it to be performed during her lifetime. This manuscript is written, revised and corrected more than most, indicating that the problem Lady Gregory had set herself in writing it and the riddle she sought to unravel was not easily solved.

Lady Gregory's preliminary summary outline for the play is also revealing of another aspect of her early life, for in it she stresses Grania's desire to be married to a great king and so to become part of the great world, for as a girl, Grania has liked best:

> Stories of great queens that had ruled the world. . . . She was always
> certain that she would like to be a great queen, to have the people
> looking at her, and the armies shouting for her and opening a way
> for her.[25]

But in the end she is punished for this desire, with the armies
jeering at her, a figure of scorn, as is Dervorgilla. In this play also,
Lady Gregory dramatizes the conflicts between wifely duty and
instinctive romance, between social and intellectual stimulation and
emotional and bodily desire; the themes of loyalty and betrayal,
and the ensuing judgement of others are again predominant, but in
Grania the question of judgement is not linked to history.
However, both plays dramatize the part played by male misogyny
and male bonding in driving women to make certain choices and in
the judgements pronounced upon them once those choices are
made. And in both, the woman heroine bravely confronts, and
almost courts, the scorn of society. For the heroines of Synge's and
Yeats's dramas, desire is not thus divided. Synge's Deirdre finds in
Naoise and the companionship of his brothers all that she desires;
to be with him is enough. It is her fear that she cannot be forever
all-in-all for Naoise which prompts her to return. Likewise, in
Yeats's *Deirdre*, it is Naoise who longs to rejoin the society of men,
not Deirdre.

Grania desires both social and sexual fulfilment, but finds she
must choose one or the other, and she is mocked and jeered at for
seeking to return to society after choosing sexual fulfilment. What
Grania learns, and the play ironically portrays, is that male passions
are aroused (and controlled) mainly in relation to the responses of
other men. It is not the relationship between himself and Grania
that matters most to Diarmiud, but the relationship between
himself and Finn. Like Deirdre, Grania flees the jealous vengeance
and repression of a man old enough to be her father, but unlike
Deirdre she finds that Finn's presence remains; his foster-son,
Diarmiud, insists on being true to his 'master', and on regarding
Grania as Finn's property to be guarded but not violated. Only the
intervention of a third male, the King of the Foreign, and the
jealousy aroused by *his* attempted transgression, leads Diarmiud to
break his word to Finn and make Grania his wife. Jealousy at
Diarmuid's violation of his property causes Finn to send Diarmiud
to his death in combat with the King of the Foreign. Nevertheless,
the dying Diarmiud can think only of Finn and reconciliation with

him: 'That would be a very foolish man would give up his dear master and his friend for any woman at all.'[26] As Elizabeth Coxhead observes, these dying words show both Grania and the audience that this drama was not 'in the strict sense a love-story at all':

> It is a play in which a woman is ousted from an emotional relationship between two men. The 'love' is that of man for man, of brother for brother: it is loyalty to the warrior band, and a corresponding resentment of the woman who takes away the warrior's freedom, makes trouble with his comrades, distracts him from his purposes in life . . . Its continuing validity was borne out by all Lady Gregory had observed in the world around her, the world of the 'loveless Irishman', the peasant society which relegated women to serfdom, the middle-class intellectual society which left them only the donkey work.[27]

As Coxhead goes on to point out, this view of the Irish woman's role is not limited to Lady Gregory's work. Synge's heroines also try to rebel against the loveless and limited lives they are expected to lead; Joyce and O'Casey show women alone and at home while their men band together and drink and foster their self-esteem in each other's eyes. Nora's plight in *The Plough and the Stars* is perhaps O'Casey's most damning indictment of the male vanity and mutual concern for each other's self-esteem which leads them to neglect their actual wives and mothers ostensibly for that abstraction called Cathleen ni Houlihan or Ireland.

Lady Gregory differs from these writers, however, in not allowing her tragic heroines to be either mere victims, or to accept the possibility that romance and a loving domestic life will be all that they need. It is Diarmiud who imagines that they can escape into romance, a 'land of heart's desire' seen in the mists beyond the seas, while Grania insists that housekeeping is not enough:

> We are the same here as if settled in the clay, clogged with the body and providing for its hunger and its needs, and the readying of the dinner of today and the providing of the dinner for tomorrow.[28]

In contrast to her first youthful decision to marry Finn, Grania's second and final decision to become his wife is made in full awareness of what is lost and gained in that choice. It entails a rejection of the idyll of romantic marriage which experience has taught her is unviable for two reasons – the nature of men, who are more concerned with power and with equality with each other than with women, and the intellectually and socially unfulfilling nature of domesticity. It is her rejection of that ideal and of the role of woman as loyal wife only, that brings the mockery of Finn's all-male army. Faced with the terrible judgement of history, Dervorgilla has retreated into seclusion; faced with the contempt of her present male society, Grania makes a different decision – she will confront it, face it down, and become a part of it.

Lady Gregory expressed a wish to see:

> historical plays being sent by us through all the counties of Ireland. For to have a real success and to come into the life of the country, one must touch a real and eternal emotion, and history comes only next to religion in our country.[29]

In *Poets and Dreamers* she writes of Raftery and his intermingling of history, religion and politics. She frequently articulated her concern with education, and hence writing of history plays in a country where Irish history had been banned in the schools. Hazard Adams commented that her three mythological history plays (*Kincora*, *Grania*, *Dervorgilla*) cast women in pivotal roles:

> But, more important, we learn that history is made out of fundamental human relationships, of the clash of wills, of the passions of domestic life. Her mythological history rips the veil of the high romantic and reveals a dialogue between husband and wife, a hearth and those who keep it or defile it. Her kings and warriors walk our earth, live in houses or are banished from them and argue with their wives. Her heroines are those who 'meddle', who would drive their men or assert their wills, challenge destiny for better or for worse, and live with the results. An old ironic saying tells us that the Irish were all kings once. Lady Gregory's myth tells us the kings were people, and that they had wives. Her plays are expressions of a humanized mythology that grew from the life around her, but that gave back something too – the vision of great things happening among a simple and long-oppressed people.[30]

Adams's final sentence might well describe Synge's *Deirdre* also, but Synge's play differs from Lady Gregory's three in that he removes the sense of the historical or political from Deirdre's context, while Yeats removes all sense of the domestic. These differences might lead us to question Yeats's declaration that 'we were the last romantics'. Lady Gregory and Synge were both classicists; only Yeats was a romantic.

The decade following the writing of *Grania* brought Lady Gregory personal triumph as well as deep personal grief and political change. She twice toured America with the Abbey Players under her supervision, and there found herself a celebrity fêted by President Theodore Roosevelt and other eminent Americans. She also discovered herself as a public speaker whose lectures were well received, as an organizer in full command of the demanding tour and all its arrangements, and as a capable and forceful defender of the group and its right to perform Synge's *The Playboy of the Western World* despite the vociferous attacks in the press, court injunctions to be fought, and the threat of riots. But then, a year after her third tour of America, her dear nephew Sir Hugh Lane was drowned when the *Lusitania* was sunk in 1915. In 1916, her son Robert transferred from the Connaught Rangers into the Royal Flying Corps, and in 1918 he was shot down in Italy. She was also deeply distressed by the violence and subsequent executions of the 1916 Easter Rising, and then by the atrocities perpetrated by the Black and Tans, and by both sides in the Civil War, during which her old family home Roxborough was burned, and Coole Park threatened.

During these years Lady Gregory's political views increasingly diverged from Yeats's. They had been close allies in the founding and development of an Irish Literary Theatre, her friendship with Yeats had certainly encouraged Lady Gregory in those early years to become an avowed nationalist, and Yeats expressed strong indignation at the Dublin City Council's churlish reaction to Hugh Lane's offer to donate his collection of modern paintings to that city. After Hugh Lane's death, he worked closely with Lady Gregory in her struggle to retrieve the pictures from Britain. Her response to the Rising and to the executions of its leaders was in some ways similar to Yeats's, but contained perhaps deeper regret at the waste of young lives and talent and less sense of 'terrible beauty' in the face of their sacrifice. And her autobiography refers repeatedly not just to the leaders of the Rising, but also to the reactions of local people, to the consequences for the poor and powerless, the small farmers and workers who had been arrested. Of the executions she wrote to Yeats:

> My mind is filled with sorrow at the Dublin Tragedy, the death of Pearse and MacDonagh who ought to have been on our side, the side of intellectual freedom, and I keep considering whether we could not have brought them into the intellectual movement. Perhaps those Abbey lectures we often spoke of might have helped. I have a more

personal grief for Sean Connolly, whom I had not only admiration but affection for. He was shot on the roof of the City Hall – there is no one to blame – but one grieves all the same. It seems as if those leaders were what is wanted in Ireland and will be even more wanted in the future, a fearsome and imaginative opposition to the conventional and opportunist Parliamentarians who have never helped our work by intelligent opposition.[31]

As a tribute to Pearse, Lady Gregory herself translated his poem 'Mise Eire' from the Irish. She thought that she, and especially Yeats, could and should do much to help construct a new intellectual leadership, and wrote to Yeats that she was puzzled by his 'apparent indifference to Ireland' after his 'excitement about the Rising'.[32] It is interesting that she chose that particular poem of Pearse's to translate, and it may have influenced her own poem 'An Old Woman Remembers', in which the persona of the old woman becomes a voice of the 'Poor Old Woman'. And in 1919, she took the title role when *Cathleen ni Houlihan* was performed at the Abbey, declaring that all the part needed was 'a hag and a voice'. Despite the humorous self-deprecation of that comment, her taking the role, her translation, and her poem suggest that Lady Gregory had come, like Maud Gonne, to see herself as a kind of embodiment of Ireland, with the right to speak on Ireland's behalf.

Following the Sinn Fein elections in 1918, Lady Gregory became increasingly Republican in her sympathies. She admired De Valera, whom Yeats long despised, she supported the prisoners in Mountjoy Gaol when they went on hunger strike to insist on their claim to be treated as prisoners of war, and she wrote a series of anonymous articles for *The Nation* between October 1920 and January 1921 describing for an English audience the atrocities committed by the Black and Tans. Yeats also denounced the actions of the Black and Tans, and drew on Lady Gregory's articles for his speeches and also for the incident described in his poem, 'Nineteeen Hundred and Nineteen':

> A drunken soldiery
> Can leave the mother, murdered at her door,
> To crawl in her own blood, and go free.

When the Treaty was signed in 1921, Lady Gregory expressed her hope for 'peace in her time' and an end to the need for martyrdom of young men in her poem 'An Old Woman Remembers', published in the *Irish Statesman* in 1921. But her hopes were not fulfilled. Although grieved by the continuing violence on both sides, which her journals describe in great detail particularly as they affect her own part of Galway, Lady Gregory was most horrified by the harsh and repressive measures of the Free State Government. In 1922 she spoke of a plan to form a republican party 'without malice':

> I proposed my plan of a republican party, 'Gan molais', as that could take in all but all sides into itself, a badge, white, yellow, and green with a little dark spot in the corner to remain there until in the natural course of events, and with peaceful pressure a republic is in being. Russell thought it a good idea, and so did most of the party, but there was no one to start it, A.E. saying he is an anarchist, and K. Reddin who much approved being an official, and J. O'Neill the same. Yet I think the idea better than this deadlock.[33]

The journals reveal a running argument with Yeats over the efficacy of executions, which Yeats deemed unpleasant but necessary if order were to be restored, and which she believed only produced more killings in response. She disagreed with Yeats over the Government's arrest of De Valera in August 1923, and its refusal to let him speak.[34] In the 1923 elections when Yeats voted for the Free State Government, she decided not to vote 'because keeping out of this election leaves me free to join those Republicans "without malice" I hope to see organised'. She continued:

> And it is my quarrel with the Government that they did not allow De Valera to make that speech declaring his policy, I think it may probably have been on those lines and the foundation of peace. If all should join to ask for the abolition of that insincere oath it could hardly be refused. And if Ulster is coming in there is little or nothing to quarrel over.
> I am typing *The Story Brought By Brigit*, but near the end of the first act my typewriter struck work again.[35]

The Story Brought By Brigit is based on the Irish legend that the Holy Family came to Ireland when they fled from Herod and were cared for by St Brigit who thirty years later had a vision of Christ's suffering and crucifixion. First staged during Holy Week, April 1924, the play draws upon the popular connection between Irish nationalism and the Biblical yearning for a Messiah to free the Jewish people, and between the Easter Rising and the martyrdom of Christ, a connection heightened by the use of 'Kiltartanese' for the language of the characters in the play. The play opens with a debate between two 'men of the people', Joel, an ardent young nationalist 'from the mountains', and Daniel, a tramp. For Joel, freedom from Roman oppression is a sufficient end, for 'Instead of a bondwoman, our country will become a free woman'; for Daniel, a hardened cynic and materialist, 'freedom never put a penny in anyone's pocket. What is wanted is to do away with the rich, and to give their goods to the poor.'[36] And it is Daniel who prophesies accurately that the people will turn against Christ in the end: 'I've seen them come and seen them go. A great cry at the beginning for anyone with a big voice, and it's likely all turning against him at the latter end.'[37]

In the first act of this three-act Passion Play, Daniel's argument that removing the Romans in and of itself will not bring adequate change unless there is also a radical overturning of the economic system seems to carry some weight, and Joel concedes that it may be 'the moneyed people who are keeping up the foreign government'. The focus of the play shifts, however, to the collaboration between the priests and the Romans, a collaboration which may have reminded Irish audiences of the denunciation of Parnell by the Catholic clergy. In an exchange between the Roman guard, Marcus, and the Hebrew scribe, Silas, it is even suggested that 'the Rising' may have benefited the colonizers in the long run, and for this reason have been condoned by members of the clergy:

> *Marcus.* . . . To tell the clean truth, a little Rising now and then is no harm at all. It gives us an excuse to get rid of disturbers and to bring more of our armies in. A Rising too is very apt to lead to splits, and splits are a great help when you want to keep a country down.
> *Silas.* All right so. Let him stir up discontent and turn the head of the ignorant women and men that believe him to be a messenger from heaven.
> *Marcus.* Be easy now. Pilate will keep an eye on him. He will do nothing to weaken your law, so long as it will help to keep the people quiet in his hand.[38]

Later on, Marcus will become more concerned when Daniel delightedly describes Christ's attack on the traders in the Temple:

> *Marcus.* Cattle-dealers, money-lenders, merchants and moneyed people, the whole fleet of them, and he driving them before them with his scourge.

It is the attack on the moneyed classes, on property, which causes him to agree to arrange for Christ's arrest:

Silas. Will you give him leave to go stir up the whole country,
making his attack on the wealthy and well-to-do?
Marcus. He had best be silenced for a while. Pilate would not give a
clipping of his nail for that thing you call 'religion'. But to turn
around upon property, that is a thing that might spread.[39]

Given the use of the term 'a Rising', and the context of the Civil
War after which this play was written and performed, the
relevance of these lines was unlikely to be missed, and may well
have seemed heretical to both religious and nationalist political
orthodoxy. Such heresy Lady Gregory shares with Synge, Joyce
and O'Casey, all of whom saw the English state and the Roman
Catholic Church as collaborating in the oppression of Ireland. And
with O'Casey she makes the further link between colonialism,
religious division, and the preservation of the economic *status quo*.
In the last half of her play, however, Lady Gregory retreats from
the implications of the drama as she had first begun to develop it.
Daniel, the spokesman for economic change, turns out to be a
looter, himself prepared to collaborate with the priests, and it is he
who hammers the nails into Christ in exchange for money. Joel
repents his earlier defection from Christ for failing to attack Caesar,
and ends the play in anguished remorse and recriminations upon
Judas, himself, and all those who turned against one who 'if he was
not a rebel itself' will have his name 'written in the book of the
people'. Little hope for the future is offered in his despairing
summary, which echoes Daniel's earlier prophecy:

Joel. That's the way of it! All the generations looking for him and
praying for him. We wanted him, and we got him, and what we did
with him was to kill him. And that is the way it will be ever and
always, so long as leaves grow upon the trees.[40]

Only the women remain steadfast throughout the play in their
loyalty to Christ. Political debate and the motives that move the
male characters, greed and the ambition for power, leave them
unchanged in their devotion to Christ. They are present at key
moments, together with Brigit, to express sorrow and compassion.
Their refusal to participate in the struggle for power and change is
their strength; it is also a mark of the play's inability to come to
terms with the debate it has set up in the beginning, and the final
plea for forgiveness and reconciliation, though heartfelt, like the
speeches of Mrs Tancred and Juno in O'Casey's *Juno and the*

Paycock, leave unresolved the question of how the social and economic changes can be made.

Ronald Ayling notes that when Lady Gregory looked back on her life in her late years, she wrote that she had been 'a "rebel" with the nationalists all through – more than they know or my dearest realised'.[41] Her plays, her journals, her attention to language, her letters concerning the executions by the Free State Government and the plight of political prisoners, show her compassion and sympathy for 'common' life and people, her ability to see life from the perspective of others. Sean O'Casey wrote to her:

> And remember you had to fight against your birth and position and comfort, as others had to fight against their birth into hardship and poverty, and it is as difficult to come out of one as it is to come out of the other, so that power may be gained to bring fountains and waters out of the hard rocks.[42]

O'Casey's respectful and affectionate tribute may be set beside Yeats's tributes quoted at the beginning of this chapter. But Lady Gregory's strength lay perhaps most of all in her ability to acknowledge the complexity of her position as inescapably a member of her class while also sympathizing emotionally and intellectually with those who opposed it. As with the Gore-Booth and Parnell sisters and Maud Gonne, that sympathy came in part from unease in a society ordered by men who were unwilling to see her as any other than 'the lady of the house'.

CHAPTER TEN

Custom, Ceremony and Innocence:

Elizabeth Bowen's *The Last September*

> May she become a flourishing hidden tree
> That all her thoughts may like the linnet be,
> [. . .]
> O may she live like some green laurel
> Rooted in one dear perpetual place.
>
> W.B. Yeats, 'A Prayer for My Daughter'
>
> Laurels breathed coldly and close; on her bare arms the tips of leaves were timid and dank, like tongues of dead animals.
>
> Elizabeth Bowen, *The Last September*[1]

Yeats's poem, 'A Prayer for My Daughter', and Elizabeth Bowen's novel, *The Last September*, both take as their subject the relationship between the character of a young woman and the house that she inhabits, a house which simultaneously figures and reinforces a particular social and political structure and nurtures a particular feminine role. Both are set during a time of instability and menace, a time of open political and military rebellion against British colonial forces in 1919 and 1920. Elizabeth Bowen's novel was written, however, almost ten years later, in 1928, and I want to compare it not only with Yeats's 'A Prayer for My Daughter', but also with the series of poems written by Yeats between 1928 and 1931 about Lady Gregory, Coole Park and Lissadell, poems which similarly equate 'a woman's powerful character' with the great house she owned and governed. By this time, the actual political power as well as the cultural hegemony of the Republic of Ireland appeared to have passed from the hands of the Anglo-Irish Ascendancy to the Catholic middle classes and clergy.[2]

At first sight, Bowen's novel shares with Yeats's poems both similarities of subject and striking similarities in terms of imagery. The howling storm, the threatening natural world which disturb Yeats's thoughts and imagination as he meditates upon his daughter's future, or the 'great works constructed [at Coole Park] in nature's spite'[3] may be compared with the recurring sense of menace which is invested in the world beyond Danielstown, the great house in Bowen's novel. Thus it is described in one of the early chapters:

> The screen of trees that reached like an arm from behind the house – embracing the lawns, banks and terraces in mild ascent – had darkened, deepening into a forest. Like splintered darkness, branches pierced the faltering dusk of leaves. Evening drenched the trees; the beeches were soundless cataracts. Behind the trees, pressing in from the open and empty country like an invasion, the orange bright sky crept and smouldered. Firs, bearing up to pierce, melted against the brightness. Somewhere there was a sunset in which the mountains lay like glass.
>
> (*LS*, 22)

Throughout the novel, the world outside the demesne is described or perceived as sinister, and that early image of the orange sky which 'crept and smouldered' is caught up and intensified until it culminates in the final paragraph of the novel in which Danielstown and two other houses are burned, and 'a fearful scarlet ate up the hard spring darkness' (*LS*, 206):

> Here there were no more autumns, except for the trees. By next year light had possessed itself of the vacancy... Leaves, tottering down the slope on the wind's hesitation, banked formless, frightened, against the too clear form of the ruin.
>
> (*LS*, 206)

Elizabeth Bowen imagines the invasion by natural forces which is a consequence of political change, leaving no new structure but only vacancy and desolation, as does Yeats in 'Coole Park, 1929':

> When all those rooms and passages are gone,
> When nettles wave upon a shapeless mound
> And saplings root among the broken stone

But whereas Yeats's 'ancestral houses' begin by ordering and domesticating nature, and provide a vantage point from which to depict a 'paysage moralisé', for Elizabeth Bowen, an opposition between nature and the Anglo-Irish house has always been present. Bowen's essay, 'The Big House', contrasts those houses with their English or French equivalents: 'Unlike the low, warm, ruddy French and English manors, they have made no natural growth from the soil – the idea that begot them was a purely social one.' And she speaks of their appearance as four square, dominating, and lonely.[4] The tenant farmer cottages described in her novel, on the other hand, blend and melt into the landscape.

Nevertheless, that 'purely social idea that begot the Big Houses' is something Bowen can admire at the same time as she acknowledges the violence and conquest which attended their establishment. Like Yeats, she participates in the longing for 'sweetness . . . reared in stone' which in turn can offer a vision of an ordered and disciplined life, nature constrained and ordered by art. Bowen speaks of the spacious and ornate steps, halls, living rooms and staircases which 'contributed to society' and:

> raised life above the exigencies of mere living to the plane of art, or at least style. There was a true bigness, a sort of impersonality, in the manner in which the houses were conceived. After an era of greed, roughness and panic . . . these new settlers who had been imposed upon Ireland began to wish to add something to life. The security they had, by the eighteenth century, however ignobly gained, they did not use quite ignobly. They began to feel, and exert, the European idea – to seek what was humanistic, classic and disciplined.[5]

But as the big houses declined – as they did almost at once, the children of their owners grew up not to be 'mice' but, in Bowen's words:

> *Farouches*, haughty, quite ignorant of the outside world. In this struggle for life, . . . the big house people were handicapped, shadowed, and to some extent queered – by their pride, by their indignation at their decline, and by their divorce from the countryside in whose heart their struggle was carried on.[6]

For Bowen, as for Yeats, no consolation is to be found in the survival of cottages or other structures. The ruined mill, like the ruined tower, speaks only of a violent past which continues to trap both the IRA gunman who hides in it and the Anglo-Irish visitors from the great house who come upon him unawares. The accidental shot which grazes Marda not only foreshadows the later violence but also suggests its futility. Lois is appalled by the tottering structures, dead mills 'like corpses at their most horrible', roofless cottages nestling under the flank of the mill 'with sinister pathos': 'This was her nightmare; brittle staring ruins' (*LS*, 123). It is a nightmare which haunts much Anglo-Irish literature, including Somerville and Ross's *The Big House at Inver* and Yeats's *Purgatory*. Nor is any recourse to be found in the peasantry, who are seen as an alien community, speaking a distinctly different and (to the landlords) insincere language, while they harbour IRA men on the run.

For Lois Farquar, as for the grown daughter Yeats imagines, the big house and all that it stands for seems to be a bulwark against the nightmare of ruins and meaninglessness. When Marda asks her why she does not leave the house, she replies:

> 'I like to be in a pattern . . . I like to be related; to have to be what I am. Just to *be* is so intransitive, so lonely.'
> 'Then you will like to be a wife and mother,' Marda got off the writing table . . . 'It's a good thing we can always be women.'
> 'I hate women,' [Lois replies] 'But I can't think how to begin to be anything else.'
>
> (*LS*, 98–9)

At the same time, Lois would hate to be a man: 'So much fuss about doing things.'

So for Lois, custom and ceremony have a strong appeal. And indeed Elizabeth Bowen, who fought to keep her ancestral home, Bowen's Court, has much sympathy for her desire to 'live like some green laurel/ Rooted in one dear perpetual place'. Despite Bowen's clear-sighted vision of the marginalization and ossification of the Anglo-Irish landed gentry, she shares some of Yeats's contempt for the middle classes, the transient and upwardly mobile men and women who lack the elegance and courtesy of the aristocracy. The Betty Vermonts of this world are mercilessly satirized – because they are not aristocrats, because they are crude and vulgar, and because they are English. Elizabeth Bowen seems to endorse Lady Naylor's dismissal of England, and especially Surrey, as a place of villas, where everything seems new and nothing is deep-rooted. Bowen shares with Yeats what Hermione Lee describes as a 'Burkean conservatism', and an antipathy for the modern urban and industrial world which at its worst is mere snobbishness (caricatured at times in Lady Naylor's attitudes), but which derives from her ideal of the 'humanistic, classic, and disciplined' idea of living which the eighteenth-century Ascendancy builders expressed in their houses.[7]

The Last September explores the appeal of the idea 'of living raised to the place of art, or at least style'; but even more it helps us understand the oppression and unease which results from the determination of the Anglo-Irish to impose that idea in a country which insists upon their presence as alien, where laurel trees are not 'deep-rooted' and flourishing, but are kept carefully trimmed to grow as dank and oppressive shrubs. While Yeats voices the pride of the Anglo-Irish ascendancy and 'their indignation at their decline', Bowen also acknowledges their 'divorce from the country-side' and its consequences. One consequence is the creation of 'farouches'; another is the obsession with a nostalgia for the past, with the *myth* of an ordered and disciplined social construct embodied in the 'Big House'. Bowen speaks of the Anglo-Irish living 'of and for a myth'.[8]

That desire for order is also related to what Elizabeth Bowen, in a letter to V.S. Pritchett, identifies as the most important source of the motive for writing and reading:

> Perhaps one emotional reason why we may write is the need to work off, out of the system, the sense of being solitary and farouche. Solitary and farouche people don't have relationships; they are quite unrelatable . . . My writing, I am prepared to think, may be a substitute for something I have been born without – a so-called normal relationship to society. . .
>
> Shape is possibly *the* important thing . . . I shouldn't wonder if it were the shape, essentially, that the reader, the mass, the public, goes to the story for. The idea of the possibility of shape is not only magnetic, it's salutary. Shapelessness, lack of meaning, and being without direction is most people's nightmare, once they begin to think.[9]

The similarity in the language which Bowen uses to describe the Anglo-Irish and writers suggests that for her, as for Yeats, the condition of being a writer and the condition of being Anglo-Irish are comparable. Both exist in a marginalized state, although both seek to place themselves at the centre, to impose a relationship between themselves and the scene they inhabit. Moreover, the need both for the Anglo-Irish and for writers to discover a shape and meaning, to move beyond futility and mere ritual, is linked to Lois's position as a young woman, at a time of social and historical transition, and her desire to escape a condition in which she feels her futility, where, as she puts it, she feels 'so humiliated the whole time', and longs to 'do something'. In one sense Lois is the daughter who is nurtured by the Big House; and who identifies herself with it, as part of its fixed pattern of living:

> She could not try to explain the magnetism they all exercised by their being static. Or how, after every return – or awakening, even, from sleep or preoccupation – she and those home surroundings still further penetrated each other mutually in the discovery of a lack.
>
> (*LS*, 166)

Like a mother, the house provides nurture, comfort, a definition of being.[10] But it is also, as Lois herself recognizes, a kind of womb which excludes the outside world. As Lois exclaims, following an attack on an army barracks:

> How is it that in this country that ought to be full of such violent realness, there seems nothing for me but clothes and what people say? I might just as well be in some kind of cocoon!
>
> (*LS*, 49)

It is indeed a cocoon that has been consciously constructed by Sir Richard and Lady Naylor. The latter informs her guests: 'From all the talk, you might think that anything was going to happen, but we never listen. I have made it a rule not to talk either.' Similarly, Sir Richard insists when Lois tells of guns being buried in the plantation: 'I will not have the men talking, and at all accounts I won't have them listened to.'

It is also a cocoon which can become oppressive and suffocating:

> The distant ceiling imposed on consciousness its blank white oblong, and a pellucid silence, distilled from a hundred and fifty years of conversation, waited beneath the ceiling. Into the silence, voices went up in stately attenuation.
>
> (*LS*, 20)

And the portraits which fill the dining-room, also oppress: they 'cancelled time, negatived personality and made of the lower cheerfulness, dining and talking, the faintest exterior friction'. Like Auden's enemy within, Laurence longs for an end to this suffocation, and to see the house burn. Lois's attitude is more ambivalent, although she too at moments longs for the house to burn (*LS*, 98) as she envisions an unchanging future.

For Lois, marriage to the young English officer, Gerald, seems to offer an escape from that future, and from the endless humiliation of playing the role of daughter of the house. But Elizabeth Bowen makes us see that marriage to Gerald is no escape. He appeals to Lois for the same reasons that Danielstown and its tradition appeals to her, and indeed the analogy between Gerald and the Irish country house is made explicit:

> In his world affections were rare and square – four-square – occurring like houses in a landscape, unrelated and positive, though with sometimes a large bright looming – as of the sunned west face of Danielstown over the tennis courts.

> (*LS*, 40)

In her desire for certainty, for a future and an identity which is other than that offered her by Danielstown, Lois suppresses her momentary unease at the half-recognition that Gerald's love may be equally suffocating, creating for her a role and an illusion which is entirely constraining, and which insists on her being rather than doing. For Gerald, Lois is the idea which gives meaning to his life, much as Danielstown is the idea which sustains the Naylors and their visitors.

What appeals to Lois in Gerald is his genuine innocence and candour. For in Bowen's novel, the 'innocence' cultivated in the Big House is artificial, and all too difficult to sustain; it is a *refusal* of knowledge and experience, not true innocence, which grows out of custom and ceremony. The artificial innocence shared by the young women, Lois and Livvy, is signalled in the second paragraph of the novel:

> In those days, girls wore crisp white skirts and transparent blouses clotted with white flowers; ribbons, threaded through with a view to appearance, appeared over their shoulders. So that Lois stood at the top of the steps looking cool and fresh; she knew how fresh she must look, like other young girls, and clasping her elbows behind her back, tried hard to conceal her embarrassment.

> (*LS*, 7)

Gerald's innocence comes not from custom and ceremony, but from belonging to a world which is not marginalized, which conceives itself as civilized, central, and in control. It comes from being young, English and male. Gerald believes wholeheartedly in Empire, patriotism, and in the fulfilment of Lois as 'a repository for his emotions':

When he said, 'You will never know what you mean to me,' he made plain his belief in her perfection as a woman. She wasn't made to know, she was not fit for it. She was his integrity, of which he might speak to strangers but of which to her he would never speak.

(*LS*, 50)

After she has learned of his death, Lois thinks, but cannot articulate the link between Gerald's public and private consciousness: 'He loved me, he believed in the British Empire' (*LS*, 203).

Scenes and conversations which explore the relation between Gerald and Lois are frequently juxtaposed with or sandwiched between scenes and conversations which raise the issue of the relationship between English and Irish. Just before the passage quoted above, Lois has herself made the analogy between Ireland and a woman, in a way rather different from the usual nationalist trope. Speaking of the frustration the soldiers must feel at not being able to retaliate, Lois declares:

'You think we don't understand your not being there in time and not doing anything afterwards? We're not all such idiots. We know it's most terribly difficult for you and you must obey orders. It's bad luck the orders are silly. It's all this dreadful idea about self-control. When *we* do nothing it is out of politeness, but England is so moral, so dreadfully keen on not losing her temper, or being for half a moment not a great deal more noble than anyone else. Can you wonder this country gets irritated? It's as bad for it as being a woman. I never can see why women shouldn't be hit, or should be saved from wrecks when everybody complains they're superfluous.'

Gerald's reply suggests there might be other reasons for 'this country' and 'this woman' to get irritated:

'You don't understand: it would be ghastly if those things went.'
'Why? I don't see – and *I* am a woman.'
Which was, of course, exactly why it wasn't to be expected or desired she *should* understand. He smiled, too happy to answer, and tore out a handful of leaves from the privet hedge. She had this one limitation, his darling Lois; she couldn't look on her own eyes, had no idea what she was, resented almost his attention being so constantly fixed on something she wasn't aware of.

(*LS*, 49)

Unlike Gabriel Conroy in Joyce's final *Dubliners* story, Gerald will die convinced of the 'innocence' of the woman he loves, by which he means her lack of self-awareness, her transparency to him but not to herself, her identity as object rather than subject. Yet, as

Bowen's novel reveals, it is Gerald who is single-minded and unselfaware; while Lois and her particular generation of Anglo-Irishmen and women (Lois, Laurence and Marda) share a double-ness of identity and loyalty with regard to nationality and an inability to accept traditional definitions of gender roles, which result in dualities of perception and self-perception. The break in continuity of identity is signified in part by the fact that neither Lois nor Laurence is biologically daughter or son of the house's owners, although they are expected to play the roles of daughter and son.

Eavan Boland has written of her need to combat 'the association of the feminine and the national – and the consequent simplifica-tion of both'.[11] Both James Joyce and Elizabeth Bowen were aware of that association and its consequences, and both set themselves the double task of problematizing notions of nation and gender, largely through the use of multiple perspectives and dislocations of narrative. Bowen, however, uses the perspective of the daughter, rather than the wife and mother, or father and son, to raise questions of female and national identity.

In an essay on the powerful influence of Yeats in creating a myth of an Anglo-Irish aristocracy, Seamus Deane writes of the con-tinuing significance of the 'Big House' in Irish literature:

> Since the death of Parnell, modern Irish writing has been fond of providing us with the image of hero as artist surrounded by the philistine or clerically-dominated mob. This is a transposition of the political theory of aristocracy into the realm of literature, and it has had, since Yeats, a very long run in Irish writing. The Big House surrounded by the unruly tenantry, Culture besieged by barbarity, a refined aristocracy beset by a vulgar middle class – all of these are recurrent images in twentieth-century Irish fiction which draws heavily on Yeats's poetry for them. Since Elizabeth Bowen's *The Last September* (1929) to more recent novels such as Aidan Higgins, *Langrishe, Go Down* (1966), Thomas Kilroy's *The Big Chapel* (1971), John Banville's *Birchwood* (1973) and Jennifer Johnston's *How Many Miles to Babylon?*, the image and its accompanying themes have been repeated in a variety of forms.[12]

Arguably, Deane here oversimplifies Yeats's varied depictions of the Big House, and I would hesitate to conflate Coole Park and the ruined house of *Purgatory*. But the assumption that Bowen presents the 'Big House' in the same light and from the same position as does Yeats is even more questionable. As I have argued above, there *are* some similarities between Coole Park and Danielstown; nevertheless the image and significance of Coole Park is constructed in his poems by a male poet and a father; Danielstown is a fictional analogy to Bowen's Court constructed and deconstructed by a female artist who is a daughter. For Bowen, the difference is important, and it has consequences for the structuring and narrative technique of her novel.

In Yeats's Coole Park and Tower poems, the house or tower is a site from which to view and order the surrounding world. Whether standing on the battlements, or standing at the window, the poet looks out, and from his vantage point gives or acknowledges significance. A single point of view dominates the landscape, and seeks to weave a single narrative, although it may, as in 'The Tower' or 'Meditations in Time of Civil War', gather in, absorb, or reject other narratives. In *The Last September*, the perspective is constantly shifting, often in an unsettling manner for the reader, and, as Toni O'Brien Johnson has demonstrated, the emphasis on light, darkness and perception is so prevalent as to become a dominant motif in the novel.[13] Again and again, Danielstown is described as 'staring', 'blank', 'blind'. On Gerald's arrival for his last meeting with Lois, 'the house so loomed, and stared so darkly and oddly that he showed a disposition – respectful rather than timorous – to move away from the front of it' (*LS*, 170). And Daventry on his mission to announce Gerald's death, 'superciliously returned the stare of the house' (*LS*, 200). There is a repeated emphasis on the darkness and obscurity of the house, a darkness which bears a close relation to the gathering darkness of the shrubberies, and the looming forests beyond which harbour Irish gunmen and hidden guns. Reluctant to remain confined within the obscurity or artificial light of the house, Lois wanders in the darkened gardens and so comes across evidence that Sir Richard and Lady Naylor refuse to acknowledge of subversion and anti-British activity.

For the darkness of the house is a willed darkness, and the light an artificial one, both means of ignoring the natural darkness outside, and ambivalences and confusions within. Thus it is significant that Lady Naylor is trimming the lamps in the drawing-room as she dismisses Lois's proclaimed love for Gerald as nonsense:

Lady Naylor, who wished for a clear steady light these lengthening evenings, saw to the lamps personally. In big yellow gloves she accurately trimmed the wicks, between the morning's headlines and a thorough talk with the cook. But the smell of oil was repugnant to her and now she said with some sharpness:

'You have no conception of love – You are in my light.'

(LS, 167)

Her insistence on a rational concept of love, her annoyance that Lois blocks her light, and casts a shadow, her determination to keep the light steady, and the connection between that determination, the political events dramatized by 'the morning's headlines' and her desire to maintain her own domestic sphere and order as she gives instructions to the cook are all suggested in this passage. A little later, when she interviews Gerald, makes it clear that he is an unacceptable suitor and dismisses the possibility that Lois is in love with him, she is again described as manipulating light and shadow so that light – in this case a distortion of the natural – will be shed only on those things she desires illuminated, and not upon herself or her motives:

She placed herself (unaccountably, it would have to appear) on the narrow window-seat. Thus, she conceded no more to the room than an imposing silhouette of hat and boa, while Gerald, glancing round pessimistically at the chairs, remaining with elbow planted among photo-frames on the mantelpiece, was exposed to her full in the strained green light coming over the bushes.

(LS, 178)

The link between light and selective 'enlightenment' is not confined to the upper classes. Images of blindness, and examples of talk which is intended to conceal rather than enlighten, are even more prominent in the few scenes which involve the Catholic tenant farmers on the estates. Thus, when Hugo decides to stop and visit the Regans, their cottage doorway is described as yearning 'up the path like an eye-socket'. The cottage is inhabited by a half-blind man and his deaf mother.

They approached the doorway that yearned up the path like an eye-socket. A breath of peat smoke, of cold trodden earth, of the ghostly dark of white walls came out from the cottage. Dannie took form in the darkness, searching with his one eye. He stood with his white beard, helpless and eager. 'Well!' exclaimed Hugo. Then Dannie broke out: this was young Mr. Hugo, wasn't he the lovely gentleman, as fine and upstanding as ever. And here was his wife he had brought with him, the beautiful lady. And trembling and searching, he took Marda's hand. He declared that she brought back the sight of youth to his eyes.

(*LS*, 86)

Within the cottage, Dannie Regan is as obscure to Hugo and Marda as they are to him, although it is not merely his 'one-eyedness' but also their class which prevents him from seeing them as individuals (for he assumes that Marda is the much older Francie) and elicits a flattering and false image of them. The irony of the final sentence underlines his use of language which is designed to please and thus conceal, as well as the uselessness of their presence and condescending graciousness, which can do nothing to improve Dannie Regan's physical condition.

An earlier episode has portrayed in similar terms a visit by Hugo and Lois to the Connors, one of whom is 'on the run' after being involved in an ambush, and who is probably being hidden by his family. Here again, the loyalties of the family are concealed in a mixture of gushing 'stage Irish' and taciturnity. As Lois and Hugo drive away, the house 'stares' after them, its gaze reducing them to insubstantiality.[14] Lois's response, her means of controlling her unease, is to replay the scene and elaborate it in terms of melodrama, with the Connors becoming mere actors in imagined scenes. Yet, the influence of their encounter lingers, and when Lois and Hugo see Danielstown again, it appears threatened and apprehensive:

> Looking down, it seemed to Lois they lived in a forest; space of lawns blotted out in the pressure and dusk of trees. She wondered they were not smothered; then wondered still more they were not afraid. Far from here too, their isolation became apparent. The house seemed to be pressing down low in apprehension, hiding its face, as though it had her vision of where it was. It seemed to gather its trees close and in amazement at the wide, light, lovely, unloving country, the unwilling bosom whereon it was set.
>
> (*LS*, 66)

'As though it had her vision of where it was', the house and Lois are both caught in a period of transition. Like Katherine Mansfield, another 'daughter of Empire', Elizabeth Bowen is keenly aware of the interrelation between an ethos of political conquest and dominance of other lands and peoples, and the insistence on particular 'feminine' and domestic roles for women. ('He loved me; he believed in the British Empire.') Like Mansfield, she often uses adolescent 'girls' as vehicles for conveying both the appeal of those roles, and the half-realized desire for liberation from them and the 'humiliation' of always being mere daughters. Lois is caught between two female roles. One is from the past and is associated with Laura, her mother, who like her Petrarchan namesake dies young and haunts the house and Hugo Montmorency as a memory of romance, a memory which is attached to the house (and its laurel trees) and prevents him from breaking away and establishing his own home. The other is associated with Marda, who fascinates both Hugo and Lois by her refusal of illusions and romance, and her refusal of traditional femininity; she is ironic, self-aware, but not self-conscious. Her choice of marriage and home in England has to do with her awareness of her own needs, rather than confused acceptance of traditional patterns. Elizabeth Bowen's *The Last September* suggests that Lois and the Anglo-Irish must also move away from the nostalgic myths which can no longer sustain them, and create new associations and structures in keeping with changing social and political forms.

Conclusion

Synge pronounced that all art is collaboration, and *The Playboy* can be read as a dramatization of the collaboration between the Irish male artist and the folk who turn him into 'a likely gaffer in the end of all' to 'go romancing through a romping lifetime'.[1] Yet, as the play ruefully acknowledges, the benefits of the collaboration are finally one way; the community and Pegeen are left as they were, deprived of romance and material welfare. The glory and, as in Synge's case, the notoriety, go to the individual artist. Similarly the self-referential works of Joyce and Yeats repeatedly return to an exploration of the psyche of the individual artist. He may be lionized, ironized, parodied or pitied for his unhappy relationship to the society that surrounds him, and for the failures of his audience, but whether so acknowledged or not by his readers, it is the artist who is hero. As such he compares himself with political heroes such as Parnell, Emmet or Wolf Tone. For Yeats and Joyce, and sometimes Synge, women became identified with Ireland, both as images of an ideal order which they sought to restore, and as images of an Ireland that had been betrayed, or had collaborated in its own betrayal. Repeatedly in their works, the gendered discourse of colonialism and anti-colonialism explicitly or implicitly influences the characterization of the women and the structuring of plots in which the contestation of patriarchal authority is marked by the struggle to claim authority over Ireland. That struggle is further complicated by the contest between members of different classes and generations to forge the 'conscience of [their] race', and to claim that race, embodied as a female figure, as their audience. When the women who had been constructed as representing Ireland turned to hear different speakers or, worse still, spoke up for their own version of the Irish conscience, they were ridiculed, reviled, or ignored.

Many of the Irish women activists and artists discussed in these pages also believed in collaboration; indeed it was something they valued and insisted upon. Political activity and writing were for the Parnell sisters, for Lady Gregory, for the Daughters of Erin (including Maud Gonne MacBride and Constance Markievicz) part of a group enterprise, not a means of attaining personal glory and renown. Too often critics have taken the self-effacement of such women writers as an excuse for ignoring them. In seeking to recover their writings and activities and assigning them to the authors, I have been aware that in one sense I have been subverting the aims and beliefs so strongly expressed by Anna Parnell and implicit in Lady Gregory's willingness to let Yeats be named as the sole author of the plays they created jointly, that it is groups rather than individuals that matter. Nevertheless, it seemed important to reveal not only the extent of the activities which women undertook, but also to uncover the distinctiveness of what they had to say when all too often their voices had been obscured or subsumed by authors such as Yeats, and when his construction of them had been too little questioned.

Much can be gained from reading and reviewing the writings of men and women involved in the nationalist movement in the context of the historical, economic and political events which surrounded them, and especially in the context of the discourses and icons which marked the cultural nationalism of their time. Those discourses and dramatic and pictorial icons also included each other's writings, and I have sought to demonstrate that Synge, Joyce, Lady Gregory, Maud Gonne, and Elizabeth Bowen all responded to and in some sense rewrote Yeats's influential representations of the nationalist drama, paying particular attention to the role of women within that drama. Thus the plays of Synge, Maud Gonne, and Lady Gregory (in *At the Gaol Gate* and *The Rising of the Moon*) contest the abstract idealism of *Cathleen ni Houlihan*; Maud Gonne and Lady Gregory also question Synge's dismissal of Christian love and social reputation. Lady Gregory sets

Grania and Dervorgilla against 'poor sorrowing Deirdre' as more interesting heroines, who 'for good or evil . . . took the shaping of their lives into their own hands'.[2] Her insistence that women have participated in the making of history and must take responsibility for their own actions, however limited their choices, is also linked to her willingness to face the responsibility the Anglo-Irish landowning class must face for Ireland's present condition. Her heroines are no Ledas, merely caught up in the rush of history; nor can they settle for mere romance, as Synge's Deirdre might, for Grania finds the world of two lovers in a thatched cottage suffocating. She determines finally to return to a social world and have a part in it. Elizabeth Bowen's heroine, Lois, finds unbearable and humiliating the role Yeats would have her accept happily as daughter of the house. Lady Gregory and Elizabeth Bowen alike acknowledge the attractions and privileges of the life of the Great House; but they also acknowledge the unhappy consequences for those whose lives are made economically poor in order to sustain those privileges, and those whose lives are spiritually impoverished by their unwillingness to admit the injustice of that economic structure. As O'Casey admitted with regard to Lady Gregory, but was unwilling to admit with regard to Constance Markievicz or Maud Gonne MacBride, her achievement was to fight against 'birth and position and comfort', and to come out of it 'so that power may be gained to bring fountains and waters out of the hard rocks'.[3]

Notes

Introduction

1. *A Portrait of the Artist as a Young Man*, New York: Viking, 1964, pp. 220–1.
2. *Ibid.*, p. 238.
3. W.I. Thompson, *The Imagination of an Insurrection*, Oxford: Oxford University Press, 1967, p. 39. Thompson's references to Maud Gonne are insistently, and almost obsessively, derogatory. He refers to her repeatedly as 'the furious republican' and a fanatic (see, for example, pp. 46, 74, 147), and her political activity as a 'bandwagon'. Like several other critics he endorses Yeats's dismissive references to her appearance as a means of dismissing her politics: 'Seen from close up, the [Rising] is a tragicomedy, the Dublin streets a far cry from the topless towers of Ilium, and Maud Gonne's face far too old and wrinkled to launch a thousand ships' (p. 148). Similarly F.S.L. Lyons comments in a footnote that Maud Gonne and Constance Markievicz 'paid a heavy price for their deracination in personal happiness and even in personal beauty', *Culture and Anarchy in Ireland, 1890–1939*, Oxford: Clarendon Press, 1979, p. 103.
4. Even David Cairns' and Shaun Richards' groundbreaking study *Writing Ireland*, Manchester: Manchester University Press, 1988, which goes to some lengths to acknowledge the significance of gendered discourse in the cultural construction of Ireland, gives a total of two or three pages to the analysis of writing by women, compared to some eighty or ninety pages discussing writings and speeches by Irish men.

Chapter One

1. Matthew Arnold, *On the Study of Celtic Literature*, London: Smith Elder, 1891, p. 82.
2. Cited by L.P. Curtis, *Anglo-Saxons and Celts: A Study of Anti-Irish Prejudice in Victorian England*, Bridgeport, Connecticut: Conference on British Studies, 1968, p. 58.
3. Quoted in Margaret Digby, *Horace Plunkett*, Oxford: Blackwell, 1949, p. 91.
4. Cited by Curtis, p. 221: from *Fraser's Magazine*, 'Ulster and Its People', 14 New Series (August 1876), p. 80.
5. 'Belfast', *Preoccupations: Selected Prose 1968–78*, Faber: London, 1980, p. 34.
6. See Herbert Davis, 'Introduction' to Jonathan Swift, *Irish Tracts 1720–1723 and Sermons*, Oxford: Basil Blackwell, 1963, pp. ix–xi.
7. *Irish Tracts*, p. 3.
8. *Irish Tracts*, p. 4.
9. *Irish Tracts*, p. 8.
10. For a full discussion of the figure of Britannia and other female representations of nations or national virtues, see Marina Warner's *Maidens and Monuments*, London: Weidenfeld & Nicolson, 1985.
11. See L.P. Curtis, *Apes and Angels: The Irishman in Victorian Caricature*, Newton Abbot: David & Charles, 1971, for discussion of the scientific and political discourses of the time and their influence.
12. Quoted by L.P. Curtis, *Anglo-Saxons and Celts*, p. 84.
13. *Ibid.*, p. 84.
14. *Apes and Angels*, pp. 84 and 85.
15. Patricia Lysaght, *The Banshee: The Irish supernatural death messenger*, Dublin: Glendale Press, 1986, p. 217.
16. *Ibid.*, p. 205.
17. *Apes and Angels*, p. 75.
18. Richard Kearney, *Myth and Motherland*, Belfast: Dorman, 1984, pp. 20–1.
19. Thomas Kinsella, ed., *The New Oxford Book of Irish Verse*, Oxford: Oxford University Press, 1986, pp. 195–6. See also 'The Vision', *ibid.*, pp. 197–8.
20. In S.F. Gallagher, ed., *Women in Irish Legend, Life and Literature*, Irish Literary Studies 14, Gerrards Cross: Colin Smythe, 1983.
21. *Ibid.*, p. 31.
22. *Ibid.*, p. 34.
23. Kinsella, *op. cit.*, p. 274.
24. James Clarence Mangan, 'Dark Rosaleen', *The Oxford Book of Irish Verse*, ed. Thomas Kinsella, Oxford: Oxford University Press, 1986, p. 274.
25. Richard Kearney, *Myth and Motherland*, Belfast: Dorman, 1984, p. 20.
26. *Women in Irish Legend, Life and Literature*, pp. 35–6.
27. Thomas MacDonagh, *Literature in Ireland: Studies in Irish and Anglo-Irish Literature*, London: T. Fisher Unwin, 1918, p. 31.
28. Kearney, *op. cit.*, p. 19.

Chapter Two

1. The genesis of the story is given by Edith Somerville in a letter to her from [Violet] Martin Ross quoted at the end of the novel:

'Yesterday I drove to see X —— House. A great cut stone house of three stories. . .

'Perfectly empty . . . It is on a long promontory by the sea, and there rioted three generations of X ——s, living with country women, occasionally marrying them, all illegitimate four times over . . . About one hundred and fifty years ago a very grand Lady —— —— married the head of the family and lived there, and was so corroded with pride that she would not allow her two daughters to associate with the neighbours of their own class. She lived to see them marry two of the men in the yard. . .

'Yesterday as we left, an old Miss X, daughter of the last owner, was at the door in a little donkey trap. She lives near in an old castle, and since her people died she will not go into X—— House, or into the enormous yard, or the beautiful old garden.

'She was a strange mixture of distinction and commonness, like her breeding, and it was very sad to see her at the door of the great house.

'If we dared to write up that subject —— !
                              'Yours ever,
                              'Martin.'

   The Big House at Inver, London: Quartet, 1978, p. 313.
2. Brooke, p. viii; cited by Seamus Deane in *A Short History of Irish Literature*, London: Hutchinson, 1986, p. 76.
3. Deane, *op. cit.*, p. 18.
4. *Ibid.*, p. 8.
5. *Ibid.*, p. 78.
6. Donal McCartney, 'Gaelic Ideological Origins of 1916', in *1916: The Easter Rising*, edited by Owen Dudley Edwards and Fergus Pyle, London: MacGibbon & Kee, 1968, p. 41.
7. Thomas Moore, *The Poetical Works*, London: Bliss, 1888, p. 91.
8. *Ibid.*, p. 95.
9. *Ibid.*, p. 117.
10. Deane, *op. cit.*, p. 69. For a detailed exploration of Ferguson's involvement in the nineteenth-century Celtic Revival, see Paul Reade, *Samuel Ferguson and the Idea of an Irish National Literature, 1830–1850*, Ph.D. thesis, University of Kent, Canterbury, 1985.
11. A. Norman Jeffares, *Anglo-Irish Literature*, Dublin: Gill & Macmillan, 1982, p. 129.
12. Lorna Reynolds, 'Irish Women in Legend, Literature and Life', in *Women in Irish Legend, Life and Literature*, edited by S.F. Gallagher, Gerrards Cross: Colin Smythe, 1983, p. 15.
13. Marie Herbert, 'Celtic heroine? The Archaeology of the Deirdre Story', in *Gender in Irish Writing*, edited by Toni O'Brien Johnson and David Cairns, Milton Keynes: Open University Press, 1991, pp. 13–22.
14. Ashis Nandy, *The Intimate Enemy*, Delhi: Oxford University Press, 1983. See David Cairns and Shaun Richards, *Writing Ireland*,

Manchester: Manchester University Press, 1988, p. 49 for a discussion of Nandy's formulation and its relevance to Irish nationalism.

15. Elin Ap Hywel, 'Elise and the Great Queens of Ireland: "Femininity" as constructed by Sinn Fein and the Abbey Theatre, 1901–1907', in *Gender in Irish Writing*, pp. 23–39.

16. F.S.L. Lyons, *Culture and Anarchy in Ireland, 1890–1939*, Oxford: Oxford University Press, 1979, p. 9.

17. The controversy over the intervention of the Catholic clergy in Irish politics is vividly dramatized in the Christmas dinner scene in Joyce's *A Portrait of the Artist as a Young Man*.

18. E.R.R. Green, 'The Great Famine (1845–50)', in *The Course of Irish History*, edited by T.W. Moody and F.X. Martin, Cork: The Mercier Press, 1967, p. 274.

19. Lyons, *Culture and Anarchy*, p. 8.

20. Green, 'The Great Famine', p. 274.

21. J.J. Lee, 'Women and the Church Since the Famine', in *Women in Irish Society: The historical dimension*, edited by Margaret McCurtain and Donncha O' Corrain, Dublin: Arlen House, 1978, p. 40.

22. *Ibid.*, p. 40.

23. F.S.L. Lyons, *Ireland Since the Famine*, London: Fontana, 1973, p. 82.

24. *Ibid.*, pp. 90n and 93.

25. Marina Warner, *Alone of All Her Sex: The myth and cult of the Virgin Mary*, London: Picador, 1985, pp. 236 ff.

26. *Ibid.*, pp. 336–7.

27. For a detailed discussion of the economic contributions of women, see Mary Cullen, 'Breadwinners and Providers: Women in the household economy of labouring families, 1835–6', in *Women Surviving: Studies in Irish women's history in the 19th and 20th centuries*, edited by Maria Luddy and Cliona Murphy, Dublin: Poolbeg Press, 1989.

28. Lee, 'Women and the Church Since the Famine', p. 38.

29. Eileen Breathnach, 'Women and Higher Education in Ireland (1879–1914)', in *The Crane Bag*, vol. 4, no. 1, 1980, pp. 47–54.

30. Lee, 'Women and the Church Since the Famine', p. 78.

31. *Ibid.*, p. 37.

32. Quoted by Breathnach, 'Women and Higher Education in Ireland (1879–1914)', p. 47.

33. Warner, *op. cit.*, p. 250.

34. Quoted by Warner, *op. cit.*, p. 190.

Chapter Three

1. Donal McCartney, 'Gaelic Ideological Origins of 1916', in *1916: The Easter Rising*, edited by Owen Dudley Edwards and Fergus Pyle, London: MacGibbon & Kee, 1968, pp. 43–4.

2. Quoted from 'The Circus Animals' Desertion', *Yeats's Poems*, edited by A. Norman Jeffares, London: Macmillan, 1989, p. 471.
3. Seamus Deane, *A Short History of Irish Literature*, London: Hutchinson, 1986, p. 141.
4. Quoted by Philip Marcus, *Yeats and the Irish Renaissance*, Ithaca: Cornell University Press, 1970, p. 236.
5. Deane, *op. cit.*, p. 85.
6. Walter Benjamin, 'The Work of Art in an Age of Mechanical Reproduction', in *Illuminations*, translated by Harry Zohn, New York: Schocken Books, 1969, p. 242. Benjamin, of course, is using the phrase with reference to fascism and its reverence for technology, a reverence alien to Yeats, but his discussion of the tendency towards making 'the political aesthetic' as a continuation of the 'art for art's sake' emphasis, and of the distortion of political consequences inherent in such movements, seems applicable to much of Yeats's work.
7. For further discussion of Lady Gregory's role in the creation of *Cathleen ni Houlihan* see Mary Lou Kohfeldt, *Lady Gregory: The woman behind the Irish Renaissance*, London: Andre Deutsch, 1984, p. 143. See also James L. Pethica's doctoral dissertation on Lady Gregory, *A Dialogue of Self and Service*, Oxford, 1989.
8. The notebook which contains the first draft is in the Berg Collection, New York Public Library.
9. Maud Gonne's articles written for *L'Irlande Libre* place Ireland's struggles in the context of British and French imperialism and capitalism, and are in tune with Wolfe Tone's anti-imperialist and anti-aristocratic analysis. For further discussion of her writing and her political views, see Chapter Eight.
10. 'The Circus Animals' Desertion', *Yeats's Poems*, p. 471.
11. Joseph Chadwick, 'Family Romance as National Allegory in Yeats's *Cathleen ni Houlihan* and *The Dreaming of the Bones*', in *Twentieth Century Literature*, vol. 32, no. 2, Summer 1986, p. 156.
12. See Chapter Eight for further elaboration of the identification between Maud Gonne and Erin.
13. In my book *The Devil's Own Mirror: The Irishman and the African in Modern Literature*, Washington, D.C.: Three Continents Press, 1990.
14. J.M. Synge, *Plays and Poems*, edited by T.R. Henn, London: Methuen, 1963, pp. 196–7.
15. Ann Saddlemyer, 'Synge and the Nature of Woman', in *Woman in Irish Legend, Life and Literature*, edited by S.F. Gallagher, Gerrards Cross: Colin Smythe, 1983, p. 68.
16. Synge, *Plays and Poems*, p. 174.
17. J.M. Synge, *The Collected Letters*, edited by Ann Saddlemyer, Oxford: Clarendon Press, 1983, p. 76.
18. Synge, *Plays and Poems*, p. 83.
19. *Ibid.*, p. 94.
20. For a more detailed discussion of this point, see my chapter on *The Playboy* in *The Devil's Own Mirror*. See also Stephen Tifft, 'The Parricidal Phantasm: Irish nationalism and the *Playboy* riots', in

Nationalisms and Sexualities, edited by Andrew Parker *et al.*, London/
New York: Routledge, 1992.

21. 'Synge and the Nature of Woman', in *Woman in Irish Legend, Life and
Literature*, edited by S.F. Gallagher, Gerrards Cross: Colin Smythe,
1983, pp. 66–7.

22. Synge, *Plays and Poems*, p. 244.

23. W.B. Yeats, *Collected Plays*, London: Macmillan, 1952, p. 113.

24. In both the Synge and the Yeats Deirdre plays, however, the issue of
trusting Conchubar, of believing he 'may keep faith after all', is a
significant one. That this should be so in these two plays written
between 1906 and 1909 may not be unconnected to the renewed hopes
of Home Rule being granted by England through Constitutional means
following the re-election of the Liberal Party in 1906.

25. *Yeats's Poems*, p. 185.

26. Seamus O'Neill, 'Gaelic Literature', in *The Macmillan Dictionary of
Irish Literature*, edited by Robert Hogan, London: Macmillan, 1980,
p. 59.

27. Douglas Hyde. See pp. 80–1 in *Poetry and Ireland Since 1800: A
source book*, edited by Mark Storey, London: Routledge, 1988.

28. See Ruth Dudley Edwards, *Patrick Pearse: The Triumph of Failure*,
London: Faber, 1979, p. 22.

29. *Ibid.*, p. 116.

30. McCartney, *op. cit.*, p. 44.

31. *Ibid.*, p. 44.

32. *Ibid.*

33. Quoted by Ruth Dudley Edwards, *op. cit.*, p. 117.

34. Synge, *Collected Letters*, vol. 2, pp. 399–400.

35. 'The Eighteenth Brumaire of Louis Bonaparte', in Karl Marx and
Frederick Engels, *Selected Works*, New York: International Publishers,
1968, p. 101.

36. McCartney, *op. cit.*, p. 46.

37. *Ibid.*

38. Quoted by Donal Nevin, 'The Irish Citizen Army', in *1916: The Easter
Rising*, edited by Edwards and Pyle, 1968, p. 127.

39. James Connolly, *Selected Writings*, edited by P. Berresford Ellis,
Harmondsworth: Penguin, 1975, pp. 190–1.

40. *Ibid.*, pp. 193–4.

Chapter Four

1. *A Portrait of the Artist as a Young Man*, New York: Viking, 1964,
p. 183. Further references to this edition are incorporated in the text
with the title abbreviated to *PA*.

2. Compare also Yeats's admonition to Irish poets in 'Under Ben
Bulben'.

3. *Dubliners*, Harmondsworth: Penguin, p. 207.

4. In *Women in Joyce*, edited by Suzette Henke and Elaine Unkeless, Hemel Hempstead: Harvester Wheatsheaf, 1982, pp. 31–56.
5. *Ibid.*, p. 33.
6. See the previous chapter for a discussion of women in Irish society at this period, and Synge's portrayal of their plight in rural Ireland.
7. James Joyce, *Selected Letters*, edited by Richard Ellmann, London: Faber, 1975, p. 25.
8. The seminal discussion of Bloom's affirmation of love rather than war is mapped out in Richard Ellmann, *Ulysses on the Liffey*, Oxford: Oxford University Press, 1973. For a recent and fuller treatment of Bloom's pacificism and his relationship to women, see Suzette Henke, *James Joyce and the Politics of Desire*, London: Routledge, 1990, Chapter Four.
9. Maureen S.G. Hawkins, 'The Dramatic Treatment of Robert Emmet and Sarah Curran', in *Women in Irish Legend, Life and Literature*, edited by S.F. Gallagher, Gerrards Cross: Colin Smythe, 1983, pp. 125–37.
10. Dion Boucicault, 'Robert Emmet', in *Forbidden Fruit and Other Plays*, edited by Allardyce Nicoll and F. Theodore Cloak, Princeton, N.J.: Princeton University Press, 1940, p. 313.
11. Cited by Maureen S.G. Hawkins, *op. cit.*, p. 128.
12. Quoted by Ruth Dudley Edwards, *Patrick Pearse: The Triumph of Failure*, London: Faber, 1979, p. 135.
13. *Ibid.*, p. 177.
14 James Joyce, *Ulysses*, Harmondsworth: Penguin, 1986, p. 251.
15. *Ibid.*, p. 254.
16. Suzette Henke, *James Joyce and the Politics of Desire*, London: Routledge, 1990, p. 122.

Chapter Five

1. See for example, William Irwin Thompson, *The Imagination of an Insurrection*, Oxford: Oxford University Press, 1967.
2. Quoted by A. Norman Jeffares, *A Commentary on the Collected Poems of W.B. Yeats*, Stanford: Stanford University Press, 1968, p. 226.
3. David Cairns and Shaun Richards, *Writing Ireland*, Manchester: Manchester University Press, 1988, p. 112.
4. Denis Donoghue, *Yeats*, London: Fontana/Collins, 1976, p. 87.
5. John Unterecker, *A Reader's Guide to William Butler Yeats*, New York: Noonday Press, 1961, pp. 158–9.
6. *The Collected Letters of W.B. Yeats*, vol. I, 1865–1895, edited by John Kelly and Eric Domville, Oxford: The Clarendon Press, 1986, p. 161.
7. *The Letters of W.B. Yeats*, edited by Alan Wade, London: Hart-Davis, 1954, p. 821.
8. W.B. Yeats, *Autobiographies*, London: Macmillan, 1955, p. 41.

9. See discussion by Elizabeth Butler Cullingford along these lines in her forthcoming book, *Gender and History in Yeats's Love Poetry*, Cambridge: Cambridge University Press, forthcoming, Chapter Five.

10. Cairns and Richards, *Writing Ireland*, pp. 112–13.

11. 'Yeats and Ireland', in *Scattering Branches*, edited by Stephen Gwynn, London: Macmillan, 1940, pp. 31–2.

12. *The Letters*, edited by Alan Wade, p. 613.

13. *Autobiographies*, p. 234.

14. W.B. Yeats, *Memoirs*, edited by Denis Donoghue, London: Macmillan, 1972, p. 176.

15. *Autobiographies*, p. 504.

16. Jeffares, *Commentary*, p. 232.

Chapter Six

1. A. Norman Jeffares (ed.), *Yeats's Poems*, London: Macmillan, 1989, p. 760.

2. W.B. Yeats, Letter to Lady Dorothy Wellesley, 28 November 1936, *The Letters of W.B. Yeats*, edited by Alan Wade, London: Hart-Davis, 1954, p. 868.

3. Cited by A. Norman Jeffares, *A Commentary on the Collected Poems of W.B. Yeats*, Stanford: Stanford University Press, 1968, p. 370.

4. *Letters*, ed. Wade, p. 742.

5. 'Coole Park, 1929', *Yeats's Poems*.

6. See Yeats's note to *A Pot of Broth*, cited by Jeffares, in *Commentary*, p. 371.

7. *Letters*, ed. Wade, p. 786.

8. 'Crazy Jane and Jack the Journeyman', *Yeats's Poems*.

9. My discussion of this poem and others in the sequence owes much to Barbara Hardy, 'The Wildness of Crazy Jane', in *Yeats, Sligo and Ireland*, edited by A. Norman Jeffares, Gerrards Cross: Colin Smythe, 1980, pp. 31–55.

10. *Essays and Introductions*, London: Macmillan, 1961, pp. 428–9.

11. Jacques Berthoud, 'The Originality of Yeats's "Supernatural Songs"', in *Generous Converse: English Essays in Memory of Edward Davis*, edited by Brian Green, Cape Town: Oxford University Press, 1980, p. 149.

12. Letter to Olivia Shakespear, 2 March 1929, *Letters*, ed. Wade, p. 758.

13. Gloria Kline, *The Last Courtly Lover: Yeats and the Idea of Woman*, Ann Arbor: UMI Research Press, 1983, p. 141.

14. 'Consolation', *Yeats's Poems*.

15. The phrase, 'dragon thought', refers to the line in 'Michael Robartes and the Dancer': 'The half-dead dragon was her thought'. Gloria Kline, in the book cited above, links that earlier poem with this, and sees 'Her Triumph' as yet another placing of the female in the realm of the mindless and the irrational, but I would point out that it is 'we',

both lovers, who have entered that realm – one which Yeats's male
persona frequently enter or seek to enter.
16. 'A Last Confession', *Yeats's Poems*.
17. 'Meeting', *Yeats's Poems*.
18. 'From the *Antigone*', *Yeats's Poems*.
19. 'The Wife of Bath's Tale' is thought by some scholars to be of Celtic
origin and is analogous to the twelfth-century tale of Niall and the Nine
Hostages. The transformation of an old woman into a beautiful young
maiden once a man promises to obey her is also central to the Cathleen
ni Houlihan myth.
20. From 'The Hag of Beara', translated by Thomas Kinsella, *The New
Oxford Book of Irish Verse*, edited by Thomas Kinsella, Oxford:
Oxford University Press, 1986, pp. 24 and 26.
21. Elizabeth Butler Cullingford, *Gender and History in Yeats's Love
Poetry*, Cambridge: Cambridge University Press, forthcoming, Chapter Five.

Chapter Seven

1. Quoted by Margaret Ward, *Unmanageable Revolutionaries*, London:
Pluto, 1983, p. 265n.
2. Dana Hearne, 'Rewriting History: Anna Parnell's *The Tale of a Great
Sham*, in *Women in Irish Life, Legend and Literature*, edited by S.F.
Gallagher, Gerrards Cross: Colin Smythe, 1983, pp. 138–49.
3. Roy Foster, *Parnell and His Family*, Hemel Hempstead: Harvester
Wheatsheaf, 1976, p. 241.
4. *Ibid.*, p. 251.
5. The poem is printed in full by Foster, *op. cit.*, pp. 323–5.
6. Foster, *op. cit.*, p. 251.
7. Quoted by Ward, *op. cit.*, p. 14.
8. St John Ervine, *Parnell*, London: Ernest Benn, 1925, p. 158.
9. *Ibid.*, p.199, cited by Dana Hearne, *op. cit.*, p. 138.
10. F.S.L. Lyons, *Charles Stewart Parnell*, London: Collins, 1977, p. 178.
11. Quoted by Lyons, *op. cit.*, p. 178.
12. Anna Parnell, *The Tale of a Great Sham*, edited by Dana Hearne,
Dublin: Arlen House, 1986.
13. Cited by Ward, *op. cit.*, p. 23.
14. Ward, *op. cit.*, p. 23.
15. *Ibid.*
16. Ward, *op. cit.*, pp. 23–4.
17. Quoted by Ward, *op. cit.*, p. 26.
18. Ward, *op. cit.*, p. 26.
19. Ward, *op. cit.*, p. 27.
20. See Foster, *op. cit.*, p. 251.
21. Anna Parnell, *op. cit.*, p. 172.

22. Rosemary Cullen Owens, *Smashing Times: A History of the Irish women's suffrage movement, 1889–1922*, Dublin: Attic Press, 1984, Chapter I.

23. Owens, *op. cit.*, p. 40.

24. Owens, *op. cit.*, p. 27.

25. Tony Fahy, 'Nuns in the Catholic Church in Ireland in the Nineteenth Century', in Mary Cullen, ed., *Girls Don't Do Honours: Irish women in education in the 19th and 20th centuries*, Dublin: Women's Education Bureau, 1987, pp. 17–18.

26. Fahy, *op. cit.*, pp. 7–8.

27. Catriona Clear, 'Walls Within Walls – Nuns in 19th-Century Ireland', in Chris Curtin, Pauline Jackson and Barbara O'Connor, eds, *Gender in Irish Society*, Galway: Galway University Press, 1987, p. 149.

28. Fahy, *op. cit.*, p. 22.

29. Cited by Anne V. O'Connor, 'The Revolution in Girls' Secondary Education in Ireland', in Mary Cullen, ed., *Girls Don't Do Honours*, p. 36.

30. Fahy, *op. cit.*, p. 25.

31. Margaret Ann Cusack wrote in an article called 'Woman's Place in the Economy of Creation', in 1874:

    The lords of creation may rest assured that if women are not devout . . . they will soon cease to be practically obedient. There is no reason, except Divine Law, why women should be in subjection. Let men once succeed in shaking the faith of women in Divine Law (and remember that women will never rest satisfied with half-beliefs) and they will soon have friends to deal with like the women of the Commune.

    Her article concluded: 'Woman's place is (with rare exceptions) in the home and her work is domestic.' Quoted by Anne V. O'Connor, 'The Revolution in Girls' Secondary Education in Ireland, 1860–1910', in Mary Cullen, ed., *Girls Don't Do Honours*, Dublin: Women's Education Bureau, 1987, p. 36.

32. O'Connor, *op. cit.*, p. 34.

33. Eibhlin Breathnach, 'Charting New Waters: Women's Experience in Higher Education, 1879–1908', in Cullen, ed., *op cit.*, p. 60.

34. Breathnach, *op. cit.*, p. 71.

35. Breathnach, *op. cit.*, p. 74.

36. *Ibid.*

37. John Kelly and Eric Domville, eds, *The Collected Letters of W.B. Yeats*, Oxford: The Clarendon Press, 1986, p. 519.

38. A. Norman Jeffares, ed., *Yeats's Poems*, London: Macmillan, 1989, pp. 414 and 622.

39. Katharine Tynan, *Louise de La Vallière and Other Poems*, London: Kegan Paul, 1885, pp. 65–71.

40. Tynan, *op. cit.*, p. 71.

41. Katharine Tynan, *Irish Poems*, London: Sidgwick and Jackson, 1914, p. 31.

42. Tynan, *Irish Poems*, p. 106.

Chapter Eight

1. *Bean na h-Eireann*, vol. 1, no. 3, January, 1909.
2. According to Margaret Ward, their first child, George, was born in January 1890, and died when only a few months old. See *Unmanageable Revolutionaries*, London: Pluto, 1983, p. 45. According to Samuel Levenson's biography, *Maud Gonne*, London: Cassell, 1977, pp. 77–8, the child was a girl, Georgette, born in May 1889.
3. Maud Gonne MacBride, *A Servant of the Queen*, Woodbridge, Suffolk: Boydell Press, 1983, pp. 94–7.
4. The identification of Maud Gonne with Erin or Kathleen, by women as well as men, is fulsomely illustrated in a poem to her by M. Barry Delaney, published in an early issue of *The Shan Van Vocht*, vol. 1, 7 Feb. 1896, p. 33, and suggests that the play Lady Gregory and Yeats wrote for her drew upon a current identification rather than creating it. The poem is quoted in the text on p. 136.
5. *Journal des Voyages*, no. 804, 4 Dec. 1982, p. 354. There is no mention of these articles in Samuel Levenson's biography, nor have I seen them referred to elsewhere.
6. The incident is referred to in passing, and in less histrionic mode, in Maud Gonne's autobiography, *A Servant of the Queen*, p. 105, where the priest is named Father McFadden.
7. *L'Irlande Libre*, Vol. 1, no. 1, May, 1897, p. 1.
8. *Ibid.* p. 2.
9. Quoted by Margaret Ward, *Unmanageable Revolutionaries*, p. 46.
10. From Ethna Carberry, 'The Kisses of Angus', *The Shan Van Vocht*, vol. 2, no. 5, 3 May 1887, p. 1. Seel also this opening stanza from Nora Hopper's 'To Sheila ni Gara: (Ireland)':

> Out of the wind and out of the rain,
> Sheila, come to my arms again;
> Close though your grave clothes wrap you round,
> Come from your quiet underground.
> (*The Shan Van Vocht*, vol. 3, no. 3, 7 March 1898, p. 1.)

11. *The Shan Van Vocht*, vol. 1, 7 Feb. 1896, p. 33. The second stanza and the final four stanzas not quoted in the text are as follows:

Gone are the days of the Brigade, and Hoche's loyal band,
But still in distant Paris waves the banner of our land,
Upheld beside the tri-color by one fair maiden's hand!

Yet well too is she known at home, in cottages that fear
The vengeance of the evictor cursed, that ever hovers near
Well is our Maid of Erin known to solace there and cheer;

To comfort as when to her heart the voice of pity calls,
And angel-like she enters in where misery appals
The living-dead who pine within dark Portland's cruel walls!

Fair idol of our sea-girt home, our island is her throne,
Guarded not by might of sword but loving hearts alone
That throb with loyalty for one whose blood is Erin's own!

We've sworn no oath of fealty – we've registered no vow,
But did a golden circlet rest upon our darling's brow
It could not crown her more than love hath crowned her now!

Barry Delaney, Paris.

12. *Bean na h-Eireann*, vol. 1, no. 4, February, 1909, pp. 9–10.
13. *Ibid.*, p. 2.
14. *Bean na h-Eireann*, vol. 2, no. 13, November, 1909, pp. 5–6.
15. *Bean na h-Eireann*, vol. 1, no. 11, September, 1909, p. 4.
16. Quoted by Eibhlin Ni Eireamhoin, *Two Great Irishwomen*, Dublin: Fallon, 1971, pp. 53–4.

Chapter Nine

1. *Lady Gregory's Journals: 1916–1930*, edited by Lennox Robinson, London: Putnam, 1946, p. 238.
2. 'Coole Park, 1929', *Yeats's Poems*, edited by A. Norman Jeffares, London: Macmillan, 1989, p. 357.
3. Augusta, Lady Gregory, *Our Irish Theatre*, New York: Capricorn Books, 1965, p. 124.
4. For a further discussion and analysis of Lady Gregory's development of an Irish language for drama and narrative, see Robert Welch, 'A Language for Healing' in *Lady Gregory: Fifty Years After*, edited by Ann Saddlemyer, Gerrards Cross: Colin Smythe, 1987, pp. 258–73.
5. Elizabeth Coxhead, *Lady Gregory: A Literary Portrait*, revised edn, London: Secker & Warburg, 1966.
6. Coxhead, *op. cit.*, p. vi.
7. Cited by Coxhead, *op. cit.*, p. 145.
8. *Ibid.*, p. 144.
9. Una Ellis-Fermor, *The Irish Dramatic Movement*, London: Methuen, 1954, p. 162.
10. W.B. Yeats, *Autobiographies*, p. 74.
11. Coxhead, *op. cit.*, p. vi.
12. *Ibid.*, p. 114.
13. *Lady Gregory's Journals: 1916–1930*, edited by Lennox Robinson, London: Putnam, 1946, p. 336.
14. Lady Gregory, *Selected Plays*, edited by Mary Fitzgerald, Gerrards Cross: Colin Smythe, 1983, p. 358.
15. Mary Lou Kohfeldt, *Lady Gregory: The woman behind the Irish Renaissance*, London: Andre Deutsch, 1985, p. 188.
16. Lady Gregory, *Selected Plays*, p. 359.
17. Lady Gregory, *Selected Plays*, p. 144.
18. *Lady Gregory's Journals: 1916–1930*, edited by Lennox Robinson, p. 340. Concerning a performance of *The Rising of the Moon* in 1925, Lady Gregory reports a letter from 'Casey' conveying Jim Larkin's request for permission to perform it in the Queen's Theatre – 'The Union is holding a concert there and Jim would like to show the work

of an Abbey playwright to many who have never been inside the Abbey Theatre.' Lady Gregory adds, 'I am giving leave – my heart goes out more to workers than to idlers' (*Journals*, p. 621).

19. Lady Gregory, *Selected Plays*, p. 359.
20. Lady Gregory, *Selected Plays*, p. 156.
21. *Ibid.*, p. 155.
22. Frank O'Connor, *The Backward Look: A survey of Irish literature*, Macmillan: London, 1967, pp. 84, 191–2.
23. MSS in the Berg collection, New York Public Library.
24. *Selected Plays*, p. 362.
25. MSS in the Berg Collection, New York Public Library.
26. Lady Gregory, *Selected Plays*, p. 212.
27. Coxhead, *op. cit.*, p. 137.
28. Lady Gregory, *Selected Plays*, p. 197.
29. Lady Gregory, *Our Irish Theatre*, p. 91.
30. Hazard Adams, *Lady Gregory*, Lewisburg: Bucknell University Press, 1973, p. 64.
31. Lady Gregory, *Seventy Years: 1852–1922: Being the Autobiography of Lady Gregory*, edited by Colin Smythe, New York: Oxford University Press, 1974, pp. 544–5.
32. *Ibid.*, p. 548.
33. *Lady Gregory's Journals*, edited by D.J. Murphy, Gerrards Cross: Colin Smythe, p. 438. See also the discussion of this incident in Elizabeth Butler Cullingford, *Yeats, Ireland and Fascism*, London: Macmillan, 1981, p. 174. See the latter also for details of other political differences between Lady Gregory and Yeats, her Republican sympathies and writings for *The Nation*, 1920/21, and her admiration for de Valera (pp. 106 ff.).
34. *Lady Gregory's Journals*, edited by D.J. Murphy, p. 472.
35. *Ibid.*, p. 473.
36. Lady Gregory, *Selected Plays*, p. 286.
37. *Ibid.*, p. 286.
38. *Ibid.*, p. 292.
39. *Ibid.*, p. 298.
40. *Ibid.*, p. 321.
41. Ronald Ayling, 'Lady Gregory and Sean O'Casey: An Unlikely Friendship Revisited', in *Lady Gregory: Fifty Years After*, edited by Ann Saddlemyer and Colin Smythe, p. 168.
42. Quoted by David Krause, *Irish Literary Supplement*, Spring, 1990, p. 6.

Chapter Ten

1. Elizabeth Bowen, *The Last September*, Harmondsworth: Penguin, 1982, p. 33. (First published, 1929.) All further references to the 1982 Penguin edition are included in the text, with the title abbreviated to *LS*.

2. Statistics quoted by Carol Coulter in a paper given at the IASAIL Conference in Leiden, July 1991, indicate that Protestant families in the Republic of Ireland continue to wield considerable economic power despite their apparent political eclipse.

3. W.B. Yeats, 'Coole Park, 1929', *Yeats's Poems*, edited by A.N. Jeffares, London: Macmillan, 1989, p. 357.

4. Elizabeth Bowen, *The Mulberry Tree*, London: Virago, 1986, p. 26.

5. *Ibid.*, p. 27.

6. *Ibid.*

7. Hermione Lee, *Elizabeth Bowen*, London and Ottawa: Vision and Barnes & Noble, 1981.

8. Bowen, *The Mulberry Tree*, p. 28.

9. *Ibid.*, p. 223.

10. For a detailed discussion of maternal associations with the 'Big House' in this novel, see Phyllis Lassner, *Elizabeth Bowen*, London: Macmillan, 1990, pp. 26–47.

11. Eavan Boland, 'Outside History', *PN Review*, vol. 17, no. 1, Sept./Oct., 1990, p. 24.

12. Seamus Deane, 'The Literary Myths of the Revival', in *Celtic Revivals: Essays in Modern Irish Literature*, London: Faber & Faber, 1985, pp. 31–2.

13. Toni O'Brien Johnson, 'Light and Enlightenment in Elizabeth Bowen's Irish Novels', in *Gender in Irish Writing*, Milton Keynes and Philadelphia: Open University Press.

14. The passage describing the farm as they leave it is worth quoting in full:

> The mountain farm, its wind-bitten firs dragged east, its furze-thatched byres, sank slowly under the curve of a hill. Looking longest after them, like an eye, a window glittered. Some grey geese that had gaped and straggled behind the trap relinquished the chase abruptly, stumbled round in a flock and went straining off in the other direction. Their backs were more than oblivious; they made the trap, the couple in it, an illusion. And indeed Lois and Hugo both felt that the pause, their talk, their passing had been less than a shadow.
>
> (*LS*, 65)

15. In her book on *The English Novelists* (1942), Elizabeth Bowen writes of 'the idea of love as a rational passion' as a concept which governs, and in some sense limits, the English novel in general. Patricia Craig suggests that in some of her later novels, such as *A House in Paris*, Bowen seeks to subvert this idea. See Patricia Craig, *Elizabeth Bowen*, Harmondsworth: Penguin, 1986, p. 68. In *The Last September*, Lady Naylor's view that Lois cannot love Gerald because it is 'inconceivable', is presented with irony. Nevertheless, Marda's 'rational' decision to marry Lesley seems to be endorsed.

Conclusion

1. J.M. Synge, *The Playboy of the Western World* in *Plays and Poems*, edited by T.R. Henn, London: Methuen, p. 229.
2. Lady Gregory, *Selected Plays*, edited by Mary Fitzgerald, Gerrards Cross: Colin Smythe, 1983, p. 362.
3. Quoted by David Krause, *Irish Literary Supplement*, Spring, 1990, p. 6.

Selected Bibliography

Adams, Hazard, *Lady Gregory*, Lewisburg: Bucknell University Press, 1973.

Arnold, Matthew, *The Study of Celtic Literature*, London: Smith Elder, 1891.

Boland, Eavan, *A Kind of Scar: The woman poet in a national tradition*, Dublin: Attic Press LIP Pamphlet, 1989.

Boland, Eavan, 'Outside History', *PN Review*, vol. 17, no. 1, Sept./Oct., 1990.

Boland, Eavan, 'The Woman, The Place, The Poet', *PN Review*, vol. 17, no. 3, Jan./Feb., 1991.

Bowen, Elizabeth, *Bowen's Court and Seven Winters*, London: Virago Press, 1984.

Bowen, Elizabeth, *The Last September*, London: Penguin, 1982.

Bowen, Elizabeth, *The Mulberry Tree*, London: Virago, 1986.

Breathnach, Eileen, 'Women and Higher Education in Ireland (1879–1914)', *The Crane Bag*, vol. 4, no. 1, 1980, pp. 47–54.

Brooke, Charlotte, *Reliques of Ancient Irish Poetry*, Dublin: George Bonham, 1789.

Brown, Terence, *Ireland: A social and cultural history, 1922–1975*, London: Fontana, 1981.

Cairns, David and Shaun Richards, *Writing Ireland: Colonialism, nationalism and culture*, Manchester: Manchester University Press, 1988.

Chadwick, Joseph, 'Family Romance as National Allegory in Yeats's *Cathleen ni Houlihan* and *The Dreaming of the Bones*', *Twentieth Century Literature*, vol. 32, no. 2, Summer, 1986.

Connolly, James, *Labour in Irish History*, Dublin: New Books Publications, 1972.

Connolly, James, *Selected Writings*, edited by P. Berresford Ellis, Harmondsworth: Penguin, 1973.

Coxhead, Elizabeth, *Daughters of Erin: Five women of the Irish Renaissance*, London: Secker & Warburg, 1965.

Coxhead, Elizabeth, *Lady Gregory: A literary portrait*, London: Secker & Warburg, 1966.

Cullen, Mary (ed.), *Girls Don't Do Honours: Irish women in education in the 19th and 20th centuries*, Dublin: Women's Education Bureau, 1987.

Cullingford, Elizabeth Butler, *Yeats, Ireland and Fascism*, London: Macmillan, 1981.

Cullingford, Elizabeth Butler (ed.), *Yeats: Poems, 1919–1935: A selection of critical essays*, London: Macmillan, 1984.

Cullingford, Elizabeth Butler, *Gender and History in Yeats's Love Poetry*, Cambridge: Cambridge University Press, forthcoming.

Curtis, Liz, *Nothing But the Same Old Story: The roots of anti-Irish racism*, London: Information on Ireland, 1984.

Curtis, L. Perry, *Anglo-Saxons and Celts: A study of anti-Irish prejudice in Victorian England*, Bridgeport, Connecticut: Conference on British Studies, 1968.

Curtis, L. Perry, *Apes and Angels: The Irishman in Victorian caricature*, Newton Abbot: David & Charles, 1971.

Deane, Seamus, *Celtic Revivals: Essays in modern Irish literature, 1880–1980*, London: Faber, 1985.

Deane, Seamus, *A Short History of Irish Literature*, London: Hutchinson, 1986.

Deane, Seamus, *et. al.* (eds), *The Field Day Anthology of Irish Literature*, London: Hutchinson, 1991.

Digby, Margaret, *Horace Plunkett: An Anglo-American Irishman*, Oxford: Basil Blackwell, 1949.

Donoghue, Denis, *Yeats*, London: Fontana/Collins, 1976.

Donoghue, Denis, *We Irish: Selected Essays*, vol. 1, Hemel Hempstead: Harvester Wheatsheaf, 1986.

Duffy, Charles Gavin (ed.), *The Spirit of the Nation*, Dublin: James Duffy, 1845.

Edwards, Owen Dudley and Fergus Pyle (eds), *1916: The Easter Rising*, London: MacGibbon & Kee, 1968.

Edwards, Ruth Dudley, *James Connolly*, Dublin: Gill & Macmillan, 1981.

Edwards, Ruth Dudley, *Patrick Pearse: The triumph of failure*, London: Faber, 1977.

Ellis-Fermor, Una, *The Irish Dramatic Movement*, London: Methuen, 1954.

Ellmann, Richard, *James Joyce*, Oxford: Oxford University Press, 1959.

Ellmann, Richard, *Ulysses on the Liffey*, Oxford: Oxford University Press, 1972.

Ferguson, Samuel, *Poems*, Dublin: W. McGee, 1880.

Field Day Company, *Ireland's Field Day*, London: Hutchinson, 1985.

Foster, Roy, *A History of Modern Ireland*, London: Allen Lane, 1990.

Foster, Roy, *Parnell and His Family*, Hemel Hempstead: Harvester Wheatsheaf, 1976.

Fox, R.M., *Rebel Irishwomen*, Dublin: Progress House, 1935.

Gallagher, S.F. (ed.), *Women In Irish Legend, Life and Literature*, Irish Literary Studies, 14, Gerrards Cross, Bucks: Colin Smythe, 1983.

Green, E.R.R., 'The Great Famine (1845–50)', in *The Course of Irish History*, edited by T.W. Moody and F.X. Martin, Cork: Mercier Press, 1967.

Gregory, Isabella Augusta, *Lady Gregory's Journals, 1916–1930*, edited by Lennox Robinson, London: Putnam, 1946.

Gregory, Isabella Augusta, *Seventy Years: 1852–1922: Being The Autobiography of Lady Gregory*, edited by Colin Smythe, New York: Oxford University Press, 1974.

Gregory, Isabella Augusta, *Lady Gregory's Journals*, vol. 1, edited by Daniel J. Murphy, Gerrards Cross: Colin Smythe, 1978.

Gregory, Isabella Augusta, *The Collected Plays* (4 vols), Coole edn, edited by Ann Saddlemyer, Gerrards Cross: Colin Smythe, 1970.

Gregory, Isabella Augusta, *Selected Plays*, edited by Mary Fitzgerald, Gerrards Cross: Colin Smythe, 1983.

Haverty, Anne, *Constance Markievicz*, London: Pandora, 1988.

Heaney, Seamus, *Preoccupations: Selected prose 1968–78*, London: Faber, 1980.

Henke, Suzette, *James Joyce and the Politics of Desire*, London, Routledge, 1990.

Henke, Suzette and Elaine Unkeless (eds), *Women in Joyce*, Hemel Hempstead: Harvester Wheatsheaf, 1982.

Hinkson, Katharine Tynan, *The Middle Years*, London: Constable, 1916.

Hinkson, Katharine Tynan, *Twenty-five Years: Reminiscences*, London: Smith Elder, 1913.

Hogan, Robert, *The Macmillan Dictionary of Irish Literature*, London: Macmillan, 1980.

Hyland, Paul and Neil Sammells (eds), *Irish Writing: Exile and subversion*, London: Macmillan, 1991.

Innes, C.L., *The Devil's Own Mirror: The Irishman and the African in modern literature*, Washington, DC: Three Continents Press, 1990.

Jeffares, A. Norman, *A Commentary on the Collected Poems of W.B. Yeats*, Stanford: Stanford University Press, 1968.

Jeffares, A. Norman, *Anglo-Irish Literature*, Dublin: Gill & Macmillan, 1982.

Jeffares, A. Norman and K.G.W. Cross (eds), *In Excited Reverie: A centenary tribute to W.B. Yeats*, New York: St. Martin's Press, 1965.

Jeffares, A. Norman (ed.), *Yeats's Poems*, London: Macmillan, 1989.

Jeffrey, Ian, Isabelle Julia and Alaine Sayag (eds), *La France: Images of woman and ideas of nation, 1789–1989*, London: South Bank Centre, 1989.

Johnson, Toni O'Brien and David Cairns, *Gender in Irish Writing*, Milton Keynes and Philadelphia: Open University Press, 1991.

Joyce, James, *Dubliners*, Harmondsworth: Penguin, 1992.

Joyce, James, *A Portrait of the Artist as a Young Man*, Harmondsworth: Penguin, 1992.

Joyce, James, *Selected Letters*, edited by Richard Ellmann, London: Faber, 1975.

Joyce, James, *Ulysses*, Harmondsworth: Penguin, 1986.

Kearney, Richard, *Myth and Motherland*, Belfast: Dorman, 1984.

Kelley, John and Eric Domville (eds), *The Collected Letters of W.B. Yeats, 1865–1895*, Oxford: Clarendon Press, 1986.

Kiberd, Declan, *Men and Feminism in Modern Literature*, London: Macmillan, 1986.

Kiberd, Declan, *Synge and the Irish Language*, London: Macmillan, 1984.

Kilroy, Robert, *The Playboy Riots*, Dublin: Dolmen, 1971.

Kinsella, Thomas (ed.), *The New Oxford Book of Irish Verse*, Oxford: Oxford University Press, 1986.

Kohfeldt, Mary Lou, *Lady Gregory: The woman behind the Irish Renaissance*, London: Andre Deutsch, 1984.

Lassner, Phyllis, *Elizabeth Bowen*, London: Macmillan, 1990.

Lee, Hermione, *Elizabeth Bowen*, London and Ottawa: Vision and Barnes & Noble, 1981.

Lee, J.J., 'Women and the Church since the Famine', in *Women in Irish Society: The historical dimension*, edited by Margaret MacCurtain and Donncha O Corrain, Dublin: Arlen House, 1978.

Levenson, Samuel, *Maud Gonne*, London: Cassell, 1977.

Loftus, Belinda, *Mirrors: William III and Mother Ireland*, Dundrum: Picture Press, 1990.

Longley, Edna, *From Cathleen to Anorexia: The Breakdown of Irelands*, Dublin: Attic Press LIP Pamphlet, 1990.

Luddy, Maria and Cliona Murphy, *Women Surviving: Studies in Irish women's history in the 19th and 20th centuries*, Dublin: Poolbeg Press, 1989.

Lyons, F.S.L, *Charles Stewart Parnell*, London: Collins, 1977.

Lyons, F.S.L, *Ireland Since the Famine*, London: Fontana, 1973.

Lyons, F.S.L, *Culture and Anarchy in Ireland, 1890–1939*, Oxford: Oxford University Press, 1979.

Lysaght, Patricia, *The Banshee: The Irish supernatural death messenger*, Dublin: Glendale Press, 1986.

Macardle, Dorothy, *The Irish Republic*, London: Victor Gollancz, 1937.

MacBride, Maud Gonne, *The Gonne-Yeats Letters, 1893–1938*, edited by Anna MacBride White and A. Norman Jeffares, London: Hutchinson, 1992.

MacBride, Maud Gonne, *A Servant of the Queen*, London: Victor Gollancz, 1938.

MacBride, Maud Gonne, 'Yeats and Ireland', in *Scattering Branches*, edited by Stephen Gwynn, London: Macmillan, 1940.

McCartney, Donal, 'Gaelic Ideological Origins of 1916', in *1916: The Easter Rising*, edited by Owen Dudley Edwards and Fergus Pyle, London: MacGibbon & Kee, 1968, pp. 41–9.

McCormack, W.J., *The Battle of the Books*, Mullingar: Lilliput Press, 1986.

MacCurtain, Margaret and Donncha O Corrain (eds), *Women in Irish Society: The historical dimension*, Dublin: Arlen House, 1978.

MacCurtain, Margaret, 'Towards an Appraisal of the Religious Image of Women', *The Crane Bag*, vol. 4, no. 1, 1980, pp. 26–30.

MacDonagh, Thomas, *Literature in Ireland: Studies in Irish and Anglo-Irish literature*, London: T. Fisher Unwin, 1918.

Markievicz, Constance, *Prison Letters of Countess Markievicz*, edited by Amanda Sebestyen, London: Virago, 1986.

Markievicz, Constance, *Women, Ideals and the Nation*, Dublin: Inghinidhe na h-Eireann, 1909.

Marreco, Anne, *The Rebel Countess*, London: Weidenfeld & Nicolson, 1967.

Meaney, Gerardine, *Sex and Nation: Women in Irish culture and politics*, Dublin: Attic Press LIP Pamphlet, 1991.

Moore, Thomas, *Poetical Works*, Edinburgh: Nimmo, Hay & Mitchell, 1888.

Nandy, Ashis, *The Intimate Enemy*, Delhi: Oxford University Press, 1983.

Nandy, Ashis, *At the Edge of Psychology*, Delhi: Oxford University Press, 1990.

Ni Chuilleanain, Eilean (ed.), *Irish Women: Image and achievement*, Dublin: Arlen House, 1985.

Ni Dhomhnaill, Nuala, 'Interview with Michael Cronin', *Graph*, 1, October 1986.

Ni Dhonnchadha, Mairin and Theo Dorgan (eds), *Revising the Rising*, Derry: Field Day, 1991.

Ni Eireamhoin, E., *Two Great Irishwomen*, Dublin: Fallon, 1971.

Norman, Diana, *Terrible Beauty: A life of Constance Markievicz*, London: Hodder & Stoughton, 1987.

O'Brien, Connor Cruise, *States of Ireland*, London: Hutchinson, 1972.

O'Casey, Sean, *Autobiography* (6 vols), London: Pan, 1972.

O'Casey, Sean, *Three Plays*, London: Macmillan, 1963.

O'Casey, Sean, *Three More Plays*, London: Macmillan, 1965.

O'Connor, Anne V., 'The Revolution in Girls' Secondary Education in Ireland', in Mary Cullen, ed., *Girls Don't Do Honours: Irish women in education in the 19th and 20th centuries*, Dublin: Women's Education Bureau, 1987.

O'Faolain, Sean, *Constance Markievicz or the Average Revolutionary*, London: Jonathan Cape, 1934.

O Tuama, Sean and Thomas Kinsella, *An Duanaire 1600–1900: Poems of the dispossessed*, Dublin, 1981.

Owens, Rosemary Cullen, *Smashing Times: A history of the Irish women's suffrage movement, 1889–1922*, Dublin: Attic Press, 1984.

Paulin, Tom, *Ireland and the English Crisis*, Newcastle upon Tyne: Bloodaxe, 1984.

Paulin, Tom, *Liberty Tree*, London: Faber, 1983.

Pethica, James, *A Dialogue of Self and Service: Lady Gregory and the Irish Renaissance*, Ph.D. thesis, Oxford University, 1989.

Reade, Paul, *Samuel Ferguson and the Idea of an Irish National Literature, 1830–1850*, Ph.D. thesis, University of Kent, Canterbury, 1985.

Ryan-Smolin, Wanda, Jenni Rogers and Patrick Murphy, *Irish Women Artists from the Eighteenth Century to the Present Day*, Dublin: The National Gallery & the Douglas Hyde Gallery, 1987.

Saddlemyer, Ann, *In Defence of Lady Gregory*, Dublin: Dolmen, 1966.

Saddlemyer, Ann (ed.), *Lady Gregory: Fifty years after*, Gerrards Cross: Colin Smythe, 1987, pp. 258–73.

Saddlemyer, Ann and Colin Smythe (eds), *Lady Gregory: Fifty years after*, Gerrards Cross: Colin Smythe, 1987.

Said, Edward, *Nationalism, Colonialism and Literature: Yeats and decolonization*, Derry: Field Day Company, 1988.

Scott, Bonnie Kime, *Joyce and Feminism*, Hemel Hempstead and Bloomington: Harvester Wheatsheaf and Indiana University Press, 1984.

Somerville, Edith and M. Ross, *The Big House at Inver*, London: Quartet, 1978.

Somerville, E. and M. Ross, *The Real Charlotte*, London: Chatto & Windus, 1972.

Storey, Mark (ed.), *Poetry and Ireland Since 1800: A source book*, London: Routledge, 1988.

Swift, Jonathan, *Irish Tracts and Sermons*, edited by Herbert Davis, Oxford: Basil Blackwell, 1963.

Thompson, William Irwin, *The Imagination of an Insurrection, Dublin 1916*, London: Oxford University Press, 1967.

Tynan, Katherine, *Louise de la Valliere and Other Poems*, London: Kegan Paul, 1885.

Tynan, Katherine, *Irish Poems*, London: Sidgwick and Jackson, 1914.

Van Voris, Jacqueline, *Constance de Markievicz in the Cause of Ireland*, Amherst: University of Massachusetts Press, 1967.

Wade, Alan (ed.), *The Letters of W.B. Yeats*, London: Hart-Davis, 1954.

Ward, Margaret, *Unmanageable Revolutionaries: Women and Irish nationalism*, London: Pluto, 1983.

Ward, Margaret, *Maud Gonne: Ireland's Joan of Arc*, London: Pandora, 1990.

Warner, Marina, *Alone of All Her Sex: The myth and the cult of the Virgin Mary*, London: Picador, 1985.

Warner, Marina, *Monuments and Maidens*, London: Weidenfeld and Nicolson, 1985.

Yeats, W.B., *Autobiographies*, London: Macmillan, 1955.

Yeats, W.B., *The Collected Plays*, London: Macmillan, 1953.

Yeats, W.B., *Poems*, edited by A.N. Jeffares, London: Macmillan, 1989.

Yeats, W.B., *Memoirs*, edited by Denis Donoghue, London: Macmillan, 1972.

Index